EXPLORING
ROMANS

EXPLORING
ROMANS

JOHN PHILLIPS

LOIZEAUX BROTHERS
Neptune, New Jersey

Originally Published by Moody Press
First Loizeaux Brothers Edition, 1991

Exploring Romans
© 1969 by John Phillips

A Publication of Loizeaux Brothers, Inc.
A Nonprofit Organization Devoted to the
Lord's Work and to the Spread of His Truth.

Library of Congress Cataloging in Publication Data

Phillips, John, 1927 –
Exploring Romans / John Phillips.
p. cm.
Originally published: Moody Press, 1969.
ISBN 0-87213-669-8
1. Bible. N.T. Romans—Commentaries. I. Title.
BS2665.3.P44 1991
227'.107—dc20   91–35605

Printed in the United States of America

10 9 8 7 6 5 4 3 2 1

CONTENTS

FOREWORD

When I was first asked to write a foreword for this book my immediate reaction was "Can it be that there is anything new to be said about Romans?" I recalled commentators whose work I have reveled in and which have been such a blessing to me. I think of names such as Godet, Moule, Westcott, Ironside, and so many more.

When I began to read through this book, however, I was immediately captivated not only by its sound and thoroughly evangelical exposition, but also by the practical application by the author by means of illustrations which are exceedingly relevant so that theology and the necessary outworking of it in practice come amazingly alive.

This is a book which every minister will find of immense value as a reference book in his library, and also every student of theology will find it an exceedingly valuable area for study. The epistle to the Romans has often been referred to as the most statesman-like presentation of the full gospel in the Bible, and this book is a most thoughtful and practical exposition of it. Here we have the heart of the whole subject of the message of full salvation wonderfully opened up. Romans 6–8 is no mere theological battleground, but here is a clear presentation of the basis for all victorious living, namely, in our union with Christ in His death and resurrection.

I find in these days so many of us as Christians have settled for only a half salvation! We have found it comparatively easy to accept the truth of Christ's death for us on the cross and the shedding of His blood as the basis for forgiveness for all our sins, and we have rejoiced in the fact that there is therefore now no condemnation to them that are in Christ Jesus (Romans 8:1).

We have, however, seemed to find it exceedingly difficult to believe that not only does the cross supply the answer to the past and give us a hope for the future, but it proclaims to us with no uncertain sound a present-day experience of deliverance.

After all, what is the value of being forgiven for our sins only to continue living in them? The death of Christ on Calvary is only half the truth; the other half is the saving life of Christ, by His Holy Spirit, reproducing His character and delivering us from the principle of sin. At the cross we have forgiveness for what we have done, in order that we may stop doing it! In His risen life indwelling us by the Spirit of God we have deliverance from what we are in order that we may become like Him—which, of course, is the whole genius and strategy of redemption.

The reader will find this message clearly sounded out in this volume. He will also find that an entry into such an experience is to be expressed in the social implications of the gospel, and the author deals with this most helpfully in his exposition of the later chapters of the epistle.

As a practical handbook on daily Christian living, I would find this volume hard to beat, and I'm sure that all who read it will be greatly blessed as I have been. It is a book which deserves a wide circulation in days when there is so much uncertainty as to what basic Christianity really is.

ALAN REDPATH

OUTLINE OF ROMANS

PROLOGUE (1:1-18)
1. The Significance of the Gospel (1:1-4)
2. The Servant of the Gospel (1:5-16)
3. The Summary of the Gospel (1:17-18)

I. THE PRINCIPLES OF THE GOSPEL (1:19—8:39)
  A. The Question of Sin (1:19—3:20)
    1. The Guilt of the Heathen (1:19-32)
    2. The Guilt of the Hypocrite (2:1-16)
    3. The Guilt of the Hebrew (2:17—3:8)
    4. The Guilt of All Humanity (3:9-20)
  B. The Question of Salvation (3:21—5:21)
    1. Salvation Is Free (3:21-31)
    2. Salvation Is by Faith (4:1-25)
    3. Salvation Is Forever (5:1-21)
  C. The Question of Sanctification (6:1—8:39)
    1. The Way of Victory Explained (6:1—7:25)
      a. Deliverance from the domain of death (6:1-11)
      b. Deliverance from the dominion of sin (6:12-23)
      c. Deliverance from the demands of law (7:1-25)
    2. The Way of Victory Experienced (8:1-39)
      a. The new law (8:1-4)
      b. The new Lord (8:5-13)
      c. The new life (8:14-39)

II. THE PROBLEMS OF THE GOSPEL (9:1—11:36)
  A. God's Past Dealings with Israel (9:1-33)
    1. Paul's Anguish for the Jewish People (9:1-3)
    2. Paul's Analysis of the Jewish Problem (9:4-33)

INTRODUCTION

"ALL ROADS LEAD TO ROME." It was a byword and a proverb in the days of Paul. From the golden milestone in Rome great arterial highways flung their tentacles across the world. From Rome, Paul could reach the world; for if all roads led *to* Rome, just as surely all roads led *from* Rome. So time and again this master strategist of Christian missions wrote "Rome" boldly at the top of his itinerary plans. And though something always hindered, he persisted in his purpose. "I must see Rome," he said. "I must see Rome."

Then, while at Corinth, Paul heard that Phebe, an active member of the church at nearby Cenchrea, was planning a visit to the city of the Caesars. "I'll write you a letter of commendation to the saints at Rome, Phebe," he said.

And so he did. By the time he came to put down his pen, however, Paul had written his theological masterpiece and one of the most important documents in the history of the world—his epistle to the Romans. The skeptic Renan is credited with the statement that when Phebe sailed away from Corinth she "carried beneath the folds of her robe the whole future of Christian theology."[1] He was right.

Romans is *the gospel according to Paul.* In his great book on Bible characters, that prince of preachers, Alexander Whyte, pictures Paul setting out for Arabia, right after his baptism, instead of returning to Jerusalem. He had come like a prince into Damascus but departed for Arabia like a pilgrim armed only with his staff and taking but his parchments and a few of life's basic needs.

[1]See James Hastings (ed.), *The Great Texts of the Bible, Acts-Romans* (Grand Rapids: Wm. B. Eerdmans Publishing Co., n.d.), p. 237.

9

At the beginning of his ministry Paul seems to have been drawn
into the silences and solitudes of Arabia as, at the end of his ministry, he was drawn increasingly toward the rush and bustle of
mighty Rome. The three years he spent beneath the shadow of
Horeb were fruitful years indeed. He took with him, as Whyte
so eloquently phrases it, "Moses and the Prophets and the Psalms
in his knapsack, and returned to Damascus with the Romans, the
Ephesians and the Colossians in his mouth and in his heart."[2]
There can be little doubt that it was Paul who thought through
the theological implications of Christianity. It was Paul who
thought through the deeper meaning of the Old Testament in the
light of Calvary and in the light of that great experience which
was his when, on the Damascus road, he came face to face with
Jesus of Nazareth and recognized Him at last as the risen,
ascended and glorified Lord. It was Paul who coined the vocabulary of the New Testament. It was Paul who did justice to the
cross. It was Paul who expounded the true meaning of Christ's
coming and His present glorified position at God's right hand. It
is in Paul's epistle to the Romans that his magnificent grasp of the
gospel is most fully displayed. All who would exercise the ministry
of a pastor, evangelist or teacher, engage in personal work or have
an intelligent understanding of the work of God in a human soul
must have a good grasp of Romans—*the gospel according to Paul*.

[2]See Alexander Whyte, *Bible Characters—Stephen to Timothy* (London:
Oliphants, n.d.), pp. 121-130.

PROLOGUE
1:1-18

I. THE SIGNIFICANCE OF THE GOSPEL (1:1-4)
   A. Its Mandate (1:1)
   B. Its Message (1:2-4)
      1. Jesus—the Revealed One (1:2)
      2. Jesus—the Reigning One (1:3)
      3. Jesus—the Resurrected One (1:4)

II. THE SERVANT OF THE GOSPEL (1:5-16)
   A. Paul's Instructions to the Roman Christians (1:5-7)
      1. His Commission (1:5)
      2. Their Call (1:6-7)
   B. Paul's Intercession for the Roman Christians (1:8-9)
      1. His Praise for Them (1:8)
      2. His Prayers for Them (1:9)
   C. Paul's Interest in the Roman Christians (1:10-12)
      1. He Longed to See Them (1:10-11*a*)
      2. He Longed to Serve Them (1:11*b*)
      3. He Longed to Strengthen Them (1:11*c*-12)
   D. Paul's Intentions with the Roman Christians (1:13-16)
      1. How These Intentions Were Frustrated (1:13)
      2. How These Intentions Were Formulated (1:14-16)
         a. His burden—"I am debtor" (1:14)
         b. His boldness—"I am ready" (1:15)
         c. His belief—"I am not ashamed" (1:16)
            (1) The supremacy of the gospel
            (2) The sufficiency of the gospel
            (3) The simplicity of the gospel

11

III. THE SUMMARY OF THE GOSPEL (1:17-18)
    A. It Reveals God's Righteousness (1:17)
        1. Its Revelation to Us
        2. Its Revolution in Us
    B. It Reveals God's Wrath (1:18)
        1. Against the Ungodly
        2. Against the Unrighteous
        3. Against the Unbelieving

WHEN HE WROTE THIS LETTER Paul had never been to Rome, so naturally he begins with a brief description of himself and his special status in the church. True, some at Rome were his friends and converts, but to most he was a stranger. His introduction gives a picture of himself, his relationship to the Lord and to them, and a glimpse of the major theme of his letter—the gospel.

I. THE SIGNIFICANCE OF THE GOSPEL (1:1-4)

Paul announces his theme in the first verse as "the gospel" and allows it to dominate his opening remarks (vv. 1, 9, 15, 16).

A. *The Mandate of the Gospel* (1:1)

"*Paul, a servant of Jesus Christ, called to be an apostle, separated unto the gospel of God*" (v. 1). The gospel arrests men for God. And of this Paul is himself a striking example, for he describes himself as a *servant* (a bondslave) of Jesus Christ (v. 1). It is not improbable that Paul had in mind here the Hebrew servant of old who so loved his master that he chose a lifetime of bondage rather than have the freedom of independent action. Like him, Paul could say, "I love my master . . . I will not go out free" (Exodus 21:5). As that Old Testament servant's ear was pierced in token of his irrevocable surrender, so Paul could say, "I bear in my body the marks [the *stigmata*, the "slave brands"] of the Lord Jesus" (Gal. 6:17).

Nobody was more conscious of his freedom than Paul. In a day when most men were slaves, Paul enjoyed the rare and much-prized privilege of being a free-born citizen of Rome. Yet he counted it his highest honor to be the bondslave of Jesus Christ. His readers, familiar enough with the slave market, and many of

them slaves themselves, would appreciate this opening phrase of
Paul's.

The mandate of the gospel not only made Paul Christ's willing
slave, but it conferred on him a special dignity. It made him an
apostle. The word means "one who is sent" and the thought behind it is conveyed exactly in our word "missionary." Paul's calling as an apostle, however, carried extra privileges, and ranked
him with Peter, James and John (II Cor. 11:5). In discharging
his apostleship, Paul became the greatest pioneer and foremost
spokesman of the church. When he died, some thirty years after
Calvary, there was a church for Christian worship in every major
city of the western Roman Empire, largely through his efforts. He
made full proof of his apostleship (Rom. 15:19).

The mandate of the gospel did something else for Paul. It *separated* him (v. 1). The man who would be most effective in the
service of God must burn all bridges. Soon after the Spanish ad-
venturers of Cortez landed on the shores of Mexico their forceful
captain ordered their boats to be burned on the beach. From then
on it was victory or death. Paul cut himself adrift from all possibility of compromise so far as Christ and the gospel were concerned.

The Greek word for "separated" in this passage contains the
thought of "the horizon." Paul's whole horizon was dominated by
Christ. All his boundaries in life were determined by Him. Paul
was separated by God *before* his conversion (Gal. 1:15), by
Christ *at* his conversion (Acts 9:15), and by the Holy Spirit *after*
his conversion (Acts 13:2). He was "separated unto the gospel of
God."

B.   *The Message of the Gospel* (1:2-4)

Christ is at the heart of the gospel message. Paul sets Him before us in a threefold way in the next three verses. He is (1) *the
revealed One*, the One "promised afore" (v. 2), for the "gospel of
God" has its roots deep in the Old Testament.

The revelation of God is an organic whole and it reaches its
highest climax in the gospel. It was Paul's special calling to take
the things of Christ latent in the Old Testament and explain them
in the light of Calvary. Three great truths or "mysteries" were

given to Paul, and his church epistles are all related to these truths. Trace the following pattern based on II Timothy 3:16.

I. Romans: The Mystery of Christ's *Cross*
   A. I and II Corinthians—Reproof (moral failure)
   B. Galatians—Correction (doctrinal error)
II. Ephesians: The Mystery of Christ's *Church*
   A. Philippians—Reproof (practical failure)
   B. Colossians—Correction (doctrinal error)
III. I and II Thessalonians: The Mystery of Christ's *Coming*

These "mysteries" were all new revelations, yet none of them are inconsistent with what God had revealed in Old Testament times. The cross, the church, and the coming again of the Lord are all hidden away in types and shadows of the Old Testament.

The message of the gospel concerns Jesus not only as the revealed One but also as (2) *the reigning One*. He is *"Jesus Christ our Lord, which was made of the seed of David according to the flesh"* (v. 3).

The New Testament begins and ends with a reference to Jesus as the son of David (Matt. 1:1; Rev. 22:16). The Messianic line was exhausted in Him. Using the various genealogies of the Old Testament, both Matthew and Luke trace His rightful claim to the throne of David. It is significant that at Calvary no one cared to accept Isaiah's challenge and "declare his generation" (Isa. 53:8). To have done so would have been to publicly proclaim His sole right to the throne of David. He was in very fact "the King of the Jews."

Paul states Christ's right to reign in two ways. *Positionally* He is "the seed of David." *Personally* He is "Jesus Christ our Lord." The world at large may deny Him His throne rights as the seed of David during this age, but every believer is duty bound to own Him as both Lord and Christ.

The message of the gospel has to do with a third aspect of Christ's advent. He is (3) *the resurrected One*, the One *"declared to be the Son of God with power, according to the spirit of holiness, by the resurrection from the dead"* (v. 4).

The expression "spirit of holiness" suggests that the Lord Jesus lived a life of victory over the *power of sin*, and indeed, His life was perfectly holy. He never looked with lust; He never uttered a hasty, unkind, untrue or frivolous word; and He never entertained an impure thought. He was never accused by conscience, never inflamed by wrongful passion, never out of step with the will of God. His time was never wasted, His talents never debased for selfish ends, His influence never bad, His judgment never wrong. He never had to apologize for anything He did or retract a single word He said. He was never too late or too soon; never upset; never insipid, shallow or afraid. He lived on earth approximately twelve thousand days and every one of them was a marvel of holiness. He was "holy, harmless, undefiled, separate from sinners" (Heb. 7:26). From the summit of the Mount of Transfiguration He could have stepped straight into glory. He had absolute victory from the moment He first drew breath in that Bethlehem barn until the moment He closed His eyes in death on the cross of Calvary. He was "declared to be the Son of God with power, according to the spirit of holiness."

The expression "by the resurrection from the dead" suggests His victory over the *penalty of sin*. He rose from the dead. During the time of the French Revolution, a certain M. Lepeau complained to Tallyrand that a new religion of his, one he considered a great improvement over Christianity, had failed to catch on with the people. He asked Tallyrand for some suggestions. Tallyrand dryly said, "M. Lepeau, to insure success for your new religion, all you need do is have yourself crucified and then rise from the dead on the third day!"

It was this very thing about Christ which impressed Paul—His resurrection! Paul first met Jesus as the risen and ascended Lord from heaven on the Damascus road (Acts 9:1-6). The fact that Jesus Christ was indisputably alive and glorified convinced Paul that He was indeed the Son of God.

See Him there on the cross in utter weakness as He bows His head and dies. Now stand by that open grave on the third morning. "Ho guards, arrest Him! See how they roll away the stone and break proud Caesar's seal. In the name of imperial Rome, seize the arm of that lone Man as He marches from the tomb. Lay hold on Him!" But no, those guards are as dead men upon the ground. Christ staked everything upon this—"I have power to lay down my life, and I have power to take it again" (John 10:18); and He has taken it again. He has conquered death! He lives

forever in the power of an endless life. According to the flesh, He
is the seed of David; but according to the spirit of holiness, He is
the Son of God.

II. THE SERVANT OF THE GOSPEL (1:5-16)

The most frequently used words in this section are Paul's personal pronouns "I," "me" and "my." He here lays bare his chief
reasons for writing to Rome.

A. *Paul's Instructions to the Roman Christians* (1:5-7)

He begins by stating (1) *his commission.* "*We have received
grace and apostleship, for obedience to the faith among all nations, for his name*" (v. 5). Grace comes before apostleship, salvation before service. Jesus says, "Come unto me," before He
says, "Go ye into all the world." Commitment to the truth comes
before commitment to the task. Many well-meaning people have
failed to see this. John Wesley was on his way to the mission field
before discovering that he himself was an unconverted man in
need of a Saviour.

Paul's whole life revolved around the words, "obedience to the
faith among all nations, for his name," and he repeats them almost word for word at the end of the epistle (16:26). Our *attitude* must be "obedience to the faith"; our *assignment* is "all nations"; our *authority* is "His name." Paul keeps before us the
pressing need for world evangelism.

Having stated his commission, he next discusses (2) *their call.*
"*Ye are also the called of Jesus Christ*" (v. 6). Later in the epistle
Paul discusses in detail what is involved in this call (8:28-30), but
at this point he mentions only three things.

The called of God are *located* by Him. In the case of Paul's
readers, they were "*in Rome*" (v. 7). But whether it be in ancient
Rome or modern New York or Chicago, the called of God are
located by Him. He knows where each one is. "The Lord knoweth
them that are his" (II Tim. 2:19).

The called of God are also *loved* by Him; they are "*beloved of
God*" (v. 7). They are *lifted* by Him; they are "*called to be saints*"
(v. 7). During this age (Acts 15:14) God is calling out from the
world a select society of people called "the church." (The very
word for "church" in the New Testament is *ecclesia*—"an assembly

of called-out ones.") These called-out ones are designated "saints," one of the names by which the people of God are known in the New Testament. The word "saint" is not used of a special class within the church, but describes all those who have trusted Christ. The word carries a companion thought to the word "church" and means "one set apart for God."

B. *Paul's Intercession for the Roman Christians* (1:8-9)

Paul's intercession began (1) *with praise. "First, I thank my God through Jesus Christ for you all, that your faith is spoken of throughout the whole world"* (v. 8).

Paul was not cast in a jealous mold! The church at Rome would have been his pride and joy. He might well have coveted the honor of planting the church at Rome in his capacity of apostle to the Gentiles. His overall strategic concepts, however, were too great for him to be small-minded simply because others had this joy. Not all are like Paul in this. In Rome itself were those who deeply resented Paul's planned visit to their city. For when finally he did arrive as Nero's prisoner, they actually preached Christ out of envy and strife, hoping thereby to add to Paul's affliction and bonds (Phil. 1:15-16). Paul knew no such spirit.

Paul's intercession continued (2) *with prayer. "For God is my witness, whom I serve with my spirit in the gospel of his Son, that without ceasing I make mention of you always in my prayers"* (v. 9). As the fires on Israel's altars were never to be extinguished, so Paul's great heart burned unceasingly for the souls of men. The smoke of his intercession rose day and night to God. Most of us are faithless enough in praying for our own family and friends, and how much less do we pray unceasingly for those in other cities and lands whose faces we have never seen. But Paul, when he admonished the Thessalonians to "pray without ceasing" (I Thess. 5:17), was simply urging them to follow in his steps.

C. *Paul's Interest in the Roman Christians* (1:10-12)

He longed to see them, to serve them and to strengthen them. His absolute sincerity is underlined in the phrase *"by any means"* (v. 10). It was a blank check, so to speak, signed and offered to God. In effect Paul said, "Lord, I want to go to Rome, but I am absolutely at Your disposal in this regard. I will go any way You choose." God took his offer at its face value, filling in that check for the maximum amount and sending him there in chains. Paul was never ashamed of those chains, never regarded himself as the prisoner of Nero, always as the prisoner of Jesus Christ.

Paul had some specific goals in mind for Rome. *"To the end,"* he says, explaining his longing, *"that ye may be established"* (v. 11). He was confident that his coming would be a source of blessing to them and that their fellowship would be an inspiration to him (v. 12). He was right! Writing later, during his first captivity in Rome, to his friends at Philippi, Paul could say: "But I would ye should understand, brethren, that the things which happened unto me have fallen out rather for the furtherance of the gospel; so that my bonds in Christ are manifest in all the palace, and in all other places; and many of the brethren in the Lord, waxing confident by my bonds, are much more bold to speak the word without fear" (Phil. 1:12-14).

D. *Paul's Intentions with the Roman Christians* (1:13-16)

Notice how Paul's plans for Rome (1) *had been frustrated.* *"Now I would not have you ignorant, brethren, that oftentimes I purposed to come unto you, (but was let hitherto)"* (v. 13). Sometimes it was Satan who hindered Paul's plans (I Thess. 2:18). But in this case it seems more likely that gospel preaching in other parts under the direction of the Holy Spirit had prevented Paul from coming to Rome.

Then notice how Paul's plans for Rome (2) *had been formulated.* They were based on three things—his burden ("I am debtor"), his boldness ("I am ready"), and his belief ("I am not ashamed of the gospel").

"I am debtor both to the Greeks, and to the Barbarians; both to the wise, and to the unwise" (v. 14). Here was *Paul's burden.* It made little difference to Paul whether a man was cultured or crude, an intellectual or an ignoramus. He would proclaim Christ with equal passion to a runaway slave like Onesimus or to a proud monarch like King Agrippa. Those who know the truth in Christ are debtors to all mankind. They are like those lepers of old who, having stumbled on vast resources when their fellows were starving in a besieged city, must say, "We do not well: this day is a day of good tidings, and we hold our peace" (II Kings

7:9). That is the spirit exactly. Those who have found the treasure of the gospel must share it with all mankind. It is a debt.

"*As much as in me is, I am ready to preach the gospel to you that are at Rome also*" (v. 15). Here was *Paul's boldness*. Rome! Says Sir Henry Rider Haggard, "Nowhere, not even in old Mexico, was high culture so completely wedded to the lowest barbarism. Intellect, Rome had in plenty; the noblest efforts of her genius are scarcely surpassed; her law is the foundation of the best of our codes of jurisprudence; art she borrowed but appreciated; her military system is still the wonder of the world; her great men remain great among a multitude of competitors. And yet how pitiless she was! What a tigress! Amid all the ruins of her cities we find none of a hospital, none I believe of an orphan school in an age that made many orphans. The pious aspirations and efforts of individuals never seem to have touched the conscience of the people. Rome incarnate had no conscience; she was a lustful, devouring beast, made more bestial by her intelligence and splendor."[1]

Paul was ready to preach the gospel at Rome. When he preached it at Jerusalem, the religious center of the world, he was mobbed. When he preached it at Athens, the intellectual center of the world, he was mocked. When he preached it at Rome, the legislative center of the world, he was martyred. He was ready for that. He was ready to preach the gospel at Rome.

"*I am not ashamed of the gospel of Christ: for it is the power of God unto salvation to every one that believeth; to the Jew first, and also to the Greek*" (1:16). Here was *Paul's belief*.

Paul's absolute confidence in the gospel was based on its *supremacy*. He knew it to be far superior to any religion or philosophy ever known on earth. The world of Paul's day was dominated by three lines of thought—the Greek, the Roman, and the Hebrew; but Greek logic, Roman law and Hebrew light all paled before the gospel. In the face of all three Paul could say, "I am not ashamed of the gospel of Christ." This was not the boast of an ignorant provincial. Paul was no illiterate but a cosmopolitan man with a world vision, a liberal education, a wide catholicity of interest and great intellectual power. It was the testimony of a man well versed in the ways of the world and out-

[1]Sir H. Rider Haggard, *Pearl Maiden* (London: Longsmans, Green and Company, 1901), p. 15.

standingly successful in proclaiming the message of the cross. Paul knew the supremacy of the gospel.

Paul's confidence in the gospel was based on its *sufficiency*. "*It is the power of God unto salvation*," he wrote. The world does not need a better system of education, more social reform, new ideas in religion. It needs the gospel. The gospel message grips the mind, stabs the conscience, warms the heart, saves the soul and sanctifies the life. It can make drunken men sober, crooked men straight and profligate women pure. It is a message sufficient to transform the life of any who believe.

Paul's confidence in the gospel was based on its *simplicity*. It is the power of God unto salvation "*to every one that believeth*." Could anything be simpler than that? The gospel call is to a simple trust in God's Son, the Lord Jesus Christ, as personal Saviour from sin.

III. THE SUMMARY OF THE GOSPEL (1:17-18)

Paul's far-reaching introduction is concluded by a brief summary of the gospel.

A. *It Reveals God's Righteousness* (1:17)

The key word "righteousness" and its cognates occur some fifty times in Romans. First, Paul spells out (1) *the revelation of that righteousness to us* with the statement, "*for therein is the righteousness of God revealed from faith to faith*" (v. 17). Righteousness means "conformity to the right," that is, to the divine claims on man. Righteousness is "that which God *is, has* and *gives*." The righteousness which God is in Himself He provides in Christ. It must be accepted by faith, for on the sole and simple condition of trust, God will reinstate man in righteousness.[2]

"For a long time," says Wuest, "Martin Luther saw only the condemning righteousness of God and hated it. When he saw that that righteousness that condemns when rejected, saves when accepted, the light of the gospel broke into his darkened soul. This righteousness, Paul says, is revealed in the good news of salvation."[3]

[2]See W. H. Griffith Thomas, *St. Paul's Epistle to the Romans* (Grand Rapids: Wm. B. Eerdmans Publishing Co., 1946), p. 62.
[3]Kenneth S. Wuest, *Romans in the Greek New Testament* (Grand Rapids: Wm. B. Eerdmans Publishing Co., 1955), p. 27. Used by permission.

God is righteous; man is unrighteous. The gospel shows how the righteousness of God can be bestowed on sinful man. It is "from faith to faith." In other words, the righteousness of God is *received* by faith and *reproduced* by faith. W. E. Vine puts it this way: " 'From faith' points to the initial act; 'to faith' to the life of faith which issues from it."[4]

Paul spells out also (2) *the revolution of that righteousness in us. "The just,"* he says, *"shall live by faith."* (Notice our likeness to God; we become "just." Notice also our life from God; we "live.")

This great statement is a quotation from Habakkuk 2:4 brought in by Paul to show that "righteousness by faith" is not a new idea propagated by him but a truth solidly founded on the Old Testament revelation. The expression occurs in two other places in the New Testament (Gal. 3:11; Heb. 10:38) and is one of the great statements of Scripture. When it reached the soul of Martin Luther it is difficult to say, but in the thinking of some at least it was as he was crawling on his knees up the staircase of St. Peter's at Rome in a vain effort to win righteousness by works of penance. It brought him down those stairs on his feet in a hurry and burned itself into his soul, until all Europe rang with the words, "The just shall live by faith."[5]

Bishop Lightfoot says of this text that the whole law was given to Moses in six hundred and thirteen precepts. David in Psalm 15 brings them all within the compass of eleven. Isaiah reduces them to six, Micah to three, and Isaiah, in a later passage, to two. But Habakkuk condenses them all into one: "The just shall live by faith."[6]

B. *The Gospel Reveals God's Wrath* (1:18)

It is a mistake to neglect the severer side of Christ's teaching. Significantly enough, He spoke more about hell than He did about

---

[4]W. E. Vine, *The Epistle to the Romans* (Grand Rapids: Zondervan Publishing House, 1948), p. 16.

[5]F. W. Boreham rightly called Romans 1:17 "Martin Luther's text" and comments, "It goes without saying that the text that made Martin Luther, made history with a vengeance." See F. W. Boreham, *A Bunch of Everlastings* (London: The Epworth Press, 1920), p. 20. Used by permission.

[6]See John Rogers Pitman, *The Whole Works of the Rev. John Lightfoot*, Vol. II (London: F. C. & J. Rivington, 1822), p. 383.

heaven.[7] In Paul's presentation of the gospel, the *bad* news of
human sin and God's wrath comes before the *good* news of salvation through Christ. *"For the wrath of God is revealed from
heaven against all ungodliness and unrighteousness of men, who
hold the truth in unrighteousness"* (v. 18). Paul states that God's
wrath is revealed from heaven for three reasons.

It is revealed because of (1) *human ungodliness*. The whole
question of ungodliness and the fact that ungodliness is inexcusable becomes Paul's first major topic in this epistle.[8]

Next, God's wrath is revealed from heaven against (2) *human
unrighteousness*. While ungodliness is chiefly sin against God,
unrighteousness is also sin against man. It is the condition of not
being straight with either God or man. Man's first sin in the
garden of Eden separated man from God; his second sin (Cain's
murder of Abel) separated man from man (Gen. 3 and 4). God
is as indignant at man's wrong treatment of his neighbor as He is
at man's wrong treatment of his Creator.

Finally, God's wrath is revealed from heaven against (3) *human unbelief*. Paul speaks of men who *"hold the truth in unrighteousness"* (v. 18) or, as other versions render the expression,
"suppress" or "stifle" the truth. God holds all men accountable for
certain basic truths and the deliberate rejection of these truths
in unbelief will be judged.

Thus Paul introduces himself and his message. The rest of
Romans is an expansion of this introduction.

---

[7]He referred to the destiny of the damned nearly twice as often as He did
to that of the blessed. In the gospel of Matthew, where we have the most
complete record of Christ's public utterances, for every verse in which He
referred to heaven there are three in which He referred to hell.

[8]It is significant that the Bible makes no attempt to prove that there is
a God. It begins with the grand statement, "In the beginning God created
. . ." The fact of God's existence is self-evident and taken for granted. The
person who says differently is bluntly called a fool (Ps. 14:1; 53:1). The
root cause of atheism is traced in both these psalms to moral rather than to
intellectual sources. It is not that a man *cannot* believe so much as that he
will not. God's wrath is kindled against those who deny Him, ignore Him
or resist Him.

I. THE PRINCIPLES OF THE GOSPEL

1:19–8:39

THE GUILT OF THE HEATHEN
1:19-32

I. The Willful Blindness of the Heathen (1:19-20)

  A. God's Witness Is Unmistakable (1:19)

  B. God's Witness Is Universal (1:20)

    1. All Men Are Exposed to It

    2. All Men Are Exposed by It

II. The Wicked Beliefs of the Heathen (1:21-25)

  A. The Inflation of Man's Own Godless Imagination (1:21)

    1. Man Has Become Consciously Irreligious (1:21*a*)

    2. Man Has Become Consequently Irrational (1:21*b*)

  B. The Influence of Man's Own Graven Images (1:22-25)

    1. The Idol Is Conceived by the Man (1:22-23)

    2. The Man Is Deceived by the Idol (1:24-25)

      a. His sensual enslavement (1:24)

      b. His spiritual enslavement (1:25)

III. The Wanton Behavior of the Heathen (1:26-32)

  A. They Become Morally Perverted (1:26-27)

    1. The Unnatural Sins of Men (1:26)

    2. The Unnatural Sins of Women (1:27)

  B. They Become Mentally Perverted (1:28-32)

    1. The Cause of Wrong Thinking (1:28)

    2. The Consequences of Wrong Thinking (1:29-32)

      a. Debased human character

      b. Debased human conduct

      c. Debased human conversation

      d. Debased human concepts

      e. Debased human companionships

THE FIRST MAJOR DIVISION of Romans deals with the *doctrine* of the gospel (chaps. 1-8). Three themes occupy the mind and heart of Paul in these chapters—sin, salvation and sanctification.

Few chapters in the Bible deal so devastatingly with the subject of sin as the opening chapters of Romans. The scene suggests a courtroom into which are brought the heathen, the hypocrite and the Hebrew—each to be found in turn to be utterly guilty before God. Finally humanity at large is arraigned and exposed to a fearful summary of God's case against mankind. The indictment begins with God's condemnation of the heathen.

Romans 1:19-32 is a broad survey of the causes and consequences of heathenism. This section reveals that there is not only a *crude* paganism, an unblushing worship by man of graven images; but there is also a *cultured* paganism, a worship by man of his own godless imagination. Some grovel at the foot of an *idol,* others worship at the shrine of an *ideal.* At Corinth, where he was residing when he wrote this epistle, Paul had contact with both kinds of paganism and could see the shameless practice of those high-handed sins he catalogs at the end of the chapter.

The "heathen," of course, are not to be limited to those who bow down to wood and stone. All those who have no knowledge of the Lord Jesus are, in a sense, heathen. Many people in enlightened Western lands who have a vague knowledge of the things of God but who leave Him out of their lives are practicing heathen too.

Paul depicts three downward steps into paganism. First, there is willful blindness, a deliberate rejection of the truth. This is followed by wicked beliefs of either a rationalistic or religious nature. These, in turn, lead to wanton behavior.

I. THE WILLFUL BLINDNESS OF THE HEATHEN (1:19-20)

"Many missionaries point out that the heathen know more than we think," says Leith Samuel. "They know that there is a God. There are no atheists among heathen tribes. There has never been discovered upon earth a tribe of people, however small or depraved, which has not believed in some kind of god or had some system of worship. . . . The heathen found in so-called primitive tribes know that they have sinned. When a Christian comes to them and talks about sin he often finds ready acknowledgment that this is true. The heathen seem to know that their sins must be punished. They seem afraid of punishment, and afraid of death (as are most men everywhere). They know that sin must be atoned for, and they seek ways of appeasing their angry deities or deity."[1]

A. God's Witness Is Unmistakable (1:19)

That the heathen are not without a witness to the true God is Paul's first point. *"That which may be known of God is manifest in them; for God hath shewed it unto them,"* he says (v. 19). Since all nations come from one original family (Gen. 10; Acts 17:26), it follows that all nations once had some knowledge of the truth originally given to mankind. Archaeology and history both demonstrate the universality of sacrifice in human religions from earliest times. Unger says that sufficient similarity exists to "demonstrate a *common origin* in a God-given revelation to the human race just after the Fall. This original source was corrupted and perverted as mankind lapsed more and more into paganism, and was reflected in the systems of sacrifice prevailing among the polytheistic neighbors of Israel."[2]

The Osiris myth in Egypt shows how much light was possessed by heathen nations. According to this myth, Osiris, the bright Spirit of Good, offered himself up for the evildoing of the human race that had dethroned him. From him and the "Divine Mother," of whom all nature is, sprang another spirit to protect the believing on earth as Osiris was their Justifier in Amenti. So ran the Osiris myth. The truth was dim and distorted but it was there.

B. God's Witness Is Universal (1:20)

God has another witness to Himself besides the primeval revelation, a witness which cannot be corrupted by man—the witness of creation. Paul declares, *"The invisible things of him from the creation of the world are clearly seen, being understood by the things that are made, even his eternal power and Godhead; so that they are without excuse"* (v. 20).

All men are (1) *exposed to this witness* of creation (often called

[1]Leith Samuel, "The Heathen—Lost?" *HIS,* student magazine of Inter-Varsity Fellowship, May, 1961, p. 2. Reprinted by permission.
[2]Merrill F. Unger, *Unger's Bible Handbook* (Chicago: Moody Press, 1966), p. 107.

"nature"). The poet Longfellow has colorfully described how nature, "God's oldest testament," speaks for God.

> And Nature, the old nurse, took
>   The child upon her knee,
> Saying: "Here is a story book
>   Thy Father has written for thee!"

> "Come, wander with me," she said,
>   "Into regions yet untrod;
> And read what is still unread
>   In the manuscripts of God!"

> And he wandered away and away
>   With Nature, the dear old nurse,
> Who sang to him night and day
>   The rhymes of the universe.[3]

God expects men to learn from nature the truth of His eternal power and the truth of godhood. These two truths, properly learned, should result in a universal desire both to praise and to please God. The heavenly hosts alone, blazing in the sky, give ample testimony to these two truths, and their witness is truly universal. Psalm 19 affirms that "the heavens declare the glory of God; and the firmament sheweth his handywork. . . . There is no speech nor language, where their voice is not heard." Abraham Lincoln once said, "I can see how it might be possible for a man to look down upon the earth and be an atheist, but I cannot conceive how he could look up into the heavens and say there is no God." One of the French revolutionaries boasted to a peasant, "We are going to pull down all that reminds you of God." Said the peasant dryly, "Citizen, pull down the stars then!"[4]

Paul, however, limits what can be learned about God from nature. Nature points to an eternal, omnipotent, omniscient, omnipresent Creator, but beyond that its voice falters and fails. "It is just here," says F. W. Boreham, "that I part company with the man who tells me he does not need a church in order to worship. He finds God in nature. We all know Ian Maclaren's friend who got more good to his soul out of one glorious sunset than out of all the sermons he ever heard. My only criticism of this man

---

[3]"The Fiftieth Birthday of Agassig," *The Complete Poetical Works of Henry Wadsworth Longfellow*, Cambridge ed. (New York: Houghton, Mifflin and Co., 1893), p. 199.

[4]See T. Sidlow Baxter, *The Best Word Ever* (London: Marshall, Morgan and Scott, n.d.), pp. 9-10.

is that he is so obviously disingenuous and dishonest. He *says* that he finds God in nature. But he *means* nothing of the kind. He practices a doctrine of mental reserve of a worst kind than is to be found in any other school of casuistry. He says that he finds God in *nature*. He means that he finds God in *violets*. But nature is not violets. Nature consists of *violets and vipers*. . . . To be perfectly honest he must worship, not only the subtle fragrance of the violets, but the horrible fangs of the viper. He must worship, not only the delightful trill of the lark, but the bloodied beak of the vulture. He must worship, not only the tender grace of the gazelle, but the dripping jaws of the wolf."[5]

Robert Louis Stevenson sums this up in stirring lines:

> There the green murderer throve and spread,
> Upon his smothering victims fed,
> And wantoned on his climbing coil.
> Contending roots fought for the soil.
> Like frightened demons, with despair,
> Competing branches pushed for air.
> Green conquerors from overhead
> Bestrode the bodies of their dead!
> And in the groins of branches, lo!
> The cancers of the orchids grow!
> So hushed the woodland warfare goes
> Unceasing, and the silent foes
> Grapple and smother, strain and clasp,
> Without a cry, without a gasp.[6]

"There is a God!" says nature, pointing to seasons, stars and suns; "He is eternal in His power." But man needs much more than that. Man needs a personal Redeemer, and nature cannot satisfy that need, for nature knows nothing of forgiveness. Its rules are relentless and ruthless, visiting swift retribution on all infringement of its laws. It teaches no moral codes. Savage tribes have dwelt with nature for ages and produced cannibals! Nature has a voice but it has no heart, and it offers no solution to man's greatest problem, that of sin. It makes no mention of a Saviour. There can be no comparison between God's witness to Himself in creation and His witness to Himself in redemption. Creation

[5]F. W. Boreham, *The Golden Milestone* (London: The Epworth Press, 1914), pp. 249-50. Used by permission.
[6]Robert Louis Stevenson, "The Woodman," *Complete Poems* (New York: Charles Scribner's Sons, 1905 ed.), p. 217.

will tell us somewhat of the work of His hands; Calvary alone
unveils His heart.

Paul points out further that all men are not only exposed *to*
God's witness in creation but also (2) *exposed by this witness* of
God to Himself. The light may be dim at times but it is always
there and always enough to establish God's "eternal power and
Godhead," leaving men without excuse. Yet despite God's unmistakable and universal witness, some men *deny* the truth and
become atheists; others sink still deeper, *distort* the truth and become idolaters. This is Paul's next theme.

II. THE WICKED BELIEFS OF THE HEATHEN (1:21-25)

One result of a willful rejection of God's revelation of Himself
is atheism and the glorification of the human intellect; another is
false religion. Men enthrone *human reasoning* and dethrone *divine revelation*. One result is the worship by man of his own
ideas, and another is the worship of idols.

A. *The Inflation by Man of His Own Godless Imagination* (1:21)

"*When they knew God, they glorified him not as God, neither
were thankful: but became vain in their imaginations, and their
foolish heart was darkened*" (v. 21). Paul points out two things
in this verse. When a man dethrones God from his thinking, he
becomes (1) *consciously irreligious*. The more he learns, the
more he becomes high and mighty in his rationalism and confirmed in his unbelief. He feels that human science and philosophy make belief in God unnecessary.[7]

But then he becomes (2) *consequently irrational*. God em-
phatically declares that such a man's heart is darkened. All his
claims to wisdom notwithstanding, the man who has dethroned
God from his intellect becomes conceited and stupid or unin-
telligent (i.e., foolish). Obviously the man who reasons from the
false premise that there is no God or that God is irrelevant will
arrive at a false conclusion no matter how logical the intervening
steps may be.

A striking illustration of man's modern heathenism expressing
itself in atheism comes out of recent developments in the field of

[7]One reason the theory of evolution has such a hypnotic effect on the
mind of modern man, despite its shortcomings and continued "missing links,"
is that it gives man a working hypothesis for atheism. The unbeliever can
"explain" the universe in terms of natural causes. The theory is plausible
enough to convince those who wish to be convinced.

molecular biology. Scientists working in this field feel that they
have discovered some of the basic secrets of life itself. Working
with deoxyribonucleic acid, scientists are unfolding the basic
genetic patterns that shape every living thing on earth. Some of
the concepts involved are almost unbelievably complex. Despite
this, one British scientist made the statement, "It seems pretty
certain to me that life resulted from purely chemical events.
What's more, I feel certain that in another decade or two we ourselves will be able to create life. I no longer find it necessary to
believe in God."[8]

B. *The Influence on Man of His Own Graven Images* (1:22-25)

The next step down from atheism is idolatry. Paul shows what
happens when (1) *the idol is conceived by man.* "*Professing
themselves to be wise, they became fools, and changed the glory
of the uncorruptible God into an image made like to corruptible
man, and to birds, and fourfooted beasts, and creeping things*"
(vv. 22-23).

Wuest points out that the word for "wise" in this passage was
used by the Greeks to describe a cultured and learned man,
skilled in letters. The word for "fools" is related to the word from
which we get "moron," which gives a good understanding of what
the Greek means.[9] Idolatry is said to have commenced in ancient
Babylon.[10] From there it spread around the world, entrenched

[8]Reported by Max Gunther, "The Secret of Life," *Saturday Evening Post,*
July 3, 1965, p. 28. Used by permission. On the same page the article reports a pertinent rebuttal to this statement coming in this instance from
Msgr. George Kelly, a spokesman for Cardinal Spellman: "When a bio-
chemist is able to create matter and energy out of nothing . . . then I would
say he is approaching the power of God. And when he has the power to
endow life with an immortal soul, then I would like to talk to him." An
excellent reply!
[9]See Kenneth S. Wuest, *Romans in the Greek New Testament* (Grand
Rapids: Wm. B. Eerdmans Publishing Co., 1955), pp. 32-33.
[10]The founder of Bab-el ("the gate of God") was Nimrod. This city was
to be a center for all those wishing to rebel against God. When God judged
and overthrew the city, its name was changed to Babel ("confusion"). It is
claimed that the wife of Nimrod, the infamous Semiramis, led men into
idolatry and that from Babylon this false system of worship spread eventually
to the ends of the earth. Babylon remained the recognized center of idolatry and of a mystery religion which rejected divine revelation. Upon the
final fall of Babylon, the mysteries were transferred to Pergamos and later
to Rome. The reigning Caesar claimed to be the *Pontifex Maximus* of the
pagan religious systems and, from the time of Constantine, this title acknowledged the Caesar to be both the head of the church and the high priest of
heathendom. Afterward the title was conferred on the bishops of Rome,
and the pope retains the title as the "Sovereign Pontiff" to this day.

itself in most pagan religions and is with us to this day. It maintains its hold on even the most cultured of modern men.

Paul shows that once the idol is conceived by man, it is not long before (2) *man is deceived by the idol.* Satanic forces entrench themselves in all idolatrous systems of worship, as Scripture clearly testifies. "They . . . mingled among the heathen, and learned their works. And they served their idols: which were a snare unto them. Yea, they sacrificed their sons and daughters unto devils, and shed innocent blood, even the blood of their sons and of their daughters, whom they sacrificed unto the idols of Canaan" (Ps. 106:35-38; see also Lev. 17:7; II Chron. 11:15; I Cor. 10:19-21).

Idolatrous worship prevails in all parts of the world to this day. Education, culture and advancement do little to free men from idolatry since the problem is basically spiritual. Superstition plays a part in idolatry, but at its deepest roots is Satan, and modern education ignores him as much as it ignores God.

In India, for example, all living things are looked upon as sacred. Snakes and crocodiles, monkeys and cows are all venerated in varying degrees. To kill a cow is as bad as murder, and to eat its flesh is an act of cannibalism. India cannot feed its own starving millions, yet two hundred million head of cattle are allowed to wander far and wide competing with man for food and damaging standing crops. Not even the government of India can liberate the nation from the cow's divinity, its efforts to do so being met with stubborn opposition from the deluded people.[11]

It was the same in olden times. The Greeks were the great intellectuals of antiquity, yet their Roman conquerors sarcastically remarked that "it was easier to find a god than a man" in Athens!

False religious systems enslave people both sensually and spiritually. Paul describes the *sensual enslavement* in these words: *"God gave them up to uncleanness through the lusts of their own hearts, to dishonour their own bodies between themselves"* (v. 24).

The idolatry of the Canaanites is an example of this. "The Canaanites were enslaved by one of the most terrible and degrading forms of idolatry, which encouraged immorality. Discovered in 1929-37, Canaanite religious literature from Ras Shamra (ancient Ugarit in North Syria) reveals the worship of the immoral

[11]See *India, Ceylon, Bhutan, Nepal, The Maldives,* volume of *The World and Its Peoples* (New York: The Greystone Press, 1965), pp. 228-232.

gods El and Baal and the sacred courtesans Anath, Asherah and Astarte. This literature fully corroborates the Old Testament notices of the religious debauchery and moral degradation of the Canaanites. Cult objects, figurines and literature combine to show how sex-centered was Canaanite religion, with human sacrifice, cult of serpents, sacred courtesans and eunuch priests excessively common. The sordid depths of social degradation to which the erotic aspects of Canaanite cults led can scarcely be imagined."[12]

Paul moves on from describing the sensual enslavement to describing the *spiritual enslavement* which results from idolatry. He says that God gave up those *"who changed the truth of God into a lie, and worshipped and served the creature more than the Creator, who is blessed for ever. Amen"* (v. 25).

Originally, when a man makes an idol, his idea is to have his image represent God. He wants it to bring religious thoughts to his mind by having it remind him, in the strongest way, of holy things. But the end result is always the same. He becomes a slave to his idols. The pages of church history provide striking examples of this. As the historian Miller says, "The apologist may draw fine distinctions between images as objects of reverence and objects of devotion, but there can be no doubt that with ignorant and superstitious minds the use, the reverence, the worship of images, whether in pictures or statues, *invariably degenerates into idolatry.*"[13]

[12]Unger, p. 51.

[13]Andrew Miller, *Miller's Church History* (Finecastle, Va.: Scripture Truth Book Company, n.d.), pp. 288-289.

Miller goes on to describe the fearful hold idolatry had on the church by the time of the eighth century. Though for more than three hundred years the church was free from this snare, Helena, the mother of Constantine, finally paved the way for it. From her time on the veneration of images, pictures and relics increased. In the eighth century, the emperor Leo sought to purge the church of idolatry but was defied by pope, prelate and people alike. The most vigorous persecution could not part the people from their beloved idols. All across Europe the priests preached against the emperor, depicting him as an abandoned apostate. "He was painted . . . as one who combined in himself every heresy that ever polluted the Christian faith and endangered the souls of men" (Miller, p. 291). After Leo III's death a church council was held at Nice to decide the question of image worship. The council strongly affirmed the viewpoint that image worship was desirable. "Images," it said, "shall be treated as holy memorials, worshipped, kissed, only without that peculiar adoration which is reserved for the Invisible, Incomprehensible God . . . ." According to Miller the council was not content with its resolution in favor of image worship but broke into a long acclamation affirming that image worship was the faith of the apostles, the

The second commandment forbids the making, the worshiping and the serving of graven images (Exodus 20). God warns in connection with this commandment that the breaking of it awakens His righteous jealousy and brings penalties which have far-reaching results for posterity. The remaining verses of Romans 1 show that this is indeed so.

III. THE WANTON BEHAVIOR OF THE HEATHEN (1:26-32)

Those who abandon God find themselves abandoned by God at last. He gives men up to their own way, and a terrible way it is.

A. *They Become Morally Perverted* (1:26-27)

Paul describes in these two verses how those who turn away from God give themselves over at last to shameful horrors and unnatural vices, to the very sins of Sodom, sins which caused God to rain fire and brimstone from heaven in the days of Lot (Gen. 19). These sins ever accompany apostasy (II Peter 2:6; Jude 7). They are with us today and are becoming more blatant, more aggressive and more evident all the time.

In the United States, those who have abandoned themselves to these fearful vices are banding together and demanding public recognition for their perverted way of life. The pornographic press is circulating millions of pieces of literature every year in which off-beat sex is the theme.[14] Stories and feature articles reporting the activities of this segment of society are becoming increasingly common in even respectable periodicals.

What is true of the United States is also true of Great Britain where those who practice these disgusting vices are gaining an increasing hold on the public life of the nation. Often they are closely linked with Communist organizations. A survey of the subject made for the British Home Office reported a few years ago that a senior government official, responsible for scrutinizing appointments of staff in residential youth establishments, was deliberately choosing perverts for certain jobs.[15] The very founda-

church, the orthodox and the world and denouncing with anathemas those who call images idols (Miller, pp. 294-295). Such is the spiritual enslavement which follows in the wake of idolatry.

[14]See for example O. K. Armstrong, "Filth for Profit: The Big Business of Pornography," *The Reader's Digest*, March, 1966.

[15]See the report entitled "Something Rotten," *The Intelligence Digest*, May, 1962.

tions of society are rotten when such practices can be officially countenanced.

B. *They Become Mentally Perverted* (1:28-32)

With moral perversion comes mental perversion. Paul describes (1) *the cause of this mental perversion.* "*And even as they did not like to retain God in their knowledge, God gave them over to a reprobate mind, to do those things which are not convenient*" (v. 28). Three times in the chapter we are told that God gives up those who give up Him (vv. 24, 26, 28). This is simply righteous retribution on God's part as He allows men to pursue to its fearful end the path they have chosen. Just as moral perversion produces wholesale sins of sex, so mental perversion gives rise to all manner of wickedness.

Paul goes on to describe (2) *the consequences of this mental perversion* and does so by piling up one word after another in an attempt to show that man's wickedness knows no bounds when unrestrained. The sins described in verses 29-32 fall into several categories.

Wrong thinking results in (*a*) *debased human character.* Men become unrighteous, wicked, covetous, malicious, envious and deceitful. They become full of malignity, God haters, despiteful, proud, without natural affection, implacable and unmerciful. It results also in (*b*) *debased human conduct.* Men become guilty of fornication and murder. They defy parental authority and treat contractual obligations with contempt. Wrong thinking results in (*c*) *debased human conversation.* Men become quarrelsome, whisperers, backbiters and boasters. It results in (*d*) *debased human concepts.* Men become inventors of evil things and God says that they are without understanding. Finally, wrong thinking results in (*e*) *debased human companionships.* "*Who,*" says Paul, "*knowing the judgment of God, that they which commit such things are worthy of death, not only do the same, but have pleasure in them that do them*" (v. 32).

This then is God's case against the heathen. No wonder He says that they are "without excuse" (v. 20). Whether the "heathen" are those of Paul's day in pagan Greece and Rome, those of our day living deep in primeval jungles, or those in the privileged lands of Christendom who simply leave God out of their thinking, all are without excuse and guilty before God. As John has said, man is "condemned already" (John 3:18). His case is hopeless apart from the intervention of sovereign grace.

THE GUILT OF THE HYPOCRITE
2:1-16

I. JUDGMENT BY THE HYPOCRITE DESCRIBED (2:1-6)
   A. What He Feels (2:1-2)
   B. What He Finds 2:1, 3)
   C. What He Forgets (2:4)
   D. What He Faces (2:5-6)

II. JUDGMENT ON THE HYPOCRITE DESCRIBED (2:7-16)
   A. Judged According to His Works (2:7-10)
      1. God Weighs the Reasons for a Person's Behavior (2:7-8)
      2. God Weighs the Results of a Person's Behavior (2:9-10)
   B. Judged According to His Worth (2:11-16)
      1. God's Judgment Is Discriminating (2:11-15)
         a. He weighs a person's advantages (2:11-12)
         b. He weighs a person's attitudes (2:13-15)
      2. God's Judgment Is Devastating (2:16)

THERE IS A DIFFERENCE OF OPINION as to who is indicated in Romans 2:1-16. Some, like Scofield, see in this passage God's judgment on Gentile pagan moralizers who were really no better than other pagans. The sophisticated Gentile philosophers of Paul's day sneered at the superstitious idolatry of the less cultured pagans who thronged the temples. But for all their superior airs they had no real substitute for idolatry themselves. Moreover, while applauding virtue they practiced vice. While proclaiming lofty ideals, these moralizers were often guilty of immorality and inconsistency. Marcus Aurelius, the Roman emperor, for example, was a notable philosopher. His ideals were lofty, inspiring and enduring. Yet his reign was marked by persistent bitter and cruel persecution of Christians whose only sin, apparently, was that of proclaiming a creed greater than that of Aurelius.

Other commentators see in this passage God's condemnation

of the Jew who fondly imagined himself to be heaven's favorite
and a cut above his fellowmen. The Jew looked with lofty disdain, contempt and loathing upon his unenlightened Gentile
neighbors, whom he classed as "unclean" and labeled as "dogs."
But the Jew had a dog-in-the-manger attitude toward the truth
he professed to hold. Unwilling to enjoy the blessings offered to
him in Christ, he was nevertheless angered at any suggestion that
these blessings be offered to the Gentiles (Acts 22:21-23). He
was often a thoroughgoing hypocrite too, a point Paul makes more
than once in the opening chapters of Romans.

Probably the correct view of Romans 2:1-16 is that it describes
God's indictment of all hypocrites regardless of race or religion,
culture or creed. Both Jews and Gentiles figure in the discussion,
the Gentile often appearing in a better light than the Jew. It
would seem too, that God's formal case against the Hebrew does
not begin until we reach the words, "Behold, thou art called a
Jew" in verse 17.

I. JUDGMENT BY THE HYPOCRITE DESCRIBED (2:1-6)

Paul has just finished the indictment of God against the gross
and flagrant sins of the openly ungodly. Now he turns his attention to "respectable" sinners who, thinking themselves better
than others, fall into the selfsame sins as those they pretend to
despise.

A. *What the Hypocrite Feels* (2:1-2)

*"Therefore thou art inexcusable, O man, whosoever thou art
that judgest; for wherein thou judgest another, thou condemnest
thyself; for thou that judgest doest the same things"* (v. 1). The
hypocrite feels that other men's sins are worse than his own. He
compares himself with the drunkard, the harlot and the hoodlum,
and prides himself on his own church membership, morality and
respectability. The comparison is, of course, very flattering to
himself. The mistake this person makes, however, is very simple
and very common. He is measuring himself alongside the wrong
standard.

When God judges men it will not be by the standards they
choose; it will be by His own. God's standard is the law, and the
law especially as explained and amplified by the Lord Jesus in

the Sermon on the Mount. Those high and holy utterances of the
Lord Jesus were lived out by Him in the crush and pressure of
daily living. If people are going to measure themselves by somebody else, then they must measure themselves alongside of Christ;
and when they do that, all grounds for hypocrisy and smugness
will be swept away.

The sin of the hypocrite is that of being *indignant* at other
people's shortcomings and of being *indulgent* of his own. David
is the classical biblical example of this. David had sinned as
deeply and as shabbily as is humanly possible. He had seduced
the wife of one of his own mighty men when the woman's husband, loyal to David almost to the point of fanaticism, was on the
front line fighting David's wars. Then he had recalled the man
from the front in a futile attempt to cover up his sin. Next he had
issued sealed orders to Joab, his commanding general, to have
Uriah slain in the heat of battle. Finally, when confirmation had
arrived from the front that the man was dead, David had married
the widow.

For some time all seemed to go well and it looked as if he had
successfully covered his sin, for the king continued to dispense
judgment in Jerusalem as if nothing had happened. Then suddenly the prophet Nathan appeared at court to demand redress of
a grievous wrong. The story he told concerned a certain poor
man who owned nothing but a cherished ewe lamb. He had been
robbed of even that by a rich neighbor who used the stolen lamb
to furnish a feast for the rich man's guest. David was indignant.
"As the LORD liveth, the man that hath done this thing shall surely
die: and he shall restore the lamb fourfold, because he did this
thing, and because he had no pity," he said (II Sam. 12:5-6).
"Thou art the man" was Nathan's conscience-smiting reply.

"For wherein thou judgest another, thou condemnest thyself."
It is all too easy to be indignant at other people's sins and indulgent of our own. This is the very essence of hypocrisy. "Hypocrite" comes from a word which means "to act a part as on a
stage." The hypocrite is a playactor. He puts on a show for the
benefit of other people but, as David found and as Paul declares,
the hypocrite does not deceive God. *"But we are sure that the
judgment of God is according to truth against them which commit such things"* (2:2).

B. *What the Hypocrite Finds* (2:3)

"And thinkest thou this, O man, that judgest them which do such things, and doest the same, that thou shalt escape the judgment of God?" The hypocrite finds that his sin has a way of finding him out; he reaps what he sows. A classic Indonesian story exposing religious hypocrisy perfectly illustrates this. It is the story of the tiger's tail.

According to this tale, an Indonesian farmer was returning to his village when he suddenly stopped on the jungle trail and stared ahead with growing alarm. Lying across his path he could see a tiger's tail and, looking carefully, he could see that the tail belonged to a very large and very fierce tiger. This tiger was waiting for him. Acting on impulse the farmer put down his scythe, ran forward and seized the tiger by the tail. With an angry snarl the tiger tried to free his tail, but the more he roared and plunged, the harder the farmer held on.

The struggle went on for a while, and then, just as the farmer felt he could hang on no longer, who should come along the path but an Indonesian holy man. The holy man stopped, surveyed the scene with interest and was about to pass on when the farmer called to him.

"Dear holy man," he cried, "please take my scythe and kill this tiger. I can't hold on to it much longer."

The holy man sighed. "My friend," he replied, "that I cannot do. I am forbidden by the rites of my religion to kill any living thing."

The farmer renewed his failing grip. "But holy man," he said, "don't you see that if you fail to kill this tiger then it will kill me. Surely the life of a man is of more value than the life of a beast!"

The holy man folded his arms in the depths of his flowing robe. "About that," he said, "I cannot speak. All around me in the jungle I see things killing and being killed. I am not responsible for these things, neither can I help them. But for me to kill . . . ah, this I cannot do."

Just then the tiger gave a vicious snarl and a furious pull on its tail. Sweat poured from the farmer. The holy man prepared to leave. "Dear holy man," sobbed the farmer in despair, "don't go! If it is against the rules of your faith to kill this beast, at least come and hold its tail while I kill him."

The holy man paused and considered. "I suppose I could do that," he conceded at last. "There can be no harm in holding the animal's tail." Cautiously he approached the infuriated beast and joined the farmer in holding on to the tail. "Do you have him, holy man?" panted the farmer. "Do you have him fast?"

"Yes, yes," said the holy man, "but hurry up before he gets loose." Leisurely the farmer brushed off his clothes. Slowly he picked up his hat and put it on. With great deliberation he picked up his scythe. Then bowing to the holy man the farmer prepared to leave.

"Here, where are you going?" demanded the suddenly alarmed holy man. "I thought you were going to kill this tiger."

The farmer paused, folded his arms in the sleeve of his coat and sighed. "Dear holy man," he replied, "you are a most excellent teacher. You have completely converted me to your most noble religion. I can see now how wrong I have been all these years. I cannot kill this tiger, for it is against the rules of our holy religion. As you have taught me, all around us in the jungle we see things killing and being killed. We are not responsible for these things, but for us holy men to kill, as you say, this cannot be. I am now going into the village yonder, so you will just have to hang on to this tiger until some coarser soul comes along not so motivated by the high ideals of our holy faith. Perhaps you will be able to convert him too, as you have converted me." And with this parting shot, the farmer left!

The story strikes a chord in our hearts. Nobody likes the hypocrite. We like to think that at last his hypocrisy will find him out. God assures us that it will. "And thinkest thou, O man, that judgest them that do such things, and doest the same, that thou shalt escape the judgment of God?"

We turn from the Indonesian legend to the Word of God and we recall the case of the elder brother in the story of the prodigal son. If ever there was a pious fraud, it was he. If ever a hypocrite betrayed himself, it was he. He was so angry that the repentant younger son had been received back fully forgiven into the bosom of the family, he refused to have any part in the celebrations. When the father came out to urge him to participate, the older brother made a speech, a speech simply oozing with self-righteousness. "Lo," he cried, "these many years do I serve thee, neither transgressed I at any time thy commandment: and yet thou never gavest me a kid, that I might make merry with my friends: but as soon as this thy son was come, which hath devoured thy living with harlots, thou hast killed for him the fatted calf" (Luke 15:29-30).

Notice the "I," the "me" and the "my" in that speech. Notice also how he refused to be identified as the penitent prodigal's brother—"this thy son," he said. Notice too how he had the far country in his own deceitful, hypocritical heart all the time. He wanted to make merry too! He wanted to kick the traces, live it up and sow his wild oats! The only difference between the two boys was that the younger brother had more courage and was no hypocrite. The younger son was guilty of sins of the flesh, but the older brother, with his pride, stubbornness, bitterness and hypocrisy, was guilty of dispositional sins, sins of the spirit. He was just as much a rebel against the father as the younger brother, and much harder to win. The indictment, "Thou doest the same things," can be written in large letters across his outwardly blameless and respectable life.

Look also at the story of the publican and Pharisee at prayer (Luke 18:9-14). (The Lord Himself declared that this parable was intended to expose those "which trusted in themselves that they were righteous, and despised others.") The publican, conscious of his deep degradation, smote his breast and cried to God for mercy with downcast eye. But the Pharisee, in a speech full of personal pronouns, proceeded to tell what an exemplary man he was. "God," said the Pharisee, "I thank thee, that I am not as other men are, extortioners, unjust, adulterers, or even as this publican. I fast twice in the week, I give tithes of all that I possess." And what did the Lord say concerning this smug sinner? "He prayed thus with himself," was His pungent comment. The man was simply a hypocrite and his hypocrisy had found him out.

C. *What the Hypocrite Forgets* (2:4)

"Or despisest thou the riches of his goodness and forbearance and longsuffering; not knowing that the goodness of God leadeth thee to repentance?"

In 597 B.C. Nebuchadnezzar, the mighty king of Babylon, besieged Jerusalem and carried away the cream of Judean nobility

into captivity. He installed a puppet king in Jerusalem and retired
from the scene. This deportation was the second of three stages
in the deportation of the Jews into exile. Back in Jerusalem, despite the warnings of Jeremiah and Ezekiel, the Jews who were
left behind began to congratulate themselves. They imagined
themselves to be heaven's favorites because they had escaped the
deportation. They failed to see that they were actually guilty of
despising the goodness, forbearance and long-suffering of God,
not knowing that the goodness of God was intended to lead them
to repentance. They actually thought they *deserved* preferential
treatment. How mistaken they were! Their persistence in their
sinful ways resulted ultimately in full and final judgment. In
586 B.C. Nebuchadnezzar came back, enraged by the duplicity of
the Jews. He sacked Jerusalem, destroyed the temple, plundered
the country, ended the monarchy and deported the greater part
of the population. Divine patience, persistently abused, leads to
certain judgment.

Think of another example, an even greater marvel of divine
patience and love. Nearly two thousand years ago Jew and Gentile joined hands at Calvary in the crucifixion of the Son of God.
It was an act which cried for the unleashing of the armies of God
and the outpouring of His wrath. Yet for nearly two thousand
years the riches of God's goodness, forbearance and long-suffering
have held up His righteous retribution. The goodness of God in
this matter should lead men to repentance, yet men hypocritically
believe that the favors of God are bestowed because, somehow,
they deserve them. Because God does not exact immediate judgment, men imagine He never will; more, they persuade themselves He has nothing to avenge, so much so that when wars and
famines do break out or personal sorrows come, they accuse and
blame God for what has happened.

This attitude is perfectly expressed by Wang Lung, the central
figure in one of Pearl Buck's popular novels. Wang Lung had
prospered after the adversities of his youth. He had wide, fertile
fields and strong, healthy sons. He was looked on by his neighbors
as a man of means. Then one day Ching, his foreman, told him
that the river was in flood. Wang feared for some of his crops and
expressed his resentment against God in bitter words. "Now," he
said, "now that old man in heaven will enjoy himself, for he will

look down and see people drowned and starving, and that is what the accursed one likes." His blasphemy frightened Ching. "But," comments Pearl Buck, "since he was rich, Wang Lung was careless; and he was as angry as he liked and he muttered as he walked homeward to think of the water swelling up over his land and over his crops."[1] The goodness of God, His forbearance and long-suffering were all despised by this farmer. Far from leading him to repentance, they left him with the feeling that he had a right to that goodness and, when it was mingled with reminders of God's sovereignty, Wang Lung blasphemed.

D. *What the Hypocrite Faces* (2:5-6)

The hypocrite faces certain judgment. *"But after thy hardness and impenitent heart treasurest up unto thyself wrath against the day of wrath and revelation of the righteous judgment of God; who will render every man according to his deeds."*

The expression "treasurest up unto thyself wrath" is striking, for it pictures the sinner storing away day by day a fresh deposit of wickedness for judgment in a coming day. The judgment of God when it finally comes will be righteous judgment. He will weigh every thought and word and deed. The sins of omission as well as the sins of commission will be considered. The effect of each sin will be considered in all its aspects—its effect on the sinner, on others and on God. As a stone cast into a pond starts the ripples flowing in ever expanding circles till the disturbance reaches the furthermost shore, so sin sets in motion events over which the sinner has no control. All this will be weighed. God will render to every man according to his deeds. Thus, when the hypocrite sets out to judge others he puts himself on very thin ice indeed. He faces the judgment of God himself.

II. JUDGMENT ON THE HYPOCRITE DESCRIBED (2:7-16)

God's judgment of the hypocrite is based on His evaluation of the hypocrite's behavior, character, works and personal worth.

A. *The Hypocrite Is Judged According to His Works* (2:7-10)

This is one of the most difficult sections in Romans, because on

---

[1]Reprinted from *The Good Earth* by Pearl S. Buck by permission of The John Day Company, Inc., publishers. Copyright © 1931, 1941 by Pearl S. Buck; copyright renewed 1958 by Pearl S. Buck.

the surface it seems to teach that salvation is by works; that eternal life can be earned by patient continuing in well-doing. Such an idea, however, is foreign to the whole tenor of Scripture. To resolve the difficulty we must bear in mind that this passage has to do with God's basis of *judgment*. In the Bible judgment is according to our works; salvation is by faith. Seeking for glory, honor, incorruption and eternal life in well-doing is the outcome of faith, the evidence—not the ground—of salvation. At this point in the epistle Paul is not discussing how a person is saved and receives eternal life. That comes later. Here he is showing that Jew and Gentile are on the same ground before God in the matter of sin.

When judging a person "according to his deeds" (v. 6), God first weighs (1) *the reasons for a person's behavior*. *"To them who by patient continuance in well doing seek for glory and honour and immortality, eternal life: but unto them that are contentious, and do not obey the truth, but obey unrighteousness, indignation and wrath"* (2:7-8).

Then God weighs (2) *the results of a person's behavior*. *"Tribulation and anguish, upon every soul of man that doeth evil, of the Jew first, and also of the Gentile; but glory, honour, and peace, to every man that worketh good, to the Jew first, and also to the Gentile"* (2:9-10). The expression "to the Jew first, and also to the Gentile" highlights the fact that increased light brings increased responsibility. The hypocrite's portion will be worse than the heathen's for the simple reason his opportunities have been so much greater.

B. *The Hypocrite Is Judged According to His Worth* (2:11-16)

We must observe (1) *how discriminating God's judgment is*. First, God weighs a person's *advantages*. *"For there is no respect of persons with God. For as many as have sinned without law shall also perish without law: and as many as have sinned in the law shall be judged by the law"* (vv. 11-12). Those who have the law have much more light than those without it, says Paul. The possession of an open Bible greatly increases our ability to know God's will. But light is light regardless of how dim or how bright it might happen to be. If a person were lost in a dark forest at night, the least glimmer would attract him; and if he desired

deliverance from the darkness, he would move toward the light
and hail it with joy. However, if he had some guilt to hide, he
would not respond to the light, except to hide or flee from it, regardless of its dimness or brilliance. Doom awaits all who reject
the light; but for those who have had a greater advantage, there
is less excuse and consequently greater guilt.

God also weighs a person's *attitude*. *"For not the hearers of the
law are just before God, but the doers of the law shall be justified.
For when the Gentiles, which have not the law, do by nature the
things contained in the law, these, having not the law, are a law
unto themselves: which shew the work of the law written in their
hearts, their conscience also bearing witness, and their thoughts
the mean while accusing or else excusing one another"* (vv. 13-
15).

The law which the Gentiles had was not in *code* but in *conscience*. True, they did not have the specific injunctions codified
and spelled out in precept after precept as did the Jew in the law
of Moses. But they did have the basic moral concepts which
underlie that law, for God's general laws have been handed down
from antiquity. Indeed, they are written into the innate con-
sciousness of the soul and to them conscience bears witness.

Now, conscience is intended to be a *goad*, not a *guide*. The
man who says, "Just let your conscience be your guide," is mis-
taking the function of conscience. Conscience is God's watchdog
in the soul. Conscience can be silenced and even seared. It is
quite possible to obtain the approval of conscience on a wrong
act.[2]

Dickens, that shrewd critic of human character, has a great
passage on conscience. Mrs. Quilp has just been an unwilling
partner in one of her odious husband's schemes. Says Dickens,
"Mrs. Quilp, who was afflicted beyond measure by the recollection
of the part she had just acted, shut herself in her chamber, and
smothering her head in the bedclothes bemoaned her fault more
bitterly than many less tenderhearted persons would have

---

[2]Scripture has much to say about conscience. It speaks of a *good* conscience (I Tim. 1:5, 19; etc.), a *weak* conscience (I Cor. 8:12), a *convicting* conscience (John 8:9), a *defiled* conscience (Titus 1:15), and a
seared conscience (I Tim. 4:2). Study the conscience of Herod. First he
had a *striving* conscience, for he listened readily to John. Next he had a
silenced conscience—he shut John up in prison. Finally he had a *seared*
conscience; he murdered John and mocked at Jesus.

mourned a much greater offence; for, in the majority of cases, conscience is an elastic and very flexible article, which will bear a deal of stretching and adapt itself to a great variety of circumstances. Some people, by prudent management and leaving it off piece by piece like a flannel waistcoat in warm weather, even contrive, in time, to dispense with it altogether; but there be others who can assume the garment and throw it off at pleasure; and this, being the greatest and most convenient improvement, is the one most in vogue."[3]

It is said that when John Huss was burned at the stake, a poor widow came along bearing a faggot of wood. She requested the officials to put the faggot on the pile as close as possible to the martyr. She was a stranger to him, so John Huss asked the woman what he had ever done to her or hers that she should hate him so much. She said that John Huss had never personally injured her. Moreover, although wood was scarce and expensive and she was very poor, she had pinched and saved to buy that faggot for a purpose. He was a heretic, she said, and it was a good work to give a faggot to have him burned. Conscience said to John Huss, "Give your body to be burned." Conscience said to the widow, "Give your faggot to burn him."

So conscience is not a guide but a goad. It must be educated and monitored by the Word of God. In the work of conviction, the Holy Spirit seizes upon conscience and brings God's Word to bear upon it with mighty power. Apart from God's Word, conscience is a very uncertain faculty of the soul. While the ancient pagan would put his children into the red hot lap of Molech with the hearty endorsement of conscience, the strict Buddhist would have agonies of remorse over killing a fly. The one extreme is as wrong as the other.

Conscience is the mental faculty by which man judges his actions and passes sentence thereon. It bears witness to the fact that man lives in a moral universe and is ultimately answerable to God. Those who have the Word of God to guide their conscience are a great deal more culpable than those who, not having the advantage of a Bible to reveal to them God's will, nevertheless behave in a moral and righteous manner. So then, God's judg-

[3]Charles Dickens, *The Old Curiosity Shop* (New York: George Routledge and Sons, n.d.), p. 54.

ment is *discriminating*, taking into account a person's advantages and attitudes. All this increases the guilt of the hypocrite.

In conclusion, observe (2) *how devastating God's judgment is*. Paul speaks of the coming day *"when God shall judge the secrets of men by Jesus Christ according to my gospel"* (v. 16). The secrets of men! What a fearful day that will be when God begins to call to light the hidden works of darkness. All men have guilty secrets, things they have done which they ought not to have done, and things they have left undone which they ought to have done. They have not been overlooked nor forgotten by God. One day the hypocrite's secrets will all be exposed and he will be shown up for what he really is.

THE GUILT OF THE HEBREW
2:17—3:8

I. RELIGIOUS ORTHODOXY EXAMINED (2:17-24)
  A. A Person's Access to the Truth (2:17-20)
    1. Being Confirmed in the Truth (2:17-18)
    2. Being Confident of the Truth (2:19-20)
  B. A Person's Accountability to the Truth (2:21-24)
    1. Spiritual Insincerity Exposed (2:21*a*)
    2. Spiritual Insensitivity Exposed (2:21*b*-22)
    3. Spiritual Insolvency Exposed (2:23-24)

II. RELIGIOUS ORDINANCES EXAMINED (2:25-29)
  A. The Limited Value of Rituals (2:25-27)
    1. The Law That God Has Given (2:25)
    2. The Light That a Person Has (2:26-27)
      a. A man devoid of rituals may be more righteous than the man devoted to them (2:26)
      b. A man devoted to rituals may be more responsible than the man devoid of them (2:27)
  B. The Limitless Value of Reality (2:28-29)
    1. In Outward Appearance (2:28)
    2. In Inward Approval (2:29)

III. RELIGIOUS OBJECTIONS EXAMINED (3:1-8)
  A. Those Who Argued That Right Was Wrong (3:1-2)
  B. Those Who Argued That Wrong Was Right (3:3-8)

THE HEATHEN IS A MAN with a perverted religion; the hypocrite is a man with a pretended religion; the Hebrew represents the man with a powerless religion. Although in Romans 2:17—3:8 it is the Hebrew particularly who is on trial, his case is, nevertheless, a test case for any religious person. The Hebrew sets before us the man who is zealous for revealed religion but who is a stranger to Christ. Christendom is full of people like this who really stand convicted on the same count as their Hebrew counterparts.

Probably the religious person is the hardest to reach with the gospel. There is nobody too bad for Jesus Christ to save, but there are millions who think themselves too good. It is with this class of people that God is concerned in this section of Romans. The orthodoxy, ordinances and objections of religious people, as epitomized in the Jew, are now examined.

I. RELIGIOUS ORTHODOXY EXAMINED (2:17-24)

Few people were more orthodox than young Saul of Tarsus. "After the most straitest sect of our religion I lived a Pharisee" was his own testimony to King Agrippa (Acts 26:5). Paul knew all about religious orthodoxy and how it can make a sincere and zealous person the very enemy of Jesus Christ. "I verily thought with myself, that I ought to do many things contrary to the name of Jesus of Nazareth," he said (Acts 26:9). Paul was not indicting the Jew because he was anti-Semitic. He was a Jew himself, but a Jew wide awake to the perils and pitfalls of religion, even revealed biblical religion, when it is divorced from the person and work of the Lord Jesus.

Orthodoxy in religion presupposes two basic requirements— access to the truth and accountability to the truth. To have access to an open Bible greatly increases a person's responsibility in the sight of God.

A. *Access to the Truth* (2:17-20)

Paul's first step is to show that the Jew not only had ready access to the truth, he was (1) *confirmed* in that truth. "*Behold, thou art called a Jew, and restest in the law, and makest thy boast of God, and knowest his will, and approvest the things that are more excellent, being instructed out of the law*" (2:17-18).

There were two advantages which accrued to the Jew according to these verses. First, he had the advantage of a Hebrew *birth*. From a child he was taught in the synagogue; was made to revere and keep the Sabbath; was made aware of his need of a sacrifice; and was indoctrinated in the truth of separation. These were no trivial advantages in a day and age when most men were pagans and steeped in superstition and idolatry. When all others groped in darkness, the Jew could lean back upon the law. So he not only had the advantage of a Hebrew birth, he also had the advantage of a Hebrew *Bible*. Moreover, he was an expert in making fine hairline distinctions over trivialities connected with the truth of God which had been revealed to him.

The Jew, moreover, was (2) *confident* of that truth. *"And art confident that thou thyself art a guide of the blind, a light of them which are in darkness, an instructor of the foolish, a teacher of babes, which hast the form of knowledge and of the truth in the law"* (2:19-20).

In other words, the Jew set himself up as a teacher of others and did so with contemptuous pride and with deep scorn for the ignorance of others not so fortunate as himself. The word for "foolish" in this passage is literally "stupid." The Jew looked with infinite disdain upon his Gentile neighbors for their abysmal ignorance of even the first principles of matters made so clear to the most illiterate Hebrew in the law of God.

Thus the first point in Paul's indictment has to do with the Jews' access to the truth, an access so sadly advertised in Paul's day by the snobbish Jewish attitude toward the Gentiles.

It is a solemn thing to have access to the truth, to have been born into a family where the things of God are common knowledge and where the Bible is a well-read book. Such privileges are weighted with awesome responsibilities, and woe betide the person who takes them for granted. To have been raised in circumstances of spiritual privilege and to become a religious prig exposes a person to the searing condemnation of Romans 2.

B. *Accountability to the Truth* (2:21-24)

Paul next begins to cross-examine the Jew in order to underline the condemnation which goes with a mere head knowledge of truth divorced from a life of obedience to God. A religious experience which is all talk and no walk will not stand the test of the day of judgment.

There is, for example, the matter of (1) *spiritual insincerity.* *"Thou therefore which teachest another, teachest thou not thyself?"* (2:21). This is a common enough fault in religious circles and one into which it is easy to fall. Since true teaching has as its goal the changing of behavior, the teacher must apply his precepts to himself before applying them to others. Isaiah is a good example. This great evangelical prophet poured out his vials of judgment on *others* in chapter 5 of his book. "Woe unto them that join house to house . . . woe unto them that rise up early in the morning, that they may follow strong drink . . . woe unto them that call evil good, and good evil . . . woe unto them that are wise in their own eyes. . . ." Six times he spoke thus, but in chapter 6 he finds himself in the presence of a thrice-holy God and he cries, "Woe is *me!*" He was a wise man; he taught himself. When he saw things in their true perspective, he did not hesitate to make the application to himself. It is the height of spiritual insincerity to teach others and not to learn the lesson for oneself.

Then there was the matter of (2) *spiritual insensitivity.* *"Thou that preachest a man should not steal, dost thou steal? Thou that sayest a man should not commit adultery, dost thou commit adultery? Thou that abhorrest idols, dost thou commit sacrilege?"* (2:21-22).

A certain itinerant preacher was well known in the circles in which he ministered for the hardness of his message and the harshness of his delivery. He invariably thundered away at sin, and hell-fire was never long out of his preaching. For many years he continued in this vein, until one Sunday morning he received the shock of his life. Years before, his preaching career had taken him to a remote city where he had fallen into sin and committed adultery with an unsaved woman. When he walked into the service that Sunday morning, far from the scene of his sin, who should be there but this very woman, recently saved. Her shock was almost as great as his when she discovered that he was a preacher, and she confronted him publicly with his guilt. His harsh and bitter preaching over the years had been nothing but a cloak for a guilty conscience. He had preached to others but had remained spiritually insensitive himself, and now his sin had found him out.

Paul points out in these verses that ethically, morally, and spiritually the Jew was guilty of just such behavior. He preached the high and holy standards of the law but was not concerned that his own life was a living lie.

There was also the matter of (3) *spiritual insolvency.* *"Thou that makest thy boast of the law, through breaking the law dishonourest thou God? For the name of God is blasphemed among the Gentiles through you, as it is written"* (2:23-24). Far from being an asset, the Jew's access to the truth was a liability for which he was terribly accountable at the bar of God; for there is nothing that will turn strangers away from the truth faster than misbehavior on the part of a professed believer.

When Abraham denied his wife in Egypt and Sarai was taken into Pharaoh's harem, Abraham ceased to be a source of blessing to the Egyptians and became instead a source of cursing and plague. Eventually Pharaoh discovered the source of his troubles and demanded an accounting from Abraham. "What is this that thou hast done unto me? Why didst thou not tell me that she was thy wife? Why saidst thou, She is my sister?" To none of these indignant questions did the embarrassed Abraham have a reply. Humanly speaking, his testimony for Jehovah was finished so far as Pharaoh was concerned. The full story is in Genesis 12:10-20.

When David sinned with Bathsheba, a similar situation arose. Nathan the prophet, having wrung David's conscience with his masterly parable and its application, charged home to him the full implications of David's guilt in the unforgettable words, "Thou hast given great occasion to the enemies of the Lord to blaspheme" (II Sam. 12:14). It is a remarkable fact, too, that to this day David is held up deridingly by unbelievers as an example of "a man after God's own heart." Probably Paul had this example of David in mind when he added "as it is written" after his statement concerning the behavior of the Jews making the Gentiles blaspheme.

So then, mere orthodoxy in religion does not make one more acceptable with God. Nor does it impress men either, for they look for reality in religion and quickly detect a mere pious pose. A person's access to the truth increases his accountability to the truth. For as Paul has just finished reminding the hypocrite, "Not the hearers of the law are just before God, but the doers of the law shall be justified" (v. 13).

II. RELIGIOUS ORDINANCES EXAMINED (2:25-29)

The religious person usually feels that he has a special standing before God not only because he is orthodox in his intellectual assent to the truth but also because he is scrupulous in keeping the ordinances, the rites, and the rituals of his religion. Paul now shows that mere rituals give no preference with God.

Paul is not concerned here with the endless rituals of the countless religions of the world. Obviously they have no value, not being authorized by the Word of God. He is concerned with the ordinances required in Old Testament times under the ceremonial section of Israel's divinely inspired legal code. Particularly is he concerned with the distinctive rite of the Jew, circumcision, the outward seal of the Abrahamic covenant, an ordinance administered to every Jewish male in infancy. Like so many in Christendom today who imagine themselves members of the church of Christ and heirs of heaven because of baptism in infancy, the Jew thought that his circumcision gave him special status with God. It is this idea that a mere religious ordinance can profit the soul apart from a vital, personal, spiritual experience which Paul next condemns. He contrasts the limited value of rituals in religious matters with the limitless value of reality.

A. *The Limited Value of Rituals* (2:25-27)

The value of any divinely authorized ritual is directly related to (1) *the law that God has given. "For circumcision verily profiteth, if thou keep the law: but if thou be a breaker of the law, thy circumcision is made uncircumcision"* (v. 25). In other words, a rite or ritual is meaningful only insofar as it is the outward expression of an inward experience. No outward ceremonial act can have any value if it is not related in some way to a dynamic, personal, scriptural spiritual experience.

And there's the rub! For circumcision to be of any practical value, the Jew must keep the law of God—something humanly impossible, and to break the law is to render the ritual null and void.

The value of a divinely authorized ritual is related not only to the law that God has given, but also to (2) *the light that a person has*. A man devoid of rituals may be more righteous than a man devoted to them, and a man devoted to rituals may be more responsible in the sight of God than a man devoid of them. *"Therefore if the uncircumcision keep the righteousness of the law, shall not his uncircumcision be counted for circumcision? And shall not uncircumcision which is by nature, if it fulfil the law, judge thee, who by the letter and circumcision dost transgress the law?"* (vv. 26-27). Paul's argument here is simply, that if a religious person flouts the clear teaching of the Word of God, in effect he cancels everything for which the divinely given ritual stands. On the other hand, a person who has never received an outward ceremonial confirmation of his faith, but whose heart is right with God, is really enjoying all that for which the ritual stands.

Paul is not saying that a divinely appointed ritual is without value. He is saying that the value is limited by the condition of a person's heart. There is never anything mechanical, automatic, or superficial about a person's relationship with God, nor can a mere ceremony make up what is deficient in a person's life. Perhaps a simple illustration will help make this clear. At the age of thirteen, Hebrew boys go through a ceremony known as bar mitzvah. For when a boy reaches his thirteenth birthday, he is believed to have attained the age of responsibility and religious duty. But performing the ceremony of bar mitzvah does not make a man out of a boy. There is far more to manhood than that. Nor does performing a ceremony make a person a Christian; there is far more to it than that.

B. *The Limitless Value of Reality* (2:28-29)

"For he is not a Jew, which is one outwardly; neither is that circumcision, which is outward in the flesh: but he is a Jew, which is one inwardly; and circumcision is that of the heart, in the spirit, and not in the letter; whose praise is not of men, but of God." This was no new idea with Paul. The truth that the mere rite of circumcision did not make a man a Jew was as old as the law and the prophets (see Deut. 10:16; Ezek. 44:9). We are far too prone to be satisfied with trying to keep the letter of

the law and to ignore its deep spiritual implications. But God looks on the heart—a lesson even godly Samuel had to learn. When Samuel was sent to find a king for Israel among the sons of Jesse, he was greatly impressed by Eliab, the tall and striking eldest son. "But," we read, "the LORD said unto Samuel, Look not on his countenance, or on the height of his stature; because I have refused him: for the LORD seeth not as man seeth; for man looketh on the outward appearance, but the LORD looketh on the heart" (I Sam. 16:7). It was not until David came (whom both Saul and Goliath later discounted as a mere youth) that God said to Samuel, "Arise, anoint him: for this is he" (I Sam. 16:12; 17:33, 42, 56). The kingly qualities of David were inward, not outward.

So then, Paul indicts the Hebrew on the second count, that of putting his trust in a ritual rather than in the reality of a true experience with God. Now, nobody can attack a religious person's orthodoxy and rituals without having to face a storm of protest. So Paul next looks at typical objections raised by religious people and shows how shallow and superficial they are.

III. RELIGIOUS OBJECTIONS EXAMINED (3:1-8)

The arguments raised by the Jews in this section were just so many red herrings drawn across the path to confuse the issue. It is amazing how adept people are at this sort of thing when it comes to a question of their relationship with God. Take, for example, the woman at the well. When she felt that the truth was coming uncomfortably close to home, she raised the irrelevant issue as to which of two places was the more favored by God as a place where He should be worshiped (John 4:20). She did not mind the discussion centering on the general topic of "religion" so long as the searchlight did not come near her own soul.

It is quite clear that the religious objections raised by the Jews, and introduced here by Paul in anticipation, were shallow and superficial in the extreme.

A. *Those Who Argued That Right Was Wrong* (3:1-2)

"*What advantage then hath the Jew? or what profit is there of circumcision?*" These people were maintaining that the devastating truths marshaled by Paul were all wrong. They were wrong,

they thought, because they undermined the privileges and prerogatives which belonged to the Jew. Paul soon dealt the death-
blow to this idea. *"What advantage hath the Jew? . . . Much
every way: chiefly, because that unto them were committed the
oracles of God"* (vv. 1-2). The greatest advantage of a Jewish
birth was the exposure it gave to the Word of God from earliest
infancy.

B. *Those Who Argued That Wrong Was Right* (3:3-8)

There were two absolutely wrong positions taken in response
to Paul's simple rebuttal of the first question. The first of these
false positions was to argue that (1) *unbelief actually enhances
God's faithfulness* and should therefore be encouraged! *"For
what if some did not believe? shall their unbelief make the faith
of God without effect?"* (v. 3). Beck's translation is clearer:
"What if some were unfaithful? Will their unfaithfulness make
God unfaithful?"[1] Paul's answer was manifestly to the point:
*"God forbid: yea, let God be true, but every man a liar; as it is
written, That thou mightest be justified in thy sayings, and mightest overcome when thou art judged"* (v. 4). Paul replied that
God is never unfaithful, never goes back on His Word, and
quoted from Psalm 51, David's great penitential psalm, to ham-
mer home still further convicting truth. The psalm shows that
David was willing to condemn himself utterly so that God might
be seen to be righteous in His judgment of him; and the quotation proves Paul's point that although God had given His promises to Israel, those promises did not mean that the unrepentant
Jew could escape doom.

The second of the false positions repudiated by Paul was that
of claiming that (2) *unrighteousness actually enhances God's
forgiveness* and therefore it is commendable to sin! God ought
not to find fault with the Jew for his sin because that sin helps
magnify His own character. *"But if our wrong shows how right
God is, what'll we say? Is God wrong (I'm talking like a man)
when He's angry and He punishes"* (Beck, v. 5).[2] Once again
Paul replied with a resounding *"God forbid!"* (1:6). God is both
just and righteous, something woven into the warp and woof of

[1]William F. Beck, *The New Testament in the Language of Today* (St.
Louis: Concordia Publishing House, 1963).
[2]*Ibid.*

His Word. Since that is so, it is obviously a false assumption that man's sin enhances God's righteousness.

Paul's enemies were actually spreading the lie that Paul preached this very thing and encouraged sin as a means of enhancing God's glory. Paul indignantly denied any such false teaching and showed that his detractors by spreading this slander stood condemned in their very condemnation of him (vv. 7-8).

Thus Paul concludes his case against the Jew. God pays no attention to the Jewish claim to be exempt from judgment on the grounds that he is a Jew. Religion in itself cannot exempt anyone from the judgment of God. Jew and Gentile, religious and irreligious alike, all stand before God, exposed to His wrath on the ground that they are sinners.

THE GUILT OF ALL HUMANITY
3:9-20

I. THE CATHOLICITY OF HUMAN SIN (3:9-12)

    A. The Racial Aspect (3:9)

    B. The Religious Aspect (3:10-12)

        1. Men Are Unrighteous (3:10)

        2. Men Are Unreasonable (3:11a)

        3. Men Are Unresponsive (3:11b)

        4. Men Are Unrepentant (3:12)

II. THE CRIMINALITY OF HUMAN SIN (3:13-18)

    A. Man's Wicked Words (3:13-14)

        1. Are Like the Vileness of the Sepulcher (3:13)

        2. Are Like the Venom of the Serpent (3:13-14)

    B. Man's Wicked Ways (3:15-18)

        1. Murder (3:15)

        2. Misery (3:16-17)

        3. Mutiny (3:18)

III. THE CULPABILITY OF HUMAN SIN (3:19-20)

    A. The Law Shows Man's Condition Is Helpless (3:19)

        1. He Is Convicted

        2. He Is Condemned

    B. The Law Shows Man's Case Is Hopeless (3:20)

The place has come in the epistle for the summation of God's case against the human race. The heathen, hypocrite, and Hebrew have each in turn been arraigned and found guilty. Now humanity at large is summoned to the bar of God to hear His indictment against mankind.

I. The Catholicity of Human Sin (3:9-12)

Note the constant repetition of the words "none" and "no not one" in this section. Not a single member of Adam's ruined race is excepted; the indictment is sweeping, comprehensive, and all-inclusive. Paul begins by reviewing both the racial and religious aspects of human sin.

A. *The Racial Aspect* (3:9)

"What then? are we better than they? No, in no wise: for we have before proved both Jews and Gentiles, that they are all under sin." All men are on the same footing before God when it comes to a matter of sin. Jew and Gentile, Oriental and Occidental, red and yellow, black or white—there is no difference. All men are sinners in the sight of God.

B. *The Religious Aspect* (3:10-12)

There follows a detailed, step-by-step enumeration of the items in the indictment, each one being actually a quotation from the Old Testament. Paul shows first that in their relationship to God (1) *men are unrighteous* and supports the charge by quoting Psalm 14:3: *"As it is written, There is none righteous, no, not one"* (3:10). Man is incapable by nature of doing that which is right in the sight of God.

One of the most graphic and terrible illustrations of this comes from the days of the judges, days which were black with apostasy and foul with glaring immorality. Yet twice in the book of Judges we read, "Every man did that which was right in his own eyes" (Judges 17:6; 21:25)—did that which was *right*, mark you, not that which was wrong. Every man doing that which was right in his own eyes produced one of the darkest eras in Israel's history.

Many people think their behavior is right—and so it may be according to human standards. But God does not try men by

human standards; He tries them by His own standards of absolute
perfection. A self-righteous man once boasted to a Christian
friend of his, "You know, John, I'm not such a bad fellow. There
are many worse than I!" His friend replied, "Ivor, you are measuring yourself by the wrong standard. You measure yourself by
the harlots and drunkards you see on Skid Row and you feel
quite satisfied by comparison. But go and measure yourself
alongside Jesus Christ and see how you make out." No person's
life cuts much of a figure when placed alongside the peerless and
perfect life of Christ. The life of the Lord Jesus simply shows us
how crooked and defiled our own lives really are. It is no wonder
God says, "There is none righteous, no, not one."

Next, Paul shows that in their relationship to God (2) *men
are unreasonable. "There is none that understandeth"* (3:11a).
Writing to the Corinthians, Paul said, "The natural man receiveth
not the things of the Spirit of God: for they are foolishness unto
him: neither can he know them, because they are spiritually dis-
cerned" (I Cor. 2:14). The same truth appears in Colossians
where Paul declares that men in their natural state are alienated
from God and enemies in their mind (Col. 1:21).

Man's power to think lifts him above the beasts of the field.
In this age of scientific enlightenment and advanced technology,
we have every evidence that man has a brilliant intellect. Yet
at the same time it is strangely clouded to spiritual realities; for
despite his genius in so many realms, man betrays a most remarkable denseness when it comes to the things of God. He has no
natural understanding in this realm at all. His mind, incisive
in so many ways, is warped and twisted when it comes to eternal
and spiritual issues. The damage wrought by sin runs deep into
the very roots of the thinking processes of man. His imaginations
are often filthy; his memories often betray him; his deductions are
often false; and his conclusions are often wrong.

On the things that matter most, man is blind. For example, the
things that a person will believe in the name of religion are
astounding. One person will tell you, "It doesn't matter what
you believe so long as you're sincere"—a philosophy he would
not tolerate for a moment in a professor of mathematics teaching
him arithmetic or calculus. Another will tell you, "I'm going to
turn over a new leaf" blithely forgetting that "God requireth that

which is past" (Eccles. 3:15). Nor if he were a businessman would he accept such a philosophy from one of his debtors. Imagine his reaction on opening his mail one morning if he were to find a letter from a man who owed him five thousand dollars which read like this: "Dear Sir: I realize that I owe you five thousand dollars, but today I have turned over a new leaf in my ledger and intend from now on to pay my debts and live up to the highest standards of business integrity. Any obligations incurred from now on will be met in full. I am ignoring the past. Sincerely——" Yet the same man who would be astounded to receive a letter like that uses exactly this philosophy in matters of the soul.

"There is none that understandeth." Man is unreasonable in his attitude to God. Man does not understand how abhorrent his sin is to God. He does not understand how holy God is; nor what is involved in the alternatives of heaven or hell which lie ahead; nor at what cost God has provided the very salvation he ignores. If men understood these things they would be in a hurry to be saved. Indeed, this is exactly what happens when a man's eyes at last are opened by the convicting work of the Holy Spirit.

Then Paul shows that in their relationship to God (3) *men are unresponsive. "There is none that seeketh after God"* (3:11b). The question naturally arises, How can this be possible in view of the fact that pagan lands are filled with temples and worshipers? The Bible gives the answer: "The things which the Gentiles sacrifice, they sacrifice to demons, and not to God" (I Cor. 10:20). Paul has already shown in his indictment of the Gentiles that the Gentile world has deliberately turned its back upon the truth of God and has gone off into infidelity and idolatry. Behind the world's false beliefs is the "god of this world" (II Cor. 4:3-4), the devil. We have the Lord's own word for it, that religion apart from regeneration is vain. He said, "No man can come to me, except the Father draw him" (John 6:44).

Wuest points out that the word for "seeketh" here is *ekzēteō*, which he defines as " 'to seek out, search for' and (which) speaks of a determined search after something."[1] Most people are not that independent but tend to accept their religious convictions ready-made. Some people, it is true, shop around from one reli-

[1]Kenneth S. Wuest, *Romans in the Greek New Testament* (Grand Rapids: Wm. B. Eerdmans Publishing Co., 1955), p. 55. Used by permission.

'gious system to another until they find something that better suits their religious tastes, but apart from the drawing and convicting work of the Holy Spirit they end up in just another brand of delusion.

God says, "And ye shall seek me, and find me, when ye shall search for me with all your heart" (Jer. 29:13), something which cannot be done apart from the work of the Holy Spirit in the soul. Praise God, He has taken the initiative! Jesus said, "The Son of man is come to seek and to save that which was lost" (Luke 19:10). It is significant that the Bible likens men to lost sheep, for a sheep is an animal which is not smart, swift nor strong, and which has no power or inclination to seek its shepherd when once it has strayed. Man is so unresponsive to God that *all* the initiative in salvation has to be on God's side. And how much He has done! He has given His *Son;* He has given the *Scriptures;* and He has given the *Spirit,* and most men still will not respond. It can be truly said of the natural man, "There is none that seeketh after God."

Next, Paul shows that (4) *men are unrepentant.* "*They are all gone out of the way, they are together become unprofitable; there is none that doeth good, no, not one*" (3:12). These words rip apart all man's imagined goodness. The frequently used assertion, "I am doing the best I can," is simply not true. No man has ever done his best; there has never been a time when a good deed might not have been improved with a little more effort or concern. People who make this claim are condemned by their own religion.

God's assessment of man is that his life is "unprofitable." His good deeds do not outweigh his bad deeds; his religious assets are all consumed by the guilt of sin. Paul himself once boasted in his religious "gains" until God showed him how utterly worthless were all the things in which he was trusting. Then he was glad enough to cast them all aside in favor of Christ. "But what things were gain to me, those I counted loss for Christ" (see Phil. 3:4-9).

Remember too that throughout this indictment concerning man's unrighteousness, unreasonableness, unresponsiveness and unrepentantness, the entire human race is arraigned. Every human being is included in this exposure of the catholicity of human sin.

II. THE CRIMINALITY OF HUMAN SIN (3:13-18)

Not only are all men guilty before God, but they are deeply guilty. Paul proves this by drawing attention to the things men both say and do.

A. *Man's Wicked Words* (3:13-14)

Paul is still quoting from the Old Testament and piling up the evidence. He points out that man's speech is characterized by (1) *the vileness of the sepulcher—"Their throat is an open sepulchre"* (v. 13*a*). What an expressive way of depicting the corruption of so much of human speech! The offensive stench exhaling from an open sepulcher is due not to the grave itself but to the rottenness within. Just so, the unclean, unkind, untrue utterances of man betray a defiled, despiteful and deceitful heart.

Then Paul points out that men's speech is characterized by (2) *the venom of the serpent—"with their tongues they have used deceit; the poison of asps is under their lips: whose mouth is full of cursing and bitterness"* (vv. 13*b*-14). Newell points out that "the fangs of a deadly serpent lie, ordinarily, folded back in its upper jaw; but when it throws up its head to strike, those hollow fangs drop down, and when the serpent bites, the fangs press a sack of deadly poison hidden 'under its lips' at the root, thus injecting the venom into the wound. You and I were born with moral poison sacks like this."[2] We strike at one another with venomous words.

Foul speech is not only an offense against man, it is an offense against God. The Lord Jesus warned that "every idle word that men shall speak, they shall give account thereof in the day of judgment" (Matt. 12:36). The average articulate person uses thousands of words a day. These daily words would comprise a fair sized volume and enough volumes in a lifetime to fill a college library. Each of these volumes represents the thoughts of the speaker in his own words, and every word is open to the inspection and judgment of God. Moreover, not one of the words can be recalled nor one of the volumes withdrawn. Paul points out here that man's wicked words form an important part of God's indictment of each one of us.

[2]William R. Newell, *Romans Verse by Verse* (Chicago: Grace Publications. Copyright by William R. Newell, 1938), p. 83.

B. *Man's Wicked Ways* (3:15-18)

It is not only what we say that exposes us to judgment, it is also what we do. First, God points to (1) *murder* as a characteristic of human behavior. *"Their feet are swift to shed blood"* (v. 15). It is significant that the first recorded sin outside of Eden was murder (Gen. 4:8). Sin leaped full grown into human experience. Man's first sin separated man from God; his second sin separated man from man. Cain's religion which was too refined to slay a lamb was not too refined to murder Abel. Paul says that men are *swift* to shed blood. J. Edgar Hoover reminds us that, even in a country like the United States, there is a murder every forty minutes.

God's indictment is not exaggerated nor outdated, as recent history proves. At the close of the second World War, the Nazi war criminals were brought to justice at Nuremberg and were indicted on four counts. Count three—war crimes—included prosecution for the murder and ill-treatment of civilian populations and prisoners of war, the deportation of populations for slave labor and the killing of hostages. Count four—crimes against humanity—included prosecution for murder, extermination, enslavement, persecution on political and racial grounds.

Justice Jackson, in opening the case for the prosecution, described the rise of the party to power and then went on to tell of the crimes against the Jews. "The most savage and numerous crimes were planned and committed by the Nazis. . . . The ghetto was a laboratory for testing repressive measures. . . . Extermination of the Jews enabled the Nazis to bring a practiced hand to similar measures against Poles, Serbs, and Greeks." Sixty percent of the Jews in Nazi-dominated Europe were murdered— or about 5.7 million Jews. "History," he said, "does not record a crime perpetrated against so many victims or ever carried out with such calculated cruelty." He described the sadistic cruelty, torture, starvation and mass murder in concentration camps, and the "scientific" experiments of the most brutal and depraved nature made in the name of medicine.

During the trial films were shown visualizing acres of corpses, the torture instruments, mutilated bodies, guillotines and baskets of heads; bodies hanging from lampposts; women weeping over their dead; mass burial services; raped and murdered women;

children with heads bashed in; the crematoria and gas chambers; the piles of clothes; the bales of women's hair.

At the end of the trial, Sir Hartley Shawcross summed up for the British delegation. He spoke eloquently of the crimes committed by the defendants, crimes so frightful that the imagination staggers at their contemplation. He spoke of the great cities which had been reduced to rubble, of the millions who had been left homeless and maimed and bereaved and of the hunger and disease which stalked the world as a result of the war. He described the revival of slavery by the Nazis and told of its callousness and brutality and how women and children had been taken from their homes to be treated worse than beasts, to be starved, beaten and murdered. Describing the horrors of the extermination of the Jews, Sir Hartley Shawcross told of the cynical melting down of gold teeth into ingots for the Reichbank, of the baling of human hair for commercial purposes and of the flaying of tatooed human flesh for lampshades. "Mass murder," he said, "was becoming a state industry with by-products."[3] It must be remembered that these crimes were committed or condoned by one of the most enlightened, cultured, and advanced nations of Europe.

It is easy to be complacent and smug, to shift the blame and say, "I've never done anything like that!" That's not the point. The human heart is heir to every imaginable crime. The Lord Jesus traced adultery to the lustful look, murder to the angry thought (Matt. 5:21-22, 27-28). And where the root is, it is only God's restraining grace which prevents the full harvest of the fruit.

Next, God points to (2) *misery* as characteristic of man's wicked ways. *"Destruction and misery are in their ways: and the way of peace have they not known"* (vv. 16-17). At the Nuremberg trials, the peoples of the world united to say, "Never again!" But with what result? None whatsoever!

Today, for example, the People's Republic of China operates the most extensive and merciless slave labor system the world has even seen, utterly dwarfing the efforts of the Nazis and comparable only to that of the Soviet Union. Communist China is one

---

[3]For an interesting discussion of the Nuremberg trials, see the book *Nuremberg Diary* by G. M. Gilbert, one of the prison psychologists.

vast prison. "Reform through labor" camps are nationwide and are operated on the same style as the slave camps which supplied the forced labor for such monuments to tyranny as the pyramids of Egypt and the Great Wall of China.

In China, terror is a recognized policy of state. Families are broken up systematically as little children are taught in school to spy on their parents, other relatives and friends. Children are given a course on "Investigation and Research" (in plain language —spying) and are given specific assignments. Despite terrible conditions in mainland China, Mao Tse-tung cherishes vast schemes for ultimate aggression against mankind. He is reported as being prepared to precipitate, under certain conditions, a nuclear war which would "sacrifice the lives of 300 million mainland people and wipe out half the people of the world" so as to "establish Socialism on the debris of death." Since China is now a world nuclear power with a growing arsenal of missiles, this horrible threat becomes an increasing possibility.

In the meantime about eight thousand tons of opium is produced annually in Red China, much of which is exported for subversive purposes. In the United States, for example, a vast dope trade is carried on by Communist agencies with the deliberate intent of making as many addicts as possible.[4]

"The way of peace have they not known." From figures furnished by the United Nations organization, it is estimated that during World War II thirty-two million people were killed on the battlefields; some twenty-five million died in bombing 'raids; twenty-five million died in concentration camps; more than twenty-nine million were wounded or mutilated. When we consider enlightened twentieth century man's inhumanity to man, we put such figures out of our minds because we can no longer cope with the enormity of the statistics involved.

It is estimated that it cost $225,000 to kill an enemy soldier in World War II and that the war cost the Allies a total of $800 billion. Despite all the apparatus set up to arbitrate international problems at the conference table, man still cannot find the way of peace.

[4]The foregoing facts about China have been culled from various issues of *Intelligence Digest*, a review of world affairs produced in the Office of Strategic Studies and the Bureau of Political War Problems and published monthly by North Cerney House, Cirencester, Gloucestershire, England.

In the United States today, one of every ten persons in the labor force is engaged in defense activities. It is estimated that in the first twenty-four hours of all-out war, the United States could unleash the equivalent of sixteen billion tons of TNT—four thousand times the total dropped in World War II. If most of the "first wave" pierced the enemy defenses, 80 to 90 percent of Russia's 200 million people would die, all major cities would be devastated, and 85 percent of Soviet industry would be wiped out.

Nearly two thousand years ago there came to this world One whose name had been given as "the Prince of Peace" (Isa. 9:6). At His birth the angels chanted across the hills of Judah, "Glory to God in the highest, and on earth peace, good will toward men" (Luke 2:14). But the world united at Calvary to crucify Him, and will know nothing but "wars and rumors of wars" (Matt. 24:6) until He comes again. In the meantime, man's misery is not only something to be endured; it is something for which man is criminally liable at the throne of God.

Finally, God points to man's (3) *mutiny* as being characteristic of man's ways—*"There is no fear of God before their eyes"* (v. 18). God, whose very presence should inspire men with fear of wrongdoing, is completely ignored by men. Far from regarding Him, men treat Him as if He did not exist. In deference to the Soviet Union, for example, the United Nations organization agreed not to acknowledge God at its sessions. Yet it displays in a prominent place a statue of Zeus, the pagan thunderer of Olympus. In the world, atheism is on the march and becoming bolder every day.

III. THE CULPABILITY OF HUMAN SIN (3:19-20)

In view of the catholicity and criminality of human sin, it is little wonder that Paul concludes the indictment by hammering home to the human conscience man's blame for his condition and God's sentence of guilt. To do this, he brings to bear the law of God.

A. *Man's Condition Is Helpless* (3:19)

The law soon exposes human conduct. Man is (1) *convicted* and his conviction of sin stems from his violation of God's law.

"Now we know that what things soever the law saith, it saith to them that are under the law: that every mouth may be stopped" (v. 19). The "law" mentioned here seems to be the entire Old Testament revelation. Paul has just been referring to fourteen sweeping statements of Scripture on the subject of human sin.[5] The person who has seen himself in this picture will certainly have nothing to say in his defense. His mouth is stopped. He will take the place of a moral and spiritual leper before God, strike his hand over his mouth and say, "I am unclean!" (Lev. 13:45; cf. Isa. 6:1-5). Like the publican, he will cry, "God be merciful to me a sinner" (Luke 18:13). For those who take this position, mercy is extended, as Paul will prove next; but to those who continue to argue the point, there will be no mercy when at last their mouths are stopped at the great white throne (Rev. 6:15-17; 20:11-15).

Man is not only convicted by God's law, he is (2) *condemned* by that law. He is found "Guilty!" One reason God gave the law was that *"all the world may become guilty before God"* (v. 19). We do not have to wait until we die to find out where we shall stand in the judgment; we can know right now. John and Paul agree that we are "condemned already" (John 3:18). The verdict of God at the great white throne will merely ratify what we have in Romans 1–3. Truly, man's condition is helpless.

B. *Man's Case Is Hopeless* (3:20)

"Therefore by the deeds of the law there shall no flesh be justified in his sight: for by the law is the knowledge of sin" (v. 20). It is vain for a person to cling to the forlorn hope that somehow, even yet, his good deeds will outweigh his bad ones; that somehow he will be able to conduct himself acceptably before God. He is condemned by God's own code—the law, the chief function of which is not to save but to condemn. The best, the sincerest, the most strenuous attempts to please God by keeping His law fail—and the law itself exposes that failure. Truly man is not only helpless as to his condition, he is hopeless as to his case.

---

[5]In Romans 3:10-18 there are quotations from various parts of the Hebrew Bible. Verses 10-12 are general and are from Ecclesiastes 7:20; Psalm 14:2-3; 53:2-3 (vv. 3-4, Heb. Bible); verses 13-18 are more particular and are from Psalm 5:9 (v. 10, Heb. Bible); 140:3; 10:7; Isaiah 59:7-8; Psalm 36:1 (v. 2, Heb. Bible).

If man is to be saved, God must save him. And that is Paul's next great theme in this epistle.

SALVATION IS FREE
3:21-31

I. GOD'S PLAN OF SALVATION IS REVEALED (3:21-23)

    A. It Is Thoroughly Scriptural (3:21)
        1. It Conforms to the Standards of the Law (3:21a)
        2. It Conforms to the Statements of the Prophets (3:21b)
    B. It Is Thoroughly Suitable (3:22-23)
        1. It Is Unique in Its Approach (3:22)
        2. It is Universal in Its Appeal (3:23)

II. GOD'S PLAN OF SALVATION IS RIGHTEOUS (3:24-26)

    A. The Ruined Condition of Man (3:24-26a)
    Salvation is therefore based on
        1. A Remarkable Principle (3:24a)
        2. A Redemptive Price (3:24b-25a)
        3. A Royal Proclamation (3:25b-26a)
    B. The Righteous Character of God (3:26b)

III. GOD'S PLAN OF SALVATION IS REASONABLE (3:27-31)

    A. It Eliminates All Human Pride (3:27-28)
    B. It Eliminates All Human Prejudice (3:29-30)
    C. It Eliminates All Human Presumption (3:31)

"BUT NOW . . ." (3:21). Mark well those *buts* of the Bible! Just as great doors swing on very ordinary hinges, so dramatic changes in Scripture often hinge upon this very common word. Note, for example, the *but* in the life of Solomon (I Kings 11:1), in the lives of Uzziah (II Chron. 26:16), Pharaoh (Exodus 8:15), and Noah (Gen. 6:8), and in the story of the prodigal son (Luke 15:20).

What a black picture Paul has been painting of human sin; how heavy are the storm clouds in the sky and how fearful the lightning flashes of wrath! But look! There is a rift in the sky where the sun breaks through. God has a plan of salvation for sinners, even the chief of sinners. The first thing Paul will impress upon us about this rift of blue is that salvation is free. It is not of man's devising but of God's.

I. God's Plan of Salvation Is Revealed (3:21-23)

Salvation for man is not the product of human reasoning and effort. It is God's plan from beginning to end and is unfolded by God in His Word. Paul takes pains to show first of all that the truth concerning salvation he is about to expound is based solidly on the teaching of the Old Testament.

A. *It Is Thoroughly Scriptural* (3:21)

It conforms to (1) *the standards of the law*. *"But now the righteousness of God without the law is manifested, being witnessed by the law"* (3:21a). God cannot lower His standards. If He is to save men from the folly and ruin of sin, it must be in a way that will not violate the righteous demands so clearly revealed in the law of Moses. The Old Testament law was both moral and ceremonial. The moral law was designed to uncover sin; the ceremonial law was designed to provide temporary cover for the sinner thus exposed. God's plan of salvation given in the gospel upholds the righteousness of God as revealed in the moral law, and also provides a more satisfactory method of cleansing sin than could ever be provided by the blood of bulls and goats. The ceremonial law was a witness however, despite its evident shortcomings, to the fact that God intended to cleanse and cancel sin at infinite cost and at great personal sacrifice and in a way which would be consistent with His holiness.

God's plan of salvation conforms to (2) *the statements of the prophets*. *"Being witnessed by the law and the prophets"* (3:21b). Isaiah 53 comes at once to mind reminding us not only of the substitutionary death of Christ on our behalf (v. 6) but also of the accrediting to our account of the righteousness of Christ (v. 11).

So then, this plan of God for making sinners righteous apart from the law or human merit is thoroughly scriptural.

B. *It Is Thoroughly Suitable* (3:22-23)

Our case is hopeless, as Paul has already shown; so it follows that if we are to be saved at all it must be in a way that suits our lost condition. God Himself must "devise means that his banished be not expelled from him" (II Sam. 14:14). This He has done. Paul shows that God's plan of salvation is (1) *unique in its ap-*

proach. He speaks of *"the righteousness of God which is by faith of Jesus Christ unto all and upon all them that believe: for there is no difference"* (v. 22). Since we cannot save ourselves, God will save us by giving to us a perfect righteousness, even the righteousness of Christ, if only we will put our faith in the Lord Jesus.

It is here that God's plan of salvation parts company with every plan devised in the human heart. A study of the world's false religious systems will show that no matter how divergent their incidental doctrines may be they all have one major tenet in common. One and all they affirm that salvation must be earned, that it is by works, that man must do something to merit the favor of God. The gospel of the Lord Jesus, with its revolutionary concept of salvation by faith alone, is set sublimely and uniquely apart from all such systems. "For by grace are ye saved through faith; and that not of yourselves: it is the gift of God: not of works, lest any man should boast. For we are his workmanship, created in Christ Jesus unto good works, which God hath before ordained that we should walk in them" (Eph. 2:8-10). In the gospel, "works" do not result *in* salvation, they result *from* salvation.

Then, God's plan of salvation is suitable because it is (2) *universal in its appeal.* *"For all have sinned, and come short of the glory of God"* (v. 23). There is a universal need for the kind of salvation Paul proclaims because all men are sinners. Paul describes sin as a coming short of the glory of God. It is a failure to meet the divine standard.

Two men went to the recruiting office in London to join a guards regiment. The standard height for a guardsman was a minimum of six feet. One man was taller than the other, but when they were measured officially both were disqualified. The shorter of the two measured only five feet seven inches and was far too short; his companion measured five feet eleven and a half inches and, stretch to his utmost as he did, he could not make it any more. Nor did his pleas avail. It mattered nothing that his father was a guardsman, that he promised to be a good soldier, that he had already memorized the drills and knew army regulations by heart. He was short of the standard.

Sin is a coming short of the standard of God. Some people come far short and are obviously unfit for the kingdom of heaven.

Others, to the eye of the beholder, are moral and upright, sincere and conscientious and, by human standards, might be thought to have a good chance of winning the approval of God. However, they are not measured here by human standards but by God's; and when measured by His standards of perfection as displayed in the Lord Jesus, they still "come short of the glory of God." That is why the plan devised by God is so suitable. It is a plan devised for sinners, "and all have sinned, and come short of the glory of God."

II. GOD'S PLAN OF SALVATION IS RIGHTEOUS (3:24-26)

Paul is now going to show how God can "be just, and the justifier of him which believeth in Jesus" (v. 26). For while reaching down to the depths into which man has fallen God, in offering to men a free salvation, has in no way compromised His own inherent holiness, justice and righteousness. God's plan of salvation is righteous for two reasons. It takes into account:

A. *The Ruined Condition of Man* (3:24-26a)

The Christian Scientist's solution to the problem of sin and death is to put its head into the sand and blithely assure us they do not exist, that they are an "error of mortal mind." The Word of God is party to no such folly. Sin and sickness are dreadful facts and are not to be airily dismissed by metaphysics. God's plan of salvation does not turn a blind eye to man's lost condition. It takes it fully into account.

Because of man's ruined condition, salvation is based on (1) *a remarkable principle*. We are to be "*justified freely by his grace*" (v. 24a). Notice the words "justified," "freely" and "grace," for they summarize the principle whereby God meets ruined man in all his need.

"Justification is here the legal and formal acquittal from guilt by God as Judge, and the pronouncement of the believing sinner as righteous in His sight. The verb is in the present continuous tense and thus indicates a constant process of justification in the succession of those who believe and are justified."[1]

There is all the difference in the world between being forgiven

[1]W. E. Vine, *The Epistle to the Romans* (Grand Rapids: Zondervan Publishing House, 1948), p. 54.

and being justified. Suppose a woman were to incur a debt at a branch store of a large company over and above her means to pay. If after hearing her case the store were to cancel her debt, that would be *forgiveness*. Under these circumstances, the woman would be no longer liable for the account, but would always have a feeling of personal discomfort about the whole transaction. If, on the other hand, the legal department of the company decided to press for payment, that would be *justice*. Suppose that while awaiting trial for her undischarged account the woman were to marry the wealthy son of the store owner who personally assumed responsibility for her account and paid it in full. There would be no legal claim against her any more and in the unlikely event of her case ever getting to court, she could plead "not guilty" to all charges on the grounds that her debts had been fully paid by her husband. The court would say that she was *justified* in pleading "not guilty" and her case would be dismissed.

If a person is to be forgiven, he must plead "guilty" and sue for mercy. If a person is to be justified, he must plead "not guilty" and show that the opposition has no case against him at all. Of course both forgiveness and justification enter into our salvation, but it is the higher truth of justification that Paul is presenting in Romans. The Lord Jesus has fully discharged all our obligations so that there is no legal ground for charges to be pressed against us anymore. Moreover, He has given us a perfect standing before God so that we are fully acceptable in His sight.

We are justified "freely." That is just like God! He does not charge us for anything. He is liberal and lavish in His dealings with men. Seedtime and harvest, warm sunshine and soft, refreshing rain, everything is free from God. Nor does God charge for saving us.

The story is told of a widow whose only daughter was very sick and in need of fresh fruit. But it was winter; grapes and oranges were expensive, and the widow was poor. Walking the streets of the city, the woman found herself outside the royal palace. She looked through the gate and saw in the royal greenhouse great clusters of the most appetizing and tempting grapes. As she gazed at them wistfully, the princess came by and, taking in the situation at a glance, with her own hands cut for the widow a magnificent basketful of fruit. With trembling hands the widow offered the royal lady in payment the few coppers she had in her purse, but she received instead this noble reply, "Madam, these grapes are not for sale. My father is a king and he's much too rich to sell, and besides, you are much too poor to buy. You can have these grapes free or not at all." That's it! Our Father is a King. He does not sell. He offers salvation free or not at all.

Then there is that word "grace." Grace is unmerited favor. It is getting something we do not deserve. All we deserve from God is His eternal punishment for our high-handed rebellion; but instead He offers us salvation through His Son at the infinite cost of Calvary. So we are "justified freely by his grace." Truly God's righteous plan of salvation is based on a most remarkable principle.

It is also based on (2) *a redemptive price,* for Paul goes on to speak of *"the redemption that is in Christ Jesus: whom God hath set forth to be a propitiation through faith in his blood"* (vv. 24b-25a). Mark well those great gospel words "redemption," "propitiation," "faith" and "blood."

We are *redeemed.* The word used here for redemption suggests more than being purchased out of the slave market; it means to be delivered, to be set free. It is one thing to be purchased, but it is something else, something far better, to be set free as a result of that purchase.

In regular usage, the word *propitiation* means to appease; but this is not the biblical idea. The Bible word means to expiate by sacrifice. God has been propitiated through the work of Christ at Calvary; that is, His holiness has been so fully satisfied that He can now look again in favor on men.

The means by which we come into the benefits of this redemption and this propitiation is *faith.* W. E. Vine says: "The commas which precede and follow 'through faith' [in ASV[2]] are important. Faith is never said to be in the blood . . . the phrase 'by his blood' expresses the means of propitiation."[3] Important as the blood is to our salvation, we do not trust in it, but in Christ, a living Redeemer. Faith is in a Person. It is trusting in Christ which makes faith valid.

[2]American Standard Version (1901).
[3]Vine, p. 55.

Two common mistakes are often made about faith. Many people make a mistake concerning the amount of faith they have, and feeling that it is insufficient they never enter into the joy of their salvation. Such persons are seeking to have faith in their faith instead of having faith in the Lord Jesus Christ. The second mistake is similar and concerns the object of faith. Faith is a common enough commodity. Indeed, it is a common denominator of life, something we all possess and without which we could not live through a single day. Every day we exercise faith, quite unconsciously, in a thousand ways. We take people at their word; we believe what we read in newspapers, periodicals and books; we trust our money to the bank, and our persons to the bus driver, the doctor, the elevator operator, or the hairdresser; we eat what is set before us without suspicion, and swallow pills without question. In all these and countless other situations, we exercise faith as a normal, integral part of our lives. But such faith is not saving faith. Faith becomes saving faith when it is placed in the Lord Jesus Christ. God very reasonably declares, "If we receive the witness of men, the witness of God is greater: for this is the witness of God which he hath testified of his Son. He that believeth on the Son of God hath the witness in himself: he that believeth not God hath made him a liar; because he believeth not the record that God gave of his Son. And this is the record, that God hath given to us eternal life, and this life is in his Son" (I John 5:9-11).

God can offer us redemption through faith and can be propitiated because of the shedding of Christ's *blood*. Salvation is free, but it is not cheap. It cost God His only begotten and well beloved Son, and it cost the Lord Jesus a death of shame and agony on the cross. God has declared that the blood shed for us is "precious blood" (I Peter 1:18-19), and so it is. The cost of Calvary is beyond all human computation; the value of the shed blood of Jesus is beyond all our comprehension. It is no wonder that God speaks so forcibly of the punishment awaiting those who treat this blood as of no account. "He that despised Moses' law died without mercy under two or three witnesses: of how much sorer punishment, suppose ye, shall he be thought worthy, who hath trodden under foot the Son of God, and hath counted the blood of the covenant, wherewith he was sanctified, an unholy thing, and hath done despite unto the Spirit of grace?" (Heb. 10:28-29).

The great object lesson of redemption through blood in the Old Testament was, of course, given in the Passover instituted on the night of the exodus from Egypt (Exodus 12). The blood of the slain Passover lamb was to be sprinkled on the two side posts of the door of each house and on the upper door post. No blood was to be sprinkled on the door step or threshold for the simple reason that there was to be no trampling on the blood.

This salvation, then, so eminently suited to the ruined condition of man, is based on a remarkable principle and on a redemptive price. It is also based on (3) *a royal proclamation*. Paul puts it this way: *"To declare his righteousness for the remission of sins that are past, through the forbearance of God; to declare, I say, at this time his righteousness"* (vv. 25b-26a).

The cross is the public declaration that God is righteous in the way He has handled the sin question. During the Old Testament era it looked as if God dealt lightly and superficially with sin. Animal sacrifices could not remove sin, and there were times when it seemed that God overlooked sin altogether ("winked at" it, is the way Paul puts it in Acts 17:30); but Calvary reveals that this was not really true. The entire sacrificial system of the Old Testament declared that God is holy, and Calvary reveals how a holy God has righteously dealt with sin. The royal proclamation then declares that God has found a way of being just while in the very act of justifying the believer, which is Paul's next point. Salvation not only meets the need of ruined man, it takes into account:

B. *The Righteous Character of God* (3:26b)

"That he might be just, and the justifier of him which believeth in Jesus." God does not overlook sin, but He forces it out into the open where He can deal with it in a way that honors His own righteous character.

Two of the great Old Testament offerings can be taken together to illustrate perfectly the transaction which takes place when a sinner accepts Christ as Saviour. These were the sin offering and the burnt offering. To some extent the ritual was similar in both sacrifices, for in both cases the offerer brought his lamb and placed his hands upon it to identify himself with the sacrifice.

The typical meaning of the two sacrifices, however, was very different. In the sin offering, all *the vileness of the sinner* was transferred to *the substitute;* but in the burnt offering, all *the virtue of the substitute* was transferred to *the sinner.* Probably Paul had this in mind when, reminding the Corinthians of the significance of Calvary, he wrote: "For he hath made him to be sin for us, who knew no sin; that we might be made the righteousness of God in him" (II Cor. 5:21). The cross of Calvary makes it possible for God to be both just and the Justifier.

Justification, however, is only for "him which *believeth in Jesus.*" This cannot be overemphasized. God justifies only those who believe in Jesus. Everybody believes in something or someone. Some people provide themselves with a stock of beliefs deliberately and systematically; others do so casually, even absentmindedly. F. W. Boreham warns of the danger of selecting the articles of our faith on the same principle that we select articles of furniture. There is a possibility that we will just gather together a few agreeable conclusions, a fairly comfortable creed, a neat little stock of congenial beliefs and then lean back and congratulate ourselves on our discernment and good taste.[4] There is danger in believing a thing simply because it is convenient. The only belief that counts with God is belief in the Lord Jesus Christ.

III. GOD'S PLAN OF SALVATION IS REASONABLE (3:27-31)

It is reasonable because it casts all upon a God who cannot fail and reduces all men to the same level of dependence on Him.

A. *It Eliminates Human Pride* (3:27-28)

Suppose God were to take people to heaven on the basis of human merit. Human nature, being what it is, the saved person would soon be boasting in heaven. One person would parade some great deed he had done or some tremendous sacrifice he had made. Another would have all men listen to a list of his virtues. Boasting is the outward, verbal expression of pride; and pride was the original sin, the sin of Satan in a distant past (Isa. 14:12-17; Ezek. 28:12-19). The reemergence in heaven of pride in the form of boasting would call for action on the part of God similar to that taken before. The boaster would be cast out of

[4]See F. W. Boreham, *The Uttermost Star* (London: The Epworth Press, 1919), pp. 210-11. Used by permission.

heaven. God has eliminated such a possibility, for He levels human pride to the dust and denies the possibility of salvation by works.

Thus Paul writes, *"Where is boasting then? It is excluded. By what law? of works? Nay: but by the law of faith. Therefore we conclude that a man is justified by faith without the deeds of the law"* (vv. 27-28).

No wonder the saints have sung for a century:

> I stand upon His merit,
> I know no other stand,
> Not e'en where glory dwelleth
> In Immanuel's land.[5]

B. *It Eliminates Human Prejudice* (3:29-30)

No nation or people, no church or denomination has a monopoly on God. The Jew, indeed, by virtue of God's special promises to Abraham and David, occupies a unique position, but it is a mistake to think that God reserves His love for one nation alone.[6] J. B. Phillips exposes the false notion some people have that God is especially partial to them and their brand of belief. Discussing the skepticism of the unchurched individual toward the various denominations, he says, "What sticks in his throat about the Christianity of the churches is not merely their differences in denomination, but the spirit of 'churchiness' which seems to pervade them all. They seem to have captured and tamed and trained Something that is really far too big ever to be forced into little man-made boxes with neat labels upon them. . . . 'If,' the churches appear to be saying to him, 'you will jump through our particular hoop or sign on our particular dotted line then we will introduce you to God. But if not, then there's no God for you.'

---

[5]Anne Ross Cousin, "Immanuel's Land."

[6]The Anglo-Israelites fall into this error. They recount the singular blessings of God on the Anglo-Saxon nations and try to account for these blessings by maintaining that the British and American peoples are really the "lost" ten tribes of Israel. To support this theory, they make an unwarranted distinction between the terms "Israelite" and "Jew." There are many weaknesses in the theory, not the least of which is that Israel, outside the promised land of Canaan, is out of the sphere of blessing completely. Moreover, God's blessings are channeled through the church not Israel, in this dispensation. In addition to this, God loves the world, not just one nation, as John 3:16 so clearly declares.

This seems to him to be nonsense, and nasty arrogant nonsense at that."[7]

Paul puts it this way: *"Is he the God of the Jews only? is he not also of the Gentiles? Yes, of the Gentiles also: seeing it is one God, which shall justify the circumcision by faith, and uncircumcision through faith"* (vv. 29-30).

C. *It Eliminates Human Presumption* (3:31)

There are some who feel that somehow the doctrine of justification *by faith alone* undermines the authority of the law and divine authority too. Paul discounts the notion. *"Do we then make void the law through faith? God forbid: yea, we establish the law"* (v. 31). As Scofield points out, "the sinner establishes the law in its right use and honor by confessing his guilt, and acknowledging that by it he is justly condemned. Christ, on the sinner's behalf, establishes the law by enduring its penalty, death."[8] A person who has truly seen the seriousness of his own sin and the significance of his redemption is not going to presume upon the grace of God. He realizes he is saved *from* sin, not saved *to* sin—something Paul will discuss at length later in the epistle.

So then, God's free salvation is based on a plan which is revealed, righteous and reasonable. It calls for instant, unconditional and joyful acceptance.

SALVATION IS BY FAITH
4:1-25

I. THE QUESTION OF TRYING FOR SALVATION (4:1-15)

    A. People Who Depend on Their Own Righteousness (4:1-8)
    This practice is refuted by
        1. The Case of Abraham—Founder of the Hebrew Racial Family (4:1-5)
            a. The appeal to Abraham's case (4:1-3)
            b. The application of Abraham's case (4:4-5)
        2. The Case of David—Founder of the Hebrew Royal Family (4:6-8)
            a. Salvation freely bestowed (4:6)
            b. Sin forever banished (4:7-8)

[7]J. B. Phillips, *Your God Is Too Small* (New York: Copyright © The Macmillan Co., 1958), p. 37.

[8]C. I. Scofield, *The Scofield Reference Bible* (New York: Oxford University Press, 1909), p. 1195.

B. People Who Depend on Their Own Religiousness (4:9-15)
  1. Trusting in the Rites of Religion (4:9-12)
     a. Note when Abraham was given the rite (4:9-10)
     b. Note why Abraham was given the rite (4:11-12)
  2. Trusting in the Rules of Religion (4:13-15)
     a. The promise of the Lord saves (4:13)
     b. The precepts of the law slay (4:14-15)

II. THE QUESTION OF TRUSTING FOR SALVATION (4:16-25)
  A. The Principle of Faith Is Expounded to Us (4:16)
     1. Faith Brings Us into God's Favor
     2. Faith Brings Us into God's Family
  B. The Principle of Faith Is Explained to Us (4:17-22)
     1. How Abraham Received God's Word (4:17-18)
     2. How Abraham Believed God's Word (4:19-22)
  C. The Principle of Faith Is Experienced by Us (4:23-25)
     1. For the Same Purpose (4:23-24a)
     2. By the Same Process (4:24b)
     3. On the Same Principle (4:25)

ROMANS 4 is the great Bible chapter on salvation by faith alone. Many claim to believe in salvation by faith, but not in salvation by faith *alone*. The word "alone" is the watershed which divides the Catholic from the Protestant, and it was the watchword of the Reformation. The Romanist, for example, believes in salvation by faith, but not by faith *alone*; he believes in the value of the blood of Christ, but not in the value of that blood *alone*; he accepts the fact that Christ is Mediator between God and man, but not that Christ is Mediator *alone*; he acknowledges the authority of the Scriptures, but not their authority *alone*. In Romans 4 Paul demonstrates that salvation is by faith alone apart from any work or merit of man.

I. THE QUESTION OF TRYING FOR SALVATION (4:1-15)

Before coming to grips with the implications of salvation by faith alone, Paul deals with the whole question of works as a means of salvation. He shows how unscriptural such an idea is by pointing to two biblical characters, Abraham and David, and

by discussing the fallacy of depending on one's own righteousness and religiousness.

A. *People Who Depend on Their Own Righteousness* (4:1-8)

One of the most cherished of all fallacies is that man has some
spark of goodness which needs only to be fanned into flame. To
refute this idea, Paul appeals to the case of *Abraham*, the greatest
of the patriarchs and one of the chiefest of Old Testament *saints*,
to show that no human being may be exalted in this matter of
salvation; and to *David*, the greatest of the kings and one of the
chiefest of Old Testament *sinners*, to show that no human being
need be excluded.

Paul begins with (1) *the case of Abraham*, founder of the Hebrew racial family (4:1-5). If ever a man was canonized in the
thinking of his fellows, that man was Abraham. It was particularly fitting that Paul should select him as his first illustration, for
if Abraham could not be saved by works then nobody can.
Notice the *appeal* to Abraham's case (4:1-3). *"What shall we
say then that Abraham our father, as pertaining to the flesh, hath
found? For if Abraham were justified by works, he hath whereof
to glory; but not before God"* (vv. 1-2). In other words, a man's
works might earn him the applause of men, but never the applause of God, for God's standards are higher and holier than
anything conceived by man. Abraham, however, did not trust
in his own merits. In any case, when God called him out of Ur
of the Chaldees, Abraham was a pagan idolater.

Imperfection characterizes all man's works whether of a moral,
spiritual or even physical nature. Perfection characterizes all the
works of God. A simple illustration will make this clear. Compare the edge of the sharpest razor man can hone with the sting
of a bee, or the surface of the finest vellum with the texture of
a leaf. Put the work of man beneath a microscope and at once
its flaws and imperfections appear, but put the work of God to
the same test and increasing glories of perfection appear. It is
the same in the moral and spiritual spheres. When put to the
test and examined by the all-seeing eye of God, man's efforts are
full of flaws. But the finished work of Christ reveals more beauties the more it is examined. So at once we are told that Abraham
had nothing of which to boast before God.

"For what saith the scripture? Abraham believed God, and it was counted unto him for righteousness" (v. 3). If imperfection marks salvation by works, *imputation* characterizes salvation by faith. The word "reckon" ("impute" or "count") occurs eleven times in this chapter. In God's system of bookkeeping it depicts sin being transferred *from* our account and righteousness being transferred *to* our account.

Abraham did the only thing a person can do without doing anything—he believed God (Gen. 15:6). Galatians 3:16 makes it clear that Abraham's belief in what God had to say concerning the promised Seed was, in the last analysis, a belief in Christ.

Then comes the *application* of Abraham's case. Paul drives home his point with the words, *"Now to him that worketh is the reward not reckoned of grace, but of debt. But to him that worketh not, but believeth on him that justifieth the ungodly, his faith is counted for righteousness"* (vv. 4-5). Under a system of works, everything depends on the sinner; under grace, everything depends on the Saviour. Under the first, God gives a fair trial, but under the second He gives a free pardon. The expression "Him that justifieth the ungodly" is one full of hope for those who realize that the fairer the trial, the more certain we are of judgment. It is of importance to note that it is the *ungodly* that God justifies. God's justification is extended to the individual as a sinner, not as a saint. His growth in grace and in the knowledge of God as a saint does not increase that justification nor do his failures decrease it. But to obtain a pardon and to sue for mercy in a court, a person must first plead guilty. The man who pleads "not guilty" can hope only for a fair trial. The man who pleads "guilty" can hope only for mercy. God does not take sinners to heaven because they deserve it, but because of His grace.

Next Paul deals with (2) *the case of David,* founder of the Hebrew royal family (4:6-8). The case of David is far different from that of Abraham. Here Paul quotes from Psalm 32, which was written by David after the public exposure of his secret sins (II Sam. 11-12). In connection with Bathsheba, David had coveted, committed adultery, and murdered, breaking three of the Ten Commandments. His seduction of Bathsheba and his camouflaged murder of Uriah exposed David to the death penalty on two counts, and according to the strict letter of the Mosaic law, there was no hope for him. The sacrificial system of the Old Testament made no provision for willful sin. This is why David cried in another of the penitential psalms, born in this same period, "For thou desirest not sacrifice; else would I give it: thou delightest not in burnt-offering. The sacrifices of God are a broken spirit: a broken and a contrite heart, O God, thou wilt not despise" (Ps. 51:16-17). David's desperate case cast all on God. Out of this experience, however, David learned two vital truths concerning salvation, truths which he wrote into Psalm 32 and which Paul picks up here to further his argument.

The first of these truths is that *salvation is freely bestowed.* *"Even as David also describeth the blessedness of the man, unto whom God imputeth righteousness without works"* (v. 6). David discovered the way to true happiness and to true holiness—without works. What could David do to restore to Bathsheba her chastity and to Uriah his life? What could he do to restore his own lost innocence? Nothing! His case was hopeless. But then God stepped in and in sovereign grace freely cancelled David's sin and counted him righteous! Simple faith in the naked promise of God, "The Lord also hath put away thy sin; thou shalt not die" (II Sam. 12:13), was all that David had, but that was enough. Salvation is freely bestowed.

David learned moreover that cancelled *sin is forever banished.* *"Blessed are they whose iniquities are forgiven, and whose sins are covered. Blessed is the man to whom the Lord will not impute sin"* (vv. 7-8). David had discovered a way to have his sins not only forgiven but forgotten; not only covered but cancelled.

Some years ago a wealthy English businessman purchased a Rolls Royce and soon afterward took his new car to France. When in the south of France, it broke down and he phoned the Rolls Royce people in Britain. The manufacturer flew a mechanic to France and the man's car was repaired. He expected to receive a sizable bill for this unprecedented service, but as months passed and no invoice arrived the businessman wrote to the Rolls Royce company asking for his account to be rendered. By return mail he received a courteous note from the company assuring him that they had no record of anything having gone wrong with his car! In other words, the Rolls Royce company refused to acknowledge any imperfection in their product. That is exactly

what happened to David in a spiritual sense. "Blessed is the
man to whom the Lord will not impute sin." When God forgives,
He blots out the record.

Dr. Moon dramatically underlines this in the film *Time and
Eternity*. After showing the various relationships of time, Dr.
Moon concludes, "All of us have looked up, on a clear night, and
seen the sparkling, twinkling stars. But how many of us have
realized that we cannot see the stars as they now are? Every
time we look, we are looking into the past, seeing them as they
were. . . . But this works both ways. If you were on one of the
stars you would, assuming an adequate telescope, see the earth
as it was sometime in the past. From the star Sirius, you could
see what you were doing nine years ago, because in a profoundly
true scientific sense you are still doing it. Yes, everything you
have ever done, you are still doing. The ghost of your past
haunts the universe. But remember, we have noted that God is
omnipresent. This means that, for God, every sin you have ever
committed, every evil thing you have ever done, you are still
doing, and will continue to do forever, apart from God's forgiveness. Only the omnipotent, eternal God, who controls all the
factors of time, space and matter, could ever remove sin. God
says: 'I, even I, am he that blotteth out thy transgressions for
mine own sake, and will not remember thy sins' (Isa. 43:25)."[1]
When God cancels sin, He wills it out of existence; it is not only
forgiven and forgotten, it is annihilated.

B. *People Who Depend on Their Own Religiousness* (4:9-15)

Those who are *trying* for salvation often lean on two crutches—
their own imagined goodness is the first, and some kind of religious observance is the second. Paul has just taken away the first
of these false props and he now removes the other by showing
the folly of depending on either the rites of religion or the rules
of religion. Of course he was well qualified to deal with the
error of trusting in one's own religiousness. He could say of his
unconverted days, "I . . . profited in the Jew's religion above
many my equals in mine own nation" (Gal. 1:14). Moreover,
the Jew's religion was the only "religion" ever given divine sanc-
tion.

[1]Irwin A. Moon, *Time and Eternity* (Los Angeles: Moody Institute of
Science, Inc., 1962), pp. 14-15.

Paul shows then the folly of (1) *trusting in the rites of religion* (4:9-12). He returns to Abraham at this point to prove that religious rites do not bestow salvation and he focuses on the most important religious rite of the Jew—circumcision. He emphasizes *when* Abraham was given the rite, and this is one of the most important points in the argument. *"Cometh this blessedness then upon the circumcision only, or upon the uncircumcision also? for we say that faith was reckoned to Abraham for righteousness. How was it then reckoned? when he was in circumcision, or in uncircumcision? Not in circumcision, but in uncircumcision"* (vv. 9-10). Circumcision, of course, was the sign of the Abrahamic covenant (Gen. 17:7-14). In Paul's day, many Jewish Christians maintained salvation was impossible apart from the administration of this rite (Acts 15:1-29; Gal. 2:1-14) and wanted all Gentile converts to be circumcised. Nowadays people tend to think that salvation is impossible apart from the administration of the rites of the church. Paul's argument here is devastating to such a view. Abraham was a justified man fourteen years before the rite of circumcision was imposed (Gen. 15:6; 17:10). The rite had nothing to do with his redemption at all.

Next Paul points out *why* Abraham was given the rite. It did not confer righteousness, it merely confirmed the righteousness Abraham already had. Circumcision to the Jew was a pledge of nationality but it was more than that. Paul tells us that there were two reasons for the rite as it was given to Abraham. It was given *"first, that Abraham might be the spiritual father of all who since that time, despite their uncircumcision, show the faith that is counted for righteousness. Then, secondly, that he might be the circumcised father of all those who are not only circumcised, but are living by the same sort of faith which he himself had before he was circumcised"* (vv. 11-12).[2] "Paul has turned the Jews' boast upside down. It is not the Gentile who must come to the Jew's circumcision for salvation; it is the Jew who must come to a Gentile faith, such a faith as Abraham had long before he was circumcised."[3]

Having shown the folly of trusting in the rites of religion, Paul

[2]J. B. Phillips, *The New Testament in Modern English* (New York: The Macmillan Company. Copyright © by J. B. Phillips, 1958), p. 324.
[3]James M. Stifler, *The Epistle to the Romans* (Chicago: Moody Press, 1960), pp. 76-77.

next shows the folly of (2) *trusting in the rules of religion* (4:13-15). The sinner, trying to work his way to heaven, tries hard to live up to the rules of his religion. Paul shows that the only valid rule for salvation is the rule of faith. He contrasts the promise of the Lord with the precepts of the law. *The promise of the Lord* was not contingent in any way on Abraham's adherence to the Mosaic law. How could it be when that law was not given until centuries after Abraham's death? *"For the promise, that he should be the heir of the world, was not to Abraham, or to his seed, through the law, but through the righteousness of faith"* (v. 13). While many of the promises in the Bible are conditional, those made to Abraham and his seed were unconditional and are guaranteed by the faithfulness of God, not the faithfulness of man (Gal. 3:17-18; Rom. 4:13-18).

The rules and requirements given to the Jews in the Mosaic law at a later date do not affect in any way the original unconditional promise. The Mosaic law had to do with the behavior of a redeemed people already in a covenant relationship with God, and were aimed at securing their health, happiness and holiness as God's people. Paul has already made it clear that Abraham's true seed were those who walked in Abraham's steps and exercised faith as Abraham did (v. 12). We can draw a parallel here. The practical requirements of the epistles which are incumbent on Christians today do not add to our salvation. They have to do rather with our spiritual peace, prosperity and power as God's sons.

In contrast with the promise of the Lord are *the precepts of the law*. Paul makes two very sobering observations about these. First, the law undermines faith. *"For if they which are of the law be heirs, faith is made void, and the promise made of none effect"* (v. 14). In other words, if the Jew could inherit the promises by his own efforts, that is, by keeping the rules of the Mosaic law, then the unconditional promise of God is made invalid. A promise is either unconditional or it isn't; there is no middle ground. If salvation is on a basis of "trying," then it is not on a basis of "trusting." But it is faith, not works; grace, not law; belief, not behavior, which is the basis and foundation of all that God gives.

The law not only undermines faith, it also underlines failure.

"Because the law worketh wrath: for where no law is, there is no transgression" (v. 15). The practical outcome of the law of Moses was to condemn not save, for it showed just how far a person had come short of God's standards. A soul awakened by the thunderings of the law surely should flee back to the promise, not try to scale the quaking, fire-bathed sides of Sinai.

So then, Paul has cut away all the ground from underneath the feet of those who insist on trying for salvation. They have no righteousness acceptable to God. Their religious exercises are futile, for neither the rites nor rules even of religion can save. Salvation is by faith and by faith alone, as Paul has already declared and will now conclusively prove.

II. THE QUESTION OF TRUSTING FOR SALVATION (4:16-25)

Paul now hammers hard at the truth that salvation is by faith alone.

A. *The Principle of Faith Is Expounded to Us* (4:16)

First of all (1) *faith brings us into God's favor.* Since human effort cannot do this, it is obvious that if we are to be saved there must be another way. *"Therefore it is of faith,"* says Paul, *"that it might be by grace"* (v. 16a). We have already noted that grace is unmerited favor. It is faith which links us to that grace, that unmerited favor of God. It is the hand of faith reaching up into the unseen that is grasped by the kindly outstretched hand of God. Faith indeed might be described as a kind of sixth sense. Its function is to make tangible and real the verities of the spiritual world. By faith we appropriate the benefits and blessings God would bestow on us. As the writer of Hebrews puts it, "Faith is the substance of things hoped for, the evidence of things not seen" (Heb. 11:1).

Then (2) *faith brings us into God's family.* Paul says, *"Therefore it is of faith, that it might be by grace; to the end the promise might be sure to all the seed; not to that only which is of the law, but to that also which is of the faith of Abraham; who is the father of us all"* (v. 16). All who believe, be they Jew or Gentile, are the spiritual children of Abraham and members of the family of God.

There is nothing uncertain about faith! The man who is uncertain about his salvation is not looking at the finished work of Christ with the eye of faith; he is looking with doubt at his own works—and well he might. Paul says that it is of faith so that the promise might be *sure*. It is sure because the promise is divine, and faith lays hold of that.

An incident in the lives of Abraham and Jacob illustrates how different is the security when God is the Guarantor than when man is. In Genesis we are told how Abraham purchased a piece of real estate for a family burial ground. The deal having been made, we read, "And the field, and the cave that is therein, were made sure unto Abraham for a possession of a burying place by the sons of Heth" (Gen. 23:20). How sure was that transaction and guarantee? Some years later, Abraham's grandson Jacob had to regain possession of this same burial plot by repurchase (Gen. 33:19; Acts 7:16). Our salvation does not rest on the uncertain promise of man, but on the mighty covenant of God. Faith delights that this is so.

B. *The Principle of Faith Is Explained to Us* (4:17-22)

Paul points out next how Abraham received and believed God's word. Notice (1) how Abraham *received* God's word. Paul goes back to Genesis 17 and the giving of the Abrahamic covenant. *"As it is written, I have made thee a father of many nations, before him whom he believed, even God, who quickeneth the dead, and calleth those things which be not as though they were. Who against hope believed in hope, that he might become the father of many nations; according to that which was spoken, So shall thy seed be"* (vv. 17-18). Our attention is drawn to the *intelligence* of Abraham's faith. His faith was in a God who could "quicken" (make alive) the dead. He counted on the omnipotence of God. The context in Genesis 15 shows that just before the promise "so shall thy seed be" was given, God had directed Abraham's attention to the countless stars of space. To a God who could create a hundred million universes, nothing is impossible. Had Abraham looked at his own dead body, he would have found it impossible to believe. But he looked up to the stars. He looked at a God who could create stars out of nothing and command death to blossom into life. His was an intelligent faith.

Our attention is drawn further to the *intensity* of Abraham's faith, for against hope Abraham believed in hope. Humanly speaking, his case *was* hopeless; but his case had been taken out of human hands altogether. Now that it was in God's hands, hope could add again its glorious tint of optimism to the spectrum of Abraham's life.

So much then for the way Abraham received God's word. Paul now probes a little deeper and shows us (2) how Abraham *believed* God's word. He believed God's word in two ways. First, by exercising faith in God's *promise*. *"And being not weak in faith, he considered not his own body now dead, when he was about an hundred years old, neither yet the deadness of Sarah's womb: he staggered not at the promise of God through unbelief: but was strong in faith, giving glory to God"* (vv. 19-20). He weighed the *human* impossibility (of becoming a father) against the *divine* impossibility (of God being able to break His word) and decided that if God was God, then nothing was impossible. His faith was strong not only because he exercised faith in God's promise but also because he exercised faith in God's *power*. *"And being fully persuaded that, what he had promised, he was able also to perform. And therefore it was imputed unto him for righteousness"* (vv. 21-22).

Thus the principle of faith is explained to us. It is simply taking God at His word and allowing God to be God in any and every situation.

C. *The Principle of Faith Is Experienced by Us* (4:23-25)

Paul concludes this great discussion on salvation by faith by making application of the truths of which he has been speaking. He brings the principle up to date and makes it practical and meaningful for us today, for the principle of salvation by faith, so effective in the case of Abraham, is to be experienced by us (1) *for the same purpose. "Now it was not written for his sake alone, that it was imputed to him; but for us also"* (vv. 23-24a). But for us also! God's method of saving Abraham and counting him righteous is also God's way of saving us and counting us righteous. Abraham was put into a situation where only faith could avail, and so are we.

This principle is experienced by us not only for the same purpose but also (2) *by the same process*. Paul says that it is for us also *"to whom it shall be imputed, if we believe on him that raised up Jesus our Lord from the dead"* (v. 24b). Abraham was faced with the impossibility of death being transformed to life, yet he resolutely believed that even this was no impossibility for God. We are faced with basically the same "impossibility," for we have to believe that God has raised Jesus from the dead (Rom. 10:9). When Paul preached this doctrine at Athens, the cultural and intellectual capital of the world, he was mocked (Acts 17:32). To this day there are many who refuse to believe that the Lord Jesus is supernaturally alive from the dead. Yet it is at the very heart of the faith. We believe it, and God imputes to us the righteousness of Christ in return (Rom. 10:9).

Finally, salvation is made good to us (3) *on the same principle*. The salvation of God in Old Testament times was substantially the same as in New Testament times. It was based on the same principle of faith. For Paul says of the Lord Jesus that He was *"delivered for our offences, and was raised again for our justification"* (v. 25). Abraham was saved the same way as we are. He looked forward by faith to the finished work of Christ; for Jesus said to the unbelieving Jews of His day, "Your father Abraham rejoiced to see my day: and he saw it, and was glad" (John 8:56). We look back by faith to the finished work of Christ and enjoy the same salvation Abraham enjoyed.

Thus the two ways are compared and contrasted—salvation by *trying* and salvation by *trusting*. What Abraham found, what David found, Paul found, and we must find. Salvation is by faith and by faith alone.

SALVATION IS FOREVER
5:1-21

I. How GOD HAS LIFTED US (5:1-5)

  A. As to Our Standing (5:1-2)

    1. We Have Acceptance (5:1)

    2. We Have Access (5:2)

  B. As to Our State (5:3-5)

    1. How Maturity Is Displayed by Us (5:3a)

SINCE THE DOCTRINE of the eternal security of the believer is in disfavor with many sincere Christians, and since it appears to be the topic of Romans 5, a few preliminary remarks need to be made about the subject in general. First, no one would deny that there are several warning passages in the New Testament which seem to imply that there is a possibility of loss of salvation. These passages are prominent in the non-Pauline epistles and especially in Hebrews, an epistle which in some ways is a companion piece to Romans. One satisfactory explanation of these passages is that they apply not to true believers but to false professors of Christianity. A full discussion of all these passages can be found in Ironside's booklet on the subject.[1] These passages are absent from Romans, the gospel according to Paul.

Secondly, some sincere Bible teachers believe there is something inherently dangerous in the doctrine of eternal security. Tell a person he is saved and can never be lost, they maintain, and the door is opened to all kinds of license and loose living.

[1]See H. A. Ironside, *The Eternal Security of the Believer* (New York: Loizeaux Brothers, 1924).

Since this particular view is one of the great themes of Romans 6, it will be considered further in the next chapter.

Thirdly, it should be recognized that a distinction is made in the Bible between a person's *standing* as a Christian and his *state* as a Christian. Our standing is perfect, immutable and guaranteed by the Word of God, the work of Christ and the witness of the Spirit. Our state is imperfect, changeable and, in a large measure, dependent on us. Our standing before God is the subject of Romans 5; our state is the subject of Romans 6-8.

I. How God Has Lifted Us (5:1-5)

Paul begins at once with the fact that we have peace with God through the work of Christ. Peace simply means that the war is over; the arms of rebellion have been laid down; God's terms of amnesty have been accepted.

A. *A Preview of Our Standing* (5:1-2)

There are two words which sum up Paul's teaching in these two verses—"acceptance" and "access." In the first place, then, we have (1) *acceptance. "Therefore being justified by faith, we have peace with God through our Lord Jesus Christ"* (v. 1). Paul is simply saying here that, in view of the finished work of Christ which he has just been presenting to us (4:24-25), we can be quite sure of our standing before God. The believer is justified. The word in the original is in the aorist tense "and indicates the definite time at which each believer, upon the exercise of faith, was justified in the sight of God."[2] He is at peace with God. He is no longer striving to earn his salvation and no longer struggling in rebellion and self-will. He is justified. He has something the world cannot give and cannot take away—peace with God.

The believer's standing before God gives him even more than acceptance. It gives him (2) *access.* Paul says: *"By whom also we have access by faith into this grace wherein we stand, and rejoice in hope of the glory of God"* (v. 2). The word "access" means "a bringing in, an introduction." "Here in Romans 5:2 the thought is rather that of our acceptance with God and the enjoyment of His grace, as those who have been justified."[3]

[2]W. E. Vine, *The Epistle to the Romans* (Grand Rapids: Zondervan Publishing House, 1948), p. 72.
[3]*Ibid.*, p. 73.

A little boy once stood outside the gates of Buckingham palace in London. He wanted to talk to the king but was sternly repulsed by the guard at the gate. He rubbed a grimy hand to his cheek to wipe away a tear. Just then along came a well-dressed man who asked the little fellow to explain his trouble. When he heard the story, the man smiled and said, "Here, hold my hand, sonny. I'll get you in. Just you never mind those soldiers." The little boy took the proffered hand and, to his surprise, saw the soldiers leap to attention and present arms as his new-found friend approached. Past the guard he was led, along carpeted halls, through wide-flung doors and on through a glittering throng right up to the throne of the king. He had taken the hand of the Prince of Wales, the king's son! Through him he had gained access.

It is a glorious thing to have acceptance, to know that the war is over and that God no longer looks upon us with disfavor and wrath. It is far better to have access. And those who have taken the pierced hand of the King's Son have access indeed. What a standing!

B. *A Preview of Our State* (5:3-5)

Our standing is perfect; our state is progressive. This is Paul's theme in the next few verses. "On to maturity!" is his cry. He shows (1) *how maturity is displayed by us.* "We glory in tribulations," he says (v. 3). The cross and the crown go together; the grief and the glory go hand in hand. To glory in tribulations is a real sign of maturity.

But how is such maturity attained? Paul goes on to explain (2) *how maturity is developed in us.* There is a melting process, a mellowing process, a molding process and a maturing process. "*Knowing,*" says Paul, "*that tribulation worketh patience; and patience, experience; and experience, hope; and hope maketh not ashamed*" (vv. 3b-5a). This was no mere theory with Paul, for he knew much about tribulation and its ability, when accepted in the right spirit, to develop Christian character in the believer. Tearing a page or two from his diary, he could write, "We are handicapped on all sides, but we are never frustrated; we are puzzled, but never in despair. We are persecuted, but we never have to stand it alone; we may be knocked down but we are never knocked out! Every day we experience something of the death of Jesus, so that we may also know the power of the life of Jesus in these bodies of ours" (II Cor. 4:8-10).[4]

The maturing power of tribulation is well illustrated in the case of Job. In the book of Job we see this righteous man first in the hands of Satan, then in the hands of men, and finally in the hands of God. At the hand of Satan, Job received tribulation and it wrought in him patience. At the hand of man his patience was sorely tried, but through it all he gained experience. It was far easier for Job, for example, to triumph over the calamities he received at the hand of Satan than to triumph over the criticisms he received from his friends. In the hands of God, Job came triumphantly through at last to that hope which maketh not ashamed. It is a far more righteous Job we meet at the end of the book than the one we meet at the beginning.

Then Paul shows (3) *how maturity is determined for us*. *"The love of God is shed abroad in our hearts by the Holy Ghost which is given unto us"* (v. 5b). Here we have the first mention of love and the first formal mention of the Holy Spirit in the epistle. God's purpose is to give full assurance of salvation to each believer, and the Agent for this is His Spirit. God's purpose is also to make each of His own into His own likeness, to bring each one to complete maturity, and for this great work too He has given His own Spirit to each one. "Being confident of this very thing, that he which hath begun a good work in you will perform it until the day of Jesus Christ" (Phil. 1:6). There are no half measures with God; our state will one day be as perfect as our standing.

II. How God Has Loved Us (5:6-11)

It is the love of God that guarantees our eternal security. That same love that planned our redemption in the far reaches of a past eternity, that yielded up the Lord Jesus to the death of the cross will fling wide at last the gates of glory to welcome us home.

A. *The Proof of God's Love* (5:6-8)

The proof of love is ever in its gift. "For God so loved the world, that he *gave* his only begotten Son" (John 3:16). "Christ loved the church, and *gave* himself for it" (Eph. 5:25). "He loved

---

[4]J. B. Phillips, *The New Testament in Modern English* (New York: The Macmillan Company. Copyright © by J. B. Phillips, 1958), p. 385.

me, and *gave* himself for me" (Gal. 2:20). Whether the Bible talks of the love of God for the *world*, for the *church*, or for *me*, the measure and manifestation of that love is always the same. The gift of Christ is ever and always the proof of God's love. Paul shows us that (1) *God's love is unconditional.* "*For when we were yet without strength, in due time Christ died for the ungodly*" (v. 6).

Christ died for the *ungodly*. There is an old poem which illustrates this. The verses tell of a young man who gave his love to a vicious woman who demanded of him as proof of his love that he bring to her his mother's heart to feed to her dog. The young man took a knife, slew his mother, and cut out her heart. As he was running back to the evil woman, the young man stumbled and fell, and his mother's heart flew from his grasp. As it rolled by, that mother's heart was heard to cry in a still, small voice, "Are you hurt, my child, are you hurt at all?"[5]

Christ died for the ungodly! If a mother's love can be so depicted, what of the love of God as manifested at Calvary? Those iron bolts of Rome in the pierced hand of the crucified Christ could well have become thunderbolts of wrath. He could have hurled His anathemas across a guilty world, summoned from the ramparts of heaven twelve shining legions with drawn and flaming swords, and marched to Armageddon then and there. Instead yon lovely Man cried, "Father, forgive them, for they know not what they do." Christ died for the ungodly. This is the proof of God's love; it is unconditional.

Moreover, (2) *God's love is incomparable.* "*For scarcely for a righteous man will one die: yet peradventure for a good man some would even dare to die. But God commendeth his love toward us, in that, while we were yet sinners, Christ died for us*" (vv. 7-8). While we were yet sinners! Jesus said, "I am not come to call the righteous, but sinners to repentance" (Matt. 9:13). "Christ Jesus came into the world to save sinners" (I Tim. 1:15). It isn't that we deserve God's help and salvation, for we merit nothing but His undiluted wrath and unmitigated punishment. Look at what sin has done to that fair and lovely world, the world upon which God uttered His benediction in the day of creation (Gen. 1:31).

[5]Jean Richepin, "A Mother's Heart," poem quoted in James Hastings, *The Great Texts of the Bible*, Vol. XIV: *Romans VIII-XVI* (Grand Rapids: Wm. B. Eerdmans Publishing Co., n.d.), p. 149.

Sin has outraged God and defiled both heaven and earth. It has introduced rebellion and ruin where once He reigned supreme. The world is haunted by demons, disease, and death, and dotted with graveyards, hospitals, prisons, and mental institutions. It is ruined by vileness and squalor, misery and hatred, war and famine, blight and pestilence, death and decay—all products of sin.

And man is hand in glove with sin. When God sent forth His Son to be their Saviour, men spat into the face of Jesus, plowed His back with a scourge, spiked Him naked and thorn-crowned to a tree, sneered and mocked Him in His anguish until the sun hid its blushing noonday face in shame and the earth quaked in terror and the bedrock granite rent wide in protest. Yet despite it all, God has "made peace through the blood of his cross" (Col. 1:20), surely one of the most astounding statements in the Word of God. We could understand if it were to read that God had made war over that precious, outpoured blood and that cursed cross; but we read instead that He made *peace* through that very blood. God's love is incomparable.

B. *The Provision of God's Love* (5:9-10)

God's love has provided for our salvation. Paul tells how (1) *Christ gave His life for us* (vv. 9-10a). "*Much more then, being now justified by his blood, we shall be saved from wrath through him. For if, when we were enemies, we were reconciled to God by the death of his Son, much more, being reconciled, we shall be saved by his life*" (vv. 9-10). We are both justified and reconciled. "Not once in the Bible is God said to be reconciled. The enmity is alone on our part. It was we who needed to be reconciled to God, not God to us; and it is propitiation which His righteousness and mercy have provided that makes reconciliation possible to those who receive it."[6] We are "saved from wrath," says Paul. Christ gave His life for us. Hallelujah! As the hymn writer puts it:

> God will not payment twice demand,
> First at my Saviour's bleeding hand
> And then again at mine.

[6]W. E. Vine, *An Expository Dictionary of New Testament Words* (London: Oliphants, Ltd., 1940), p. 261.

Mark well the expression "much more," which occurs repeatedly in this great chapter. The work of Christ did more than restore what Adam lost. This fact is illustrated by the trespass offering required under the Mosaic law. It was mandatory that the trespasser not only make good the actual loss he had inflicted on his victim but he must add a fifth to it by way of restitution. The injured party thus became a gainer. The work of Christ at Calvary has not only brought infinite glory to God but great gain to the believing sinner. It would have been possible for man to have remained in innocence in the garden of Eden indefinitely and still have remained a son of Adam only. Because of Calvary, however, we become the sons of God and enjoy a relationship to God far closer than that enjoyed by Adam.

Christ gave His life for us. We are "justified by his blood" and "saved from wrath through him." We have been "reconciled to God by the death of his Son." But there is more to it than that. Paul tells us how (2) *Christ gives His life to us.* "*Being reconciled, we shall be saved through his life*" (v. 10*b*). In other words, if God's love reached us *before,* when we were in our sins, how much more *now* when we are vitally linked with His Son. Our union with Him guarantees a continuing salvation and an ultimate arrival at glory. Christ giving His life *for* us saves us from the *penalty* of sin; Christ giving His life *to* us saves us from the *power* of sin, as it will one day save us from the *presence* of sin.

C. *The Products of God's Love* (5:11)

The first fruit of sin in human experience was an aversion to God and to His company. Adam and Eve flew to hide at the first sound of God's voice after they had eaten of the forbidden fruit. By contrast, the first fruit of salvation is the very opposite—it is exultation in God. Paul says, "*We also joy in God through our Lord Jesus Christ, by whom we have now received the atonement*" (v. 11). The word "atonement" here is "reconciliation" as in verse 10. One can imagine the prodigal son returned from the far country reconciled and restored, exulting in his father. "Behold and see," he might have exclaimed to all who would hear his story; "behold and see whether there be any father like unto my father!" How much more should we exult in God!

III. HOW GOD HAS LOOSED US (5:12-21)

Salvation is forever. Having dealt with the *fruits* of sin (its guilt and its outworking in the life), Paul now goes on to deal with its *root*. He goes back to the origin of sin, to Adam and the fall. He sees in Adam the representative of *ruined* humanity and contrasts him with Jesus, the last Adam, the Representative of *redeemed* humanity. In Adam all men are *sinners*; in Christ they are *saints*. In Adam's family, *death* reigns; in Christ's family, *deliverance* reigns. In the case of Adam, God places the emphasis on *his offense;* in the case of Jesus, God places the emphasis on *His obedience*. In Christ, God has dealt with *sin,* root and branch, and has devised a means of taking the believer out of Adam's family and of placing him into the family of God.

Dr. R. E. D. Clark, in his important apologetic against evolution, has an interesting chapter with the intriguing title "Men Within Men." The chapter deals with "preformationism," one of the views which tries to explain how a human being, or any other creature for that matter, can be born from an egg.

"Preformation," says Dr. Clark, "soon found its place in theology and philosophy. Swammerdam, as a result of a suggestion made by Malebranche, used it to explain original sin. He said that if we were present inside our parents when they sinned, it followed that we, being a part of them, must have sinned too. . . . He even went so far as to produce a delightful proof of preformation from the Bible. According to Hebrews 7:9-10, Levi paid tithes before he was born, and must, therefore, have existed as a tiny fellow inside Abraham when the latter gave tithes to Melchizedek, king of Salem!"[7]

[7] See Robert E. D. Clark, *Darwin: Before and After* (Chicago: Moody Press, 1967), pp. 18-26. According to this view, "the embryo is present all the time, though too small to be seen, until, in the process of growth, it unfolds itself and becomes visible." Clark describes the development of the theory and shows how some preformationists "went to extremes and brought the whole doctrine into disrepute—a disrepute from which it is only now beginning to recover." Dr. Clark gives illustrations of extreme ideas and suggestions which began to cluster around the theory and says, "In time the inevitable happened. These fantastic speculations and calculations served to bring preformationism into disrepute. The sound common sense and appreciation of scientific principles upon which this doctrine had been based were forgotten and in time the very word 'preformation' served to conjure up the image of the absurd *embroisement* theory. . . .

"Yet today, after a long lapse of time, there is no doubt that the preformationist was right. The attitude adopted by modern embryologists is well

Actually there are good theological grounds for taking this literally (Rom. 3:23; 5:12). The doctrine of the hereditary nature of sin is deeply written into the Word of God. So far as the human race is concerned, sin had its rise in Adam, and has been transmitted by him to all his posterity. The theory of evolution strikes hard at this biblical doctrine, far closer to the heart of the Christian faith indeed than most people realize. Banish Adam from the scheme of things, and Romans 5 must be torn from the Word of God and with it the very heart of the Bible's teaching on the cause, nature and consequences of sin.

A. *The Problem of Sin Is Stated* (5:12-14)

The problem concerns (1) the *presence* of sin. Paul says, *"By one man sin entered into the world"* (v. 12). The story of Adam and Eve is no mere myth, folklore or legend but an actual event in human history. Scripture puts the full blame for human sin on the shoulders of Adam, the father of the human race. All the unborn generations of men were "in Adam," so to speak, when Adam fell. Theologians speak of man as being in Adam "federally and seminally." That is, Adam both represented us and contained us. He was created in the image and likeness of God (Gen. 1:26-27). However, when Adam's family began to arrive after the fall, we are expressly told that "Adam . . . begat a son in his own likeness, after his image" (Gen. 5:3). Adam's descendants do not bear the image and likeness of God, but the image and likeness of fallen Adam.

Then there is the problem of (2) the *penalty* of sin. *"By one man sin entered into the world, and death by sin"* (v. 12). "Thou shalt surely die" was God's clear word (Gen. 2:17). "Ye shall not surely die" was the serpent's blatant lie (Gen. 3:4). The moment Adam sinned he died spiritually; years later he died physically as well. The dread decree, "Dust thou art, and unto dust shalt thou return" (Gen. 3:19) embraces all mankind. *"So death passed upon all men, for that all have sinned"* (v. 12). Death was imputed immediately from Adam to each individual descendant of

summarized by Huxley and de Beer, who remark that we are now vigorously preformationists as regards heredity, but rigorously epigenetic as regards embryological development." Dr. Clark anticipates the day when "science will have returned completely to the old preformationist view, almost in the form that Malpighi taught it."

his. All sinned in Adam and death was imputed immediately and directly from Adam to each individual human being.

Finally Paul reminds us of (3) the *power* of sin. *"For until the law sin was in the world: but sin is not imputed when there is no law. Nevertheless death reigned from Adam to Moses, even over them that had not sinned after the similitude of Adam's transgression, who is the figure of him that was to come"* (vv. 13-14). The remarkable fact is that although sin was in the world for centuries, it was not formally charged to men's accounts until Moses came, because it was not until then that the law was given. Yet men died. They died primarily not because they had sinned but because Adam had sinned. While sin was not charged to their account, so to speak, men died just the same, and for this fearful state of affairs Adam was responsible. The death of an infant is proof enough that death reigns even over an "innocent" babe. Such is the power of sin introduced by Adam to his race.

Here then is the problem of sin. Adam, by the fall, introduced to his race, as yet unborn, the deadly virus of sin. We are not sinners because we sin; we sin because we are sinners. And because we sinned in Adam, death is imputed to us. Therefore we die, some younger, some older, but sooner or later we die.

B. *The Problem of Sin Is Studied* (5:15-21)

Is there any solution to this problem of sin? There is indeed— a second Man is the answer, a last Adam; One who through His obedience can restore all that which the first Adam threw away by willful rebellion against the command of God. The solution is twofold. It is found in (1) the *gift* of God. *"But not as the offence, so also is the free gift. For if through the offence of one many be dead, much more the grace of God, and the gift by grace, which is by one man, Jesus Christ, hath abounded unto man"* (v. 15). This tells us that God's gift releases us from *bankruptcy*. The thought is brought out better in the Phillips' translation which reads: "But the gift of God through Christ is a very different matter from the 'account rendered' through the sin of Adam. For while as a result of one man's sin death by natural consequence became the common lot of men, it was by the generosity of God, the free giving of the grace of the one man Jesus Christ, that the love of God overflowed for the benefit of all men."[8] The "account rendered" of sin leaves us bankrupt indeed; but by contrast, the gift of God makes us sons of God and joint heirs with Jesus Christ.

God's gift, moreover, releases us from *blame*. "*And not as it was by one that sinned, so is the gift: for the judgment was by one to condemnation, but the free gift is of many offences unto justification*" (v. 16). Phillips is helpful here too: "Nor is the effect of God's gift the same as the effect of that one man's sin. For in the one case one man's sin brought its inevitable judgment, and the result was condemnation. But, in the other, countless men's sins are met with the free gift of grace, and the result is justification before God."[9] Sin's awful guilt is gone.

In addition, God's gift releases us from *bondage*, that is, from bondage to death. "*For if by one man's offence death reigned by one; much more they which receive abundance of grace and of the gift of righteousness shall reign in life by one, Jesus Christ*" (v. 17). Or again as J. B. Phillips puts it: "For if one man's offence meant that men should be slaves to death all their lives, it is a far greater thing that through another man, Jesus Christ, men by their acceptance of his more than sufficient grace and righteousness should live all their lives like kings."[10] So Paul reports in glowing words the good news of the gift of God which releases us from sin's bankruptcy, blame and bondage through the finished work of Christ.

But this good news of our complete salvation is just too good, it seems, to be believed with one statement of the case. So Paul repeats this good news of the gift of God. "*Therefore as by the offence of one judgment came upon all men to condemnation; even so by the righteousness of one the free gift came upon all men unto justification of life. For as by one man's disobedience many were made sinners, so by the obedience of one shall many be made righteous*" (vv. 18-19). Praise God! The provision is as wide as the problem. He has not only lifted us and loved us, He has loosed us from our sins. And done so freely, fully and forever, and all "without money and without price."

The solution of the problem of sin, however, depends not only on the gift of God but also on (2) the *grace* of God. Grace made

---

[8]J. B. Phillips, *The New Testament in Modern English*, pp. 326-327.
[9]*Ibid.*, p. 327.
[10]*Ibid.*, p. 327.

that gift possible. In bringing to a close this great chapter on the security of the believer, Paul shows us something of (a) the *abundant supply* of God's grace. When God finally gave the law, it was so that the guiltiness of sin might become apparent; but then at once He manifested His grace, His unmerited favor, to guilty sinners. *"Moreover the law entered, that the offence might abound. But where sin abounded, grace did much more abound"* (v. 20). Those who have sinned the most flagrantly are often the most conscious of what this abundant supply of God's grace really means. Thus John Bunyan wrote his book *Grace Abounding*, and John Newton, the one-time slave of slaves, wrote his matchless hymn "Amazing Grace."

The grace of God is an exhaustless theme. Sam Duncannan, a simple soul with very few talents, had a great desire to do something for the Lord. So he made it his practice to cut out pictures from cards and magazines and to paste on to these pictures appropriate verses and poems, and then to give these simple gifts to those whom he felt would be blessed by them. One day, Sam came across a picture of Niagara Falls, but for a long time could find no poem appropriate for this picture. Then he heard Sankey sing a hymn and the moment he heard it, Sam Duncannan knew he had found the poem for which he had looked so long. Sankey's hymn went like this:

> Have you on the Lord believed?
>   Still there's more to follow.
> Of His grace have you received?
>   Still there's more to follow.
>
> Oh, the grace the Father shows,
>   Still there's more to follow;
> Freely He His grace bestows,
>   Still there's more to follow.
>
> More and more and more and more,
>   Always more to follow;
> Oh, His matchless, boundless love,
>   Still there's more to follow!

Underneath his picture of Niagara Falls, Sam wrote these lines and titled the picture with the appropriate words: "More to Follow!" What better illustration could there be of the abundant supply of God's grace! "Where sin abounded, grace did much more abound."

But that's not all! Paul ends this great chapter by reminding us of (*b*) the *absolute sovereignty* of God's grace. *"That as sin hath reigned unto death, even so might grace reign through righteousness unto eternal life by Jesus Christ our Lord"* (v. 21). Nothing can stand in the way of God's grace. It is absolutely sovereign. Eternal life through Jesus Christ our Lord is assured. Praise His name!

THE WAY OF VICTORY EXPLAINED
6:1—7:25

I. Deliverance From the Domain of Death (6:1-11)

    A. The Reality of Our Death with Christ (6:1-5)
        1. The Truth of It (6:1-2)
        2. The Triumph of It (6:3-5)
    B. The Reason for Our Death with Christ (6:6-7)
        1. Sin's Stronghold in the Life (6:6*a*)
        2. Sin's Stranglehold on the Life (6:6*b*-7)
    C. The Results of Our Death with Christ (6:8-11)
        1. Appreciation of the Victory of Christ (6:8-10)
        2. Appropriation of the Victory of Christ (6:11)

II. Deliverance From the Dominion of Sin (6:12-23)

    A. Sin, the Old Monarch, Is Now Defeated (6:12-14)
    B. Sin, the Old Master, Is Now Deposed (6:15-23)
        1. A New Liberty (6:15-18)
        2. A New Loyalty (6:19-20)
        3. A New Longevity (6:21-23)

III. Deliverance From the Demands of the Law (7:1-25)

    A. The Law and the Spiritual Man (7:1-6)
        1. He Knows the Law's Power Ends at Death (7:1-3)
        2. He Shows the Law's Power Ends at Death (7:4-6)
    B. The Law and the Natural Man (7:7-13)
        1. The Law Exposes the Hidden Nature of Sin (7:7-9)
        2. The Law Exposes the Hideous Nature of Sin (7:10-13)
    C. The Law and the Carnal Man (7:14-25)

THERE IS, OF COURSE, no literary break between Romans 5 and Romans 6; the one chapter continues the argument begun in the other. Paul is still dealing with the subject of *sin* rather than *sins*, but now he is going to show that Christ's victory at Calvary liberates us not only from sin's penalty but also from its power. Our security gives us no excuse to "continue in sin" (6:1). On the contrary, we who were once "dead *in* sin" are now "dead *to* sin." Far from the doctrine of eternal security of the believer resulting in freedom *to* sin, it actually sets before us our freedom *from* sin. The expression "free from sin" occurs three times in Romans 6 (vv. 7, 18, 22).

I. DELIVERANCE FROM THE DOMAIN OF DEATH (6:1-11)

According to Paul, ignorance is a key factor in hindering a life of victory. The expression "know ye not" occurs three times in this section of the epistle (6:3, 16; 7:1) and helps us divide the section into its component parts. The expression "through Jesus Christ our Lord" is another key expression and occurs once in each of these parts (6:11, 23; 7:25). The first area of ignorance with which Paul deals has to do with the domain of death. Death, once our enemy, is now actually made to minister to the believer the benefits of Christ's victory over the tomb.

A. *The Reality of Our Death with Christ* (6:1-5)

The idea that the believer has already died is so revolutionary that Paul begins by asserting (1) *the truth of it.* *"What shall we say then? Shall we continue in sin, that grace may abound? God forbid. How shall we that are dead to sin, live any longer therein?"* (vv. 1-2). Nothing can be more unresponsive than a person who is dead. Imagine someone trying to evoke a reaction from a corpse! It can be caressed, commanded, or kicked and no response will come, for the simple reason that it is dead to all such stimuli. God reckons the believer to be dead to the promptings of sin.

In a certain church was a narrow, bigoted old deacon, wedded to the old paths and suspicious of anything new. A dried up old die-hard was he, sitting in judgment on all who refused to be ruled by his view of Scripture, acid of temperament and barren of soul. Although that was not his real name, we shall call him

Macadam. To this church came a young man with the fresh dew of
God's anointing upon him, a young man of vision, gift, charm and
possessed of an unusual grasp of Scripture and a distinct measure
of wisdom. This young man's ministry was singularly blessed of
God to the salvation of souls and the quickening of many of God's
people. But, inevitably perhaps, some of his views did not coin-
cide with those of the dour old Scot who ruled the deaconate. For
years the deacon did all in his power to discourage, oppose and
criticize the younger man. One day another member of this
church asked the younger man how he managed to put up with
this deacon. "William," was the startling reply, "I died to Macadam five years ago." This young man had grasped the secret of
the believer's death with Christ. Let us grasp the truth of it—
"How shall we that are dead to sin, live any longer therein?" There
should be in our lives such an experience of the reality of our
death with Christ that sin can evoke no response from us at all.

Next Paul asserts (2) *the triumph of it;* and to drive home his
point, he gives two illustrations. *"Know ye not, that so many of us
as were baptized into Jesus Christ were baptized into his death?
Therefore we are buried with him by baptism into death: that like
as Christ was raised up from the dead by the glory of the Father,
even so we also should walk in newness of life"* (vv. 3-4).

Wuest has a helpful comment on this verse. "The word 'baptized' is not the translation of the Greek word here, but its trans-
literation, its spelling in English letters. The word is used in the
classics of a smith who dips a piece of hot iron in water, temper-
ing it; also of Greek soldiers placing the points of their swords,
and barbarians, the points of their spears, in a bowl of blood. . . .
The usage of the word as seen in the above examples resolves
itself into the following definition of the word *baptizō*, 'the introduction or placing of a person or thing into a new environment or
into union with someone else so as to alter its condition or its relationship to its previous environment or condition.' And that is
its usage in Romans 6. It refers to the act of God introducing a
believing sinner into vital union with Jesus Christ, in order that
the believer might have the power of his sinful nature broken and
the divine nature implanted through his identification with Christ
in His death, burial and resurrection; thus altering the condition
and relationship of that sinner with regard to his previous state

and environment, bringing him into a new environment, the kingdom of God."[1]

In other words, in this biographical illustration, Paul refers to our baptism into Christ. This is something that happens at conversion so far as our experience is concerned. There are others who maintain, of course, that the baptism referred to here is water baptism and not Spirit baptism.[2] Whichever view is adopted, the fact remains that Paul is driving home the reality of our death with Christ by pointing to a real and actual personal experience.

The second illustration follows. *"For if we have been planted together in the likeness of his death, we shall be also in the likeness of his resurrection"* (v. 5). The word "planted" here is literally "united together." Wuest says the word could be used of Siamese twins. Sanday translates it "united by growth" and adds, "The word exactly expresses the process by which a graft becomes united with the life of a tree. So the Christian becomes 'grafted into' Christ."[3] We become vitally united to Him. We share His very life.

In these two illustrations, the one biographical and theological and the other biological, Paul is seeking to convey the remarkable truth that Christ's death was our death; His burial was our burial; His resurrection was our resurrection. He not only died *for* me; He died *as* me! So far as God is concerned, we are already on the resurrection side of the grave and it but remains for us to realize this truth and appropriate it, and victory is assured.

---

[1]Kenneth S. Wuest, *Romans in the Greek New Testament* (Grand Rapids: Wm. B. Eerdmans Publishing Co., 1955), pp. 96-97. Used by permission.

[2]William R. Newell for example in *Romans Verse by Verse* strongly maintains that water baptism is in view in Romans 6.

Those who practice the baptism of believers by immersion maintain that water baptism is "the outward expression of an inward experience." It typifies that which has already been done in the heart by the Holy Spirit. Baptism by immersion does indeed afford a striking illustration of the believer's death, burial and resurrection with Christ. First, the believer takes his stand in water—an element foreign to his nature and which spells death to him as a natural man. Then he is immersed in this element of death, put right out of sight, buried. Finally, he is brought up from this watery grave by the power of another's arm. Then he lives on, publicly identified with Christ through this act of obedience. Baptism thus complements the Lord's Table. The one ordinance sets forth *the believer's death with Christ*; the other sets forth *Christ's death for the believer*.

[3]W. Sanday and A. C. Headlam, *A Critical and Exegetical Commentary on the Epistle to the Romans* (Edinburgh: T. and T. Clark, 1911), p. 157.

B. *The Reason for Our Death with Christ* (6:6-7)

Through our identification with Christ in this unique and wonderful way, God has broken (1) *sin's stronghold in the life.*
"Knowing this," says Paul, *"that our old man is crucified with him"*
(v. 6a). The expression "the old man" occurs in Ephesians 4:22
and in Colossians 3:9, as well as here, "and always means the man
of the old, corrupt human nature, the inborn tendency to evil in
all men. In Romans 6:6 it is the natural man himself; in Ephesians
4:22 and Colossians 3:9 his ways. *Positionally,* in the reckoning
of God, the old man is crucified, and the believer is exhorted to
make this good in *experience,* reckoning it to be so by definitely
'putting off' the old man and 'putting on' the new."[4]

The old man, then, is the man of old, the man we used to be
before our conversion. There is something we should know about
this old man: he is now dead! He has been crucified with Christ.
The figure of crucifixion is very striking, for no man can crucify
himself. In death by crucifixion the execution is of necessity at
the hands of another. At Calvary, *God* has dealt with the question
of *self* as well as the question of *sin* by putting us to death with
Christ. This is something we need to know, for without this
knowledge we can never hope to experience deliverance from all
that we are by natural birth.

Through our identification with Christ, furthermore, God has
broken (2) *sin's stranglehold on the life.* *"Knowing this, that our*
old man is crucified with him, that the body of sin might be
destroyed, that henceforth we should not serve sin. For he that
is dead is freed from sin" (vv. 6-7). "The body of sin" has been
defined as "the instrument for carrying out sin's orders." W. E.
Vine says that the word *sōma* "denotes the body as the organic
instrument of natural life; it is used here figuratively with that as
its essential significance. . . . In the phrase, 'the body of sin,' then,
sin is regarded as an organized power, acting through the members of the body, though the seat of sin is in the will."[5] The believer is to regard his body as dead so far as being an instrument
through which sin can work, is concerned.

Now, of course the body does not *feel* dead to sin, but that is
quite beside the point; God says it is. A sinner seeking salvation

[4]C. I. Scofield, *Scofield Reference Bible* (New York: Oxford University
Press, 1909), p. 1198.
[5]W. E. Vine, *The Epistle to the Romans* (Grand Rapids: Zondervan
Publishing House, 1948), p. 89.

must learn that salvation does not depend upon feelings but upon certain facts related to the work of Christ and the Word of God. These facts must be believed, and Christ must be received by faith. Then, on the authority of God's Word, the sinner can know his sins are forgiven no matter how he may *feel* in this regard. Just so with the saint. He must accept the fact that at Calvary God dealt with "the body of sin" and he must believe that God means what He says in Romans 6:6. Feelings are quite secondary and incidental.

A certain man was accustomed to rising at six o'clock to catch a train each morning at seven. His wife usually saw him off to work; but one night the little ones had been particularly restless and his wife was just settling down to a deep sleep when the alarm clock went off. "Oh, dear," she groaned, "is that six o'clock?" When her husband told her it was, she said, "It doesn't *feel* like six o'clock." Now here's the point. It didn't feel like six o'clock but the sun, the moon, and the stars, the earth on its orbit, and the whole machinery of the heavens declared that it was six o'clock. But it didn't *feel* like six o'clock! It is the same with this great biblical truth that the believer is dead with Christ. He may not feel very dead, but that is beside the point. God says that he is, and the whole machinery of redemption declares it to be a fact.

How slow we are to believe this great, basic fact which opens for us the door to victorious Christian living! The story is told of two Irishmen, Pat and Mike, who found a most unusual turtle. The animal's head had been completely severed from its body, but the turtle was still running around as though nothing had happened. Pat maintained that it was dead, but Mike denied it stoutly and the argument waxed louder and louder until presently along came O'Brien. They decided that O'Brien should arbitrate the matter and that his verdict would be final. O'Brien took one look at this remarkable turtle and said, "It's dead—but it don't believe it!" That is exactly the problem with many Christians: they are dead but they do not believe it. This is a tragedy, for it is the truth of this verse fully and unreservedly believed that breaks sin's stranglehold in the life once it is believed.

C. *The Results of Our Death with Christ* (6:8-11)

God has made death to work on our behalf. It swings open for

us now the door to victory, just as later, if the Lord has not come,
it will swing open for us the door to glory. The resurrection of
Christ from the dead is a liberating truth. We must learn to (1)
appreciate the victory of Christ. "*Now if we be dead with Christ,
we believe that we shall also live with him: knowing that Christ
being raised from the dead dieth no more; death hath no more
dominion over him*" (vv. 8-9). Paul wants us to grasp the *significance* of Christ's death and resurrection. It stands to reason,
he argues, that if we are identified with Christ in His death, then
likewise we are identified with Him in His resurrection. The two
go together. The same mighty power which raised up Christ from
the dead (1:4) is at work in the believer's life today. This statement does not refer primarily to the coming resurrection at the
last trump, but has immediate application to the present power of
the indwelling Holy Spirit who ministers to us the blessings and
the benefits of Christ's resurrection. Paul returns to this theme in
Romans 8.

Paul wants us to grasp not only the significance of Christ's
resurrection but also its *magnificence.* "Christ being raised from
the dead dieth no more; death hath no more dominion over him."
One of the great shortcomings of some churches lies in their in-
adequate concept of Christ. They present Christ either as an
infant in the arms of His mother, or as still on the cross. But
Christ is no longer in the cradle, in the arms of the Virgin, on the
cross, or in the tomb. He is alive from the dead and forever beyond the power of death. The fact that death has no more dominion over Christ is the basis for Paul's argument that sin has
no more dominion over us. "*He died unto sin once: but in that
he liveth, he liveth unto God*" (v. 10). If we are to enjoy victory
we must first appreciate the victory of Christ.

Then we must (2) *appropriate the victory of Christ.* "*Likewise
reckon ye also yourselves to be dead indeed unto sin, but alive
unto God through Jesus Christ our Lord*" (v. 11). It is one thing
"to know" (v. 9); it is something else "to reckon." Many people
have a general knowledge of the truths of these chapters but
never enter into the good of them because they fail to reckon
them true in experience. The word "reckon" is "to count, com-
pute, to take into account." To recognize it as an accounting term
will help us understand what Paul is saying.

Suppose a businessman were to say to his accountant, "What is the total sum needed to meet this month's payroll?" After some calculation his bookkeeper says, "Twenty thousand dollars, sir; but there's a balance of only five thousand dollars in the bank right now." "Make out the checks," the businessman might say, "but do not give them to the men until you receive further word from me." Then the businessman pays a call on his banker, arranges for a loan of thirty thousand dollars, and calls his accountant and says, "You can now pass out the checks. The bank has more than covered the payroll." Presently the first employee calls at the office for his paycheck. "I'm sorry," says the accountant, "I cannot let you have this check right now. The total payroll is twenty thousand dollars and there's only five thousand in the bank. Here, you can look at the ledger and see for yourself." What would that accountant be failing to do? He would be failing to *reckon*, failing to take into account the fact that adequate provision had been -made for far more than the needs of the payroll. And, of course, by failing to reckon, he would be dishonoring his employer and would be putting himself in a false position.

At Calvary God made adequate provision for the sinner. He dealt fully and forever with all aspects of the question of sin. We have to reckon this to be so. We have to take this into account in the moment of temptation. God says that the believer has died to sin. He assures us that adequate provision has been made in the death of Christ and in our identification with Him for any temptation that might arise. Thus, through Jesus Christ our Lord we have been delivered from the domain of death, and as Paul is now going to demonstrate, with that we have also been delivered from the dominion of sin.

II. DELIVERANCE FROM THE DOMINION OF SIN (6:12-23)

In the remaining verses of this chapter sin is set before us in two graphic illustrations. It is likened to an old monarch, but an old monarch who is now defeated; and it is likened to an old master, but an old master who is now deposed.

A. *Sin, the Old Monarch, Is Now Defeated* (6:12-14)

As we think of our deliverance from the dominion of sin, we discover three principles. There is (1) *a physical principle in-*

volved. *"Let not sin therefore reign in your mortal body, that ye should obey it in the lusts thereof"* (v. 12). Sin expresses itself through the organs of the body and through this channel reigns in both the natural man and the carnal man. Such a state of affairs, however, should not be characteristic of the believer; for his body is set free from the reign of sin. In order to enjoy this victory, the believer must cooperate with God and determine that by God's grace sin shall not be sovereign. Paul puts it this way in his letter to the Corinthians: "And every man that striveth for the mastery is temperate in all things. Now they do it to obtain a corruptible crown; but we an incorruptible. I therefore so run, not as uncertainly; so fight I, not as one that beateth the air: but I keep under my body, and bring it into subjection: lest that by any means, when I have preached unto others, I myself should be a castaway" (I Cor. 9:25-27). An athlete will bring his body into subjection to his will to keep fit for the fight or the race. Can the believer do any less in order to win through to victory over sin?

In addition to the physical principle, there is (2) *a moral principle involved. "Neither yield ye your members as instruments of unrighteousness unto sin"* (v. 13a). Three great words in this chapter summarize the secret of making practical in the life the principles of victory. These words are "know," "reckon" and "yield." Paul tells us that we are not to yield to sin. We are not to permit our eyes to look with lust, our ears to listen to gossip, our tongues to employ vileness and untruth. There has to be an act of the will in this regard, for as moral agents we are responsible for the use to which we put our bodily members.

Then there is (3) *a spiritual principle involved.* It is not enough to make a resolution that the members will not be yielded to sin. Many people have tried this method of living, with little or no success; for victory does not rest ultimately upon our moral resolve but upon a spiritual principle. Notice the three steps involved in translating the principle into practice. We must *give in to God's will. "Yield yourselves unto God, as those that are alive from the dead, and your members as instruments of righteousness unto God"* (v. 13b). It is only as we give in to God that we have the victory. Think for a moment of a much misquoted verse from the book of James: "Resist the devil, and he will flee from you" (James 4:7). Quoted that way, this verse is simply not true. The devil is not going to flee from us; he is not the least bit afraid of us; he is more than a match for us. What the verse actually says is this: "Submit yourselves unto God. Resist the devil, and he will flee from you." That is quite different. It is as we yield, as we submit to God, that we swing wide the door for the outpouring of His power. His Spirit is resident in every believer; but only as we submit to Him does He liberate us from the shackles of sin.

There is a very important principle here. We are so made that when we are tempted we have to give in; but notice this. We do not have to give in to the temptation. Instead, we can give in to God, and in that act of yielding know complete victory from all the power of sin.

The next spiritual principle is to *get hold of God's Word.* "For sin shall not have dominion over you" (v. 14a). That is God's Word—"sin shall not have dominion over you." We must get a firm grasp on that. It was God's original plan for man to have dominion (Gen. 1:26); but when in the garden of Eden Adam surrendered his sovereignty to Satan, he doomed his posterity to slavery to sin. Since then, however, the Lord Jesus has invaded the arena of human affairs, come to grips with our old enemy at the cross, and restored our lost dominion. "Verily, verily, I say unto you," said the Lord Jesus, "Whosoever committeth sin is the servant of sin. . . . If the Son therefore shall make you free, ye shall be free indeed" (John 8:34, 36). We need to get hold of this clear Word of God, "sin shall not have dominion over you."

Sin, the old monarch, is now deposed. There is one more step to the realization of this truth. We must *go on in God's way.* "For ye are not under the law, but under grace" (v. 14b). In other words, continuing victory for the emancipated believer does not depend on his own efforts but on the abundant supply of God's grace, sufficient for every need.

B. *Sin, the Old Master, Is Now Deposed* (6:15-23)

Paul's next illustration is that of master and slave, for emancipation from the old master brings (1) *a new liberty.* This new liberty begins with *an attitude.* Paul says, *"What then? shall we sin, because we are not under the law, but under grace? God forbid! Know ye not, that to whom ye yield yourselves servants to obey, his servants ye are to whom ye obey; whether of sin unto death, or of obedience unto righteousness?"* (vv. 15-16). No person can expect victory who doesn't really want victory. No person can expect victory who has a soft attitude toward sin. God expects sincerity as much today as He did when He said to rebellious Israel, "And ye shall seek me, and find me, when ye shall search for me with all your heart" (Jer. 29:13). God is not going to bring us into the blessedness of this new liberty unless we really want it. The attitude that grace gives us license to sin, makes deliverance from its power impossible. So long as that attitude is indulged, sin will remain the master and we shall remain the slaves.

If this new liberty commences with an attitude, it consummates in *an attainment*. *"But God be thanked, that ye were the servants of sin, but ye have obeyed from the heart that form of doctrine which was delivered you. Being then made free from sin, ye became the servants of righteousness"* (vv. 17-18). Nearly two thousand years ago the Lord Jesus came down into the slave market of sin, paid the full price of our redemption and set us free. Our decision to believe the gospel bears permanent results provided it is no mere intellectual assent to truth but "from the heart." It should be observed that the doctrine and the deliverance go together. Paul speaks of "that form of doctrine" as playing a vital part in our emancipation. The word "form" suggests a mold into which molten metal is poured so as to take its destined shape. The believer is the molten metal, the doctrine or teaching of the gospel is the mold. Wuest reminds us that it is not "that form of doctrine which was delivered you"; it is rather "that form of doctrine into which you were delivered."[6] When we were saved, God cast our inward natures into the mold described in Romans 6. The gospel not only delivers us from the penalty and power of sin; it shapes our character as well. We have been delivered from sin's mastery and delivered over to the truth. As Paul puts it, "Being then made free from sin, ye became the servants of righteousness."

Emancipation from the old master brings more than a new liberty; it brings (2) *a new loyalty*. *"I speak after the manner of men because of the infirmity of your flesh: for as ye have yielded your members servants to uncleanness and to iniquity unto iniq-*

[6]See Kenneth Wuest, *Romans in the Greek New Testament*, p. 111.

*uity; even so now yield your members servants to righteousness
unto holiness. For when ye were the servants of sin, ye were free
from righteousness"* (vv. 19-20).

The scriptural comparisons introduced by the expression "as
. . . even so" should always be noted. Think, for example, of the
parallel drawn by the Lord Jesus in His conversation with Nicodemus: *"As* Moses lifted up the serpent in the wilderness, *even so*
must the Son of man be lifted up" (John 3:14); or of the parallel
He drew in His great Olivet Discourse: "But *as* the days of Noe
were, *so* shall also the coming of the Son of man be" (Matt.
24:37). *"As,"* says Paul, "ye have yielded your members servants
to uncleanness . . . *even so* now yield your members servants to
righteousness." Once we were loyal to the old master and yielded
our members as slaves to sin. Now we must be loyal to our new
Master, who has purchased us with His own life's blood at Calvary, and yield our members as instruments of righteousness. Paul
has already driven home the significance of that word "yield."

Emancipation from the old master brings (3) *a new longevity,*
in fact, a new quality of life altogether. We are to be *ashamed
of the old way of life.* Paul says, *"What fruit had ye then in those
things whereof ye are now ashamed? for the end of those things
is death"* (v. 21). There was nothing lasting about the old life of
sin. On the contrary, it hurried us along to certain death. In contrast with this, we are to be *assured of the new way of life.* *"But
now being made free from sin, and become servants to God, ye
have your fruit unto holiness, and the end everlasting life. For the
wages of sin is death; but the gift of God is eternal life through
Jesus Christ our Lord"* (vv. 22-23). Our emancipation from sin
guarantees unqualified success in this life, "fruit unto holiness";
and unqualified security for the next life, "eternal life through
Jesus Christ our Lord." The old master shamed us and paid us the
wages of death. The new Master makes us holy and gives us life
forevermore.

III. DELIVERANCE FROM THE DEMANDS OF THE LAW (7:1-25)

Paul has already explained that victory for the believer rests
upon a different principle from that of the law (6:15). The law
emphasizes human effort. Paul is now going to underline the fact

that no system of human effort can sustain a victorious Christian
life.

A. *The Law and the Spiritual Man* (7:1-6)

Paul describes men as being either natural, carnal or spiritual.
The *natural man* is the unsaved man who can rise no higher than
his intellectual, moral or volitional powers can lift him. He is
ruled by his senses. The *carnal man* is a saved man still dominated at least partially by the power of sin and under the control
of the old nature. The *spiritual man* is the believer whose life is
controlled by the Holy Spirit. These three "men" are in view in
Romans 7.

First, Paul deals with the spiritual man and shows that he is
delivered from the law. The spiritual man (1) *knows that the law's
power ends at death.* "*Know ye not, brethren, (for I speak to
them that know the law,) how that the law hath dominion over a
man as long as he liveth? For the woman which hath an husband
is bound by the law to her husband so long as he liveth; but if the
husband be dead, she is loosed from the law of her husband. So
then if, while her husband liveth, she be married to another man,
she shall be called an adulteress: but if her husband be dead, she
is free from that law; so that she is no adulteress, though she be
married to another man*" (vv. 1-3).

Paul's marriage illustration is very graphic, for it emphasizes
how valid and vital are the claims of the law up to the time of
death. Picture for a moment an unhappy marriage in which the
marriage vows have become a hateful bondage. There is no release from this bondage until death severs the relationship. The
law rivets firm and fast the bond of the marriage vow—at least in
the sight of God. But then the husband dies and the woman is
free. The death of the husband makes void the woman's status as
a wife in the eyes of the law. Paul is driving home the truth that
the law's power ends at death. The spiritual believer knows this.
He sees it to be true both in principle and in practice.

The spiritual man, moreover, (2) *shows that the law's power
ends at death.* He is no longer "trying" for victory anymore than
he is "trying" for salvation. He has discovered (*a*) *a more thrilling way to victory.* Driving home his argument that the law's
power ends at death, Paul says, "*Wherefore, my brethren, ye also*

*are become dead to the law by the body of Christ; that ye should
be married to another, even to him who is raised from the dead,
that we should bring forth fruit unto God*" (v. 4). Because of our
identification with Christ in His death, the claims of the law are
broken.[7]

Paul's illustration is thrilling indeed. The old marriage to sin,
hateful, intimate and unbearable, and made even worse by the
law, is over. That marriage is now dissolved, not by divorce but
by death. Now the believer is "married to another." All of us as
believers can remember the day the Holy Spirit came and pointed
to God's beloved Son, urging us to link our life with His. "Will
you take this Man to be your Saviour?" He asked. "Will you take
Him for richer or for poorer, for sickness or for health, for better
or for worse, for time and for eternity?" "I will!" was the glad
reply. In that holy moment the old marriage to sin was dissolved
and the believer was married to Another, "even to him who is
raised from the dead." Now the believer is Christ's, and his love,
life and loyalty all belong to Him. He is to live on terms of
closest intimacy with that risen One who has cancelled sin and
conquered death and satisfied the law. What a thrilling way to
victory!

The spiritual man, however, in showing that the law's power
ends at death, has discovered (*b*) *a more thorough way to victory.* The failure of the flesh no longer *haunts* him. *"For when we
were in the flesh, the motions of sins, which were by the law, did
work in our members to bring forth fruit unto death"* (v. 5). This
is an argument Paul develops further in verses 7-13. The law has
a baneful influence on the fleshly nature, actually stimulating it
to action and bringing to fruition its deadly seeds. By removing us
from the law principle, God has removed all fear of such failure
now.

The letter of the law no longer *daunts* him. *"But now we are
delivered from the law, that being dead wherein we were held;
that we should serve in newness of spirit, and not in the oldness
of the letter"* (v. 6). It is not the law, of course, that has been put
to death, but the believer. Instead of seeking an outward conformity to the "letter" (the external rules of conduct prescribed

[7]Strictly speaking, the analogy calls for the death of the law, but Paul will
not press the analogy that far. Instead he simply shows that the marriage
relation is killed.

by the law), the believer, indwelt by the Holy Spirit, fulfills the spirit of the law. The Christian life does not consist in mere conformity to a list of rules and regulations; it is the very life and loveliness of the Lord Jesus being wrought out in us by the Spirit of God.

B. *The Law and the Natural Man* (7:7-13)

If the spiritual man is delivered from the law, the natural man is *doomed* by the law. It has been much debated whether in this section Paul is describing his present experience as a defeated saint or his past experience as a doomed sinner. Since the verbs are in the past tense it seems a fair assumption that he is here going back to his unconverted days. The verbs in verses 14-25 are in the present tense and refer to Paul's experiences after his conversion. In his unconverted days he sought salvation in vain efforts to keep the law. The law only condemned him. There had to come a time in his experience when he came utterly to an end of himself and all his own efforts, and he surrendered completely to Christ. This is the experience he describes in verses 7-13. The parallel he draws in verses 14-25 is clear—as a believer, he must likewise come to an end of his own efforts if he is to know victory.

As a natural man, an unsaved man, he found that (1) *the law exposed the hidden nature of sin* and did so in two ways. First of all, it *revealed* his sinful nature. *"What shall we say then? Is the law sin? God forbid. Nay, I had not known sin, but by the law: for I had not known lust, except the law had said, Thou shalt not covet"* (v. 7). The great function of the Mosaic law is to expose sin. Men try to cover sin, excuse it, and camouflage it. They call it by respectable names. A person is not a drunkard, he is an alcoholic; drunkenness is not a sin, it is a disease. A person is not a liar, he is a prevaricator or, as someone has suggested, "an extrovert with a lively imagination"! Men speak of people as having complexes, phobias and inhibitions. They speak of a book as being daring; God would call it filthy. They say a man has had "an affair"; God says he has committed adultery. This is one of the games men play, and a deadly and dangerous game it is. It would be the height of folly to take a bottle from the shelf and remove the unpleasant label with its skull and crossbones and its bold letters, "Poison," putting on instead an attractive label bear-

ing the words, "Essence of Peppermint." This would only conceal the true nature of the contents of the bottle and invite the
unsuspecting to drink and die. Such a practice would not only be
folly but criminal as well; yet this is the practice of modern man
when faced with the ugly fact of sin. The function of the law is
to give sin its proper name and to expose it for what it is.

Paul says, "I had not known sin, but by the law; for I had not
known lust, except the law had said, Thou shalt not covet." Probably in his unconverted days as a conscientious Pharisee, Paul had
little trouble with the first nine commandments of the Decalogue.
He could say, "All these have I kept from my youth up." But the
tenth commandment dealt with inward desire, and Paul knew
very well that his inward desires were often wrong. In desire, if
not in deed, Paul had become a sinner and exposed to the curse of
the law.

The law, however, did more than reveal his sinful nature; it
revived his sinful nature. *"But sin, taking occasion by the commandment, wrought in me all manner of concupiscence. For without the law sin was dead. For I was alive without the law once:
but when the commandment came, sin revived, and I died"* (vv.
8-9). Before the law came there was freedom from an accusing
conscience, a kind of false peace brought about by man's ignorance of his alienation from God. The coming of the law changed
all this. Its straight edge reveals the crookedness of human nature
and even goes a step further and forces into the open all the latent
rebellion of the human heart. As the summer sun shines on a
vacant lot and warms the soil, causing the hidden seeds to spring
to life, covering the lot with weeds, so the law of God, shining on
the human heart, causes the latent seeds of sin to germinate and
reveal themselves. The truth of this is evident enough. Does not
the sign "Keep off the grass" arouse the latent rebellion of our
hearts, prompting us to at least put a foot on the forbidden
ground? Does not the sign "Speed Limit 20 mph" provoke a desire to try to get away with driving 30 mph? Does not the sign
"Speed Checked by Radar" arouse a mild resentment that we do
not have even a sporting chance of successfully breaking the law?
The law exposes the hidden nature of sin.

A wealthy land owner once overheard his gardener blaming
Adam for the weeds which cursed the soil and for the sweat which

bathed his brow. "Curse Adam!" cried the gardener as he labored through the heat of the day. The rich man asked the gardener to explain himself. "Well," replied the gardener, "it's
Adam's fault. If Adam had not sinned there'd be no weeds to
plague me, would there?" His employer argued that had the gardener been in Adam's place he would probably have done the
same, a proposition which the laborer refused to entertain.

"Well," said the gentleman, "you come up to my place for
supper tonight and we'll see." Later in the day the gardener presented himself at the rich man's home and was ushered into the
dining room where a large table was spread with everything a
hungry man could desire. All the dishes were open, steaming hot
and filling the air with a most appetizing fragrance, except one.
In the center of the table was a large dish covered with a lid.

The gardener and his host were about to sit down to their meal
when a servant entered and summoned the land owner to the
phone. "You will excuse me," said the rich man to his guest; "I
shall be back in a few minutes. Why don't you start? You are
welcome to everything on the table except what is in the covered
dish. That dish is reserved for me and I do not want you to so
much as touch it. That's a command!"

It wasn't long before the gardener, having filled his plate from
the wide choice of good things before him, began to grow increasingly curious about that mysterious covered dish. "There
must be something exceptionally good in there," he thought. "I
wonder why I can't have some. I'd certainly like to know what
it is."

The host was a long time in returning. At last the gardener
could restrain his curiosity no longer. Reaching across the table
he lifted the cover of the dish, at least to find out what was inside.
He pulled off the lid and hundreds of tiny feathers flew out of the
dish scattering far and wide across the table. And just then the
rich man walked in. "Curse Adam!" he said with a grin!

As a natural man, Paul found moreover that (2) *the law exposed the hideous nature of sin* and again did so in two ways.
First it exposed the *seriousness* of sin. "*And the commandment,
which was ordained to life, I found to be unto death. For sin,
taking occasion by the commandment, deceived me, and by it
slew me*" (vv. 10-11). For the law contained punishments as well

as precepts. It had power to reveal sin but no power to remove
sin, for even the sacrifices of the Mosaic system were but shadows.
The law does not reward us for keeping its commands; it only
punishes us for breaking them. Who has ever been stopped by a
police officer and told to report at once to the police station to be
rewarded for driving in an orderly fashion through a speed zone
and for stopping correctly at all the marked intersections! It is
not the normal function of the law to congratulate the law-abiding
citizen, only to expose, condemn and punish the lawbreaker. The
law of God punished severely. A careful study of the Old Testament shows that the death penalty was either appended to or
associated with the breaking of every commandment in the
Decalogue.[8] That's how serious sin is in God's sight. It carries a
death penalty in this life and eternal punishment in the next.

Suppose a hot-tempered GI were to smite a fellow soldier in
the barrack room. The punishment for thus breaking the peace
would be perhaps a few *days* detention. If he were to hit a sergeant, however, his punishment would more likely be three *weeks*
detention, while for assaulting an officer he would get three
months. If, however, he were to attempt to strike the visiting
President of the United States, he would be executed on the spot
by the President's bodyguard. In each case, the act would be the
same—striking a fellow man. But as the dignity and rank of the
person assaulted increases, so the seriousness of the offense increases in proportion. Now, all sin is against God (Ps. 51:4; Luke
15:18, 21) and is therefore an act of such seriousness that it earns
eternal damnation. One of the great functions of the law is to
reveal the seriousness of sin.

Paul found, however, that the law, while exposing the hideous
nature of sin, revealed not only its seriousness but its *sinfulness* as

[8]The death penalty was attached to the commandments as follows: the
first, against worshiping false gods (Exodus 20:3; 22:20; Deut. 6:13-15);
the *second*, against idolatry (Exodus 20:4; Deut. 27:15; Exodus 32:1, 26-
28); the *third*, against profanity (Exodus 20:7; Lev. 24:15-16); the *fourth*,
enforcing the Sabbath (Exodus 20:8; Num. 15:32-36); the *fifth*, enforcing respect of parents (Exodus 20:12; 21:15, 17; Deut. 27:16; 21:18-21); the *sixth*,
against murder (Exodus 20:13; 21:12, 29); the *seventh*, against adultery
(Exodus 20:14; Lev. 20:10); the *eighth*, against theft (Exodus 20:15;
21:16); the *ninth*, against false witness (Exodus 20:16; Deut. 19:16, 19,
21); the *tenth*, against covetousness (Exodus 20:17) when it found expression in sins covered by the other commandments. See Roy L. Aldrich, "The
Mosaic Ten Commandments," *Bibliotha Sacra*, Vol. 118, July, 1961, pp.
251-258.

well. *"Wherefore the law is holy, and the commandment holy, and just, and good. Was then that which is good made death to me? God forbid. But sin, that it might appear sin, working death in me by that which is good; that sin by the commandment might become exceeding sinful"* (vv. 12-13). There are at least fifteen Hebrew words in the Old Testament for sin, covering the entire spectrum of all possible kinds of wrong attitude to God and man. There are about as many different words in the Greek New Testament too, covering such ideas as sin, wickedness, evil, ungodliness, disobedience, transgression, iniquity, error and fault. Such a rich vocabulary in both Testaments reveals fully what God thinks about sin in all its forms. It is exceeding sinful. The high and holy standard of behavior demanded by the law leaves the sinner exposed, lost and defenseless. The law cannot save—that is the prerogative of grace. Paul found, as a sinner, that his best efforts to win salvation were unavailing. He was confronted with a law which was "holy, and just, and good," the lofty pinnacles of which he could never climb. Moreover, its fires and thunders struck terror to his heart.

C. *The Law and the Carnal Man* (7:14-25)

If the spiritual man is *delivered* from the law and the natural man is *doomed* by the law, by the same token the carnal man is *defeated* by the law. Between what the law demands and what the flesh can produce, there is a great gulf fixed. Observe (1) *how clearly this gulf is to be seen.* *"For we know that the law is spiritual: but I am carnal, sold under sin"* (v. 14). The word "carnal" is not used to describe an unsaved person, but a Christian who though saved, is still in bondage to the power of the flesh. The law is spiritual. "Between the law and one who is carnal there is a lack of moral adjustment. Peter, in his attempt to walk on the water, began to sink, because he was out of the sphere suited to mere doubting man."[9] The carnal Christian cannot behave the way God expects for the simple reason he is, to use language borrowed from the slave market, "sold under sin."

The next thing to observe is (2) *how carefully this gulf has been surveyed.* Note the threefold repetition of the word "for." The gulf exists first in terms of *conflicting potentialities.* *"For that*

[9]James M. Stifler, *The Epistle to the Romans* (Chicago: Moody Press, 1960), p. 128.

*which I do I allow not: for what I would, that do I not; but
what I hate, that do I. If then I do that which I would not, I consent unto the law that it is good. Now then it is no more I that do
it, but sin that dwelleth in me"* (vv. 15-17). There is a clash of
potentialities here that is very real. Every true believer has two
natures. He has an old nature, an Adamic nature, a nature with
which he was born, which can do nothing right (see v. 18); and
he also has a new nature, the nature of God, which can do nothing
wrong (I John 3:9). These two natures are in constant conflict
(Gal. 5:17), for the simple reason they are incompatible and
irreconcilable.

The gulf exists moreover in terms of *conflicting purposes.* *"For
I know that in me (that is, in my flesh) dwelleth no good thing:
for to will is present with me; but how to perform that which is
good I find not. For the good that I would I do not: but the evil
which I would not, that I do. Now if I do that I would not, it is
no more I that do it, but sin that dwelleth in me"* (vv. 18-20). In
an earlier section of the epistle, Paul has already driven home the
fact that "there is none that doeth good, no not one." What man
applauds as being "good" is not good at all, for nothing can be
truly good that springs from a life out of touch with God. The
carnal believer finds himself at cross purposes, desiring two different qualities of life at the same time.

The gulf exists, furthermore, in terms of *conflicting principles.*
*"I find then a law, that, when I would do good, evil is present with
me. For I delight in the law of God after the inward man: but I
see another law in my members, warring against the law of my
mind, and bringing me into captivity to the law of sin which is in
my members. O wretched man that I am! who shall deliver me
from the body of this death?"* (vv. 21-24). Paul sees two spiritual
laws or authorities at work here. There is what can be called (1)
the law of Sinai, the law of God. This law is holy, just and good;
it points him heavenward. It demands absolute perfection as a
standard of behavior, for perfection is God's minimum requirement consistent with His own holiness.

Then there is an opposite law which Paul calls (2) *the law of
sin.* When Adam fell in the garden of Eden, he placed the whole
human race under this law. Paul also calls it "the law of sin and
death" (8:2). Any science of human behavior which ignores the

law of sin must ultimately wander hopelessly astray from the truth. Yet our schools and universities teach every law known to science, except the law of sin. The fact remains, however, that it is the law of sin that really explains why people do what they do. It is at the very root of all behavioral problems. Paul finds that while the law of Sinai points him heavenward, the law of sin pulls him hellward. It acts in the moral realm exactly as the law of gravity operates in the physical realm. It exerts a downward pull.

Paul next describes two principles he sees at work within himself. (1) There is what he calls *the law of my mind*. This law seems to be practically identical with the law of God in verse 22. In any case it takes sides with the law of God, for Paul confesses that "with the mind I myself serve the law of God" (v. 25). In other words, his inner man delights in God's law. Every true believer knows what Paul is talking about here. We give intellectual assent to God's laws. We read the Sermon on the Mount and say, "Yes, I should like to live like that." We study the life of Jesus and say, "Yes, I would like to be like Jesus." Mentally every believer sides with God on the question of conduct.

But there is an opposite principle which Paul defines as (2) *the law in my members* (v. 23). This law seems to be identical with the law of sin. In fact, Paul says that it is "the law of sin in my members" (v. 23). It is the law of sin asserting itself in the members of the believer's body so that often involuntarily the eyes look with lust, the tongue wags in gossip, the ears strain to hear that which is improper and impure.

The gulf between what the law demands and what the flesh can produce is vast indeed. What with conflicting potentialities, purposes, and principles the believer is well-nigh pulled apart. He cries, "O wretched man that I am! who shall deliver me from the body of this death?"

Some believe Paul is drawing an analogy here. Certain types of criminals were executed by the Romans with special brutality. Sometimes if the man had committed a murder, he was bound hand to hand, face to face with the corpse of his victim and then thrown out into the heat of the Mediterranean sun. As the corpse decayed, it ate death into the living man and became to him, in the strictest literal sense, "a body of death." Paul sees the carnal believer thus bound to the old nature and truly a wretched man.

Suppose a biologist were to perform an experiment by grafting at a given stage of development a butterfly to a spider and do so in such a way that the two creatures were fused into one and thus grew to maturity. What a clash of instincts there would be in a monstrosity like this. One part of the creature's nature would long for the clear vault of heaven, while the other part would crave a web in a dark corner and a diet of blood. What could be done with such a creature? Nothing, except put it to death. There is a sense in which, in the garden of Eden, Satan performed just such diabolical surgery on the human race. Part of his own personality, so to speak, was grafted onto the human personality and the product of this union is the "flesh." There is only one thing God can do to the flesh and that is to put it to death. This is exactly what He has done by identifying us with Christ in His death. The flesh is hopelessly corrupt and can produce nothing acceptable to God. Our hope is to escape from it in the way that God has appointed. That way, of course, is the great theme of Romans 6 and 8.

The final thing then to observe is (3) *how completely this gulf has been spanned.* What is Paul's final answer? Brought at last to a complete end of himself, he sees the way of escape. *"I thank God through Jesus Christ our Lord"* (v. 25). Just as eternal life is "through Jesus Christ our Lord," so escape from the flesh is through Him. On the cross the Lord Jesus dealt effectively not only with the problem of sin and with the problem of Satan, but with the problem of self as well. In the next chapter Paul shows how this victory, explained at such length in chapters 6 and 7, can be experienced.

THE WAY OF VICTORY EXPERIENCED
8:1-39

I. THE NEW LAW (8:1-4)

    A. No More Condemnation for Sin (8:1)

    B. No More Control by Sin (8:2)

    C. No More Continuance in Sin (8:3-4)

II. THE NEW LORD (8:5-13)

  A. The Holy Spirit Controls the Mind (8:5-7)
  B. The Holy Spirit Controls the Motives (8:8-9)
  C. The Holy Spirit Controls the Members (8:10-13)

III. THE NEW LIFE (8:14-39)

  A. The Emphasis on Sonship (8:14-27)
    1. Adoption into the Family (8:14-17)
    2. Adaption for the Family (8:18-27)
      a. As it affects the creation (8:18-22)
      b. As it affects the Christian (8:23-25)
      c. As it affects the Comforter (8:26-27)
  B. The Emphasis on Security (8:28-39)
    1. The Believer Is Predestinated for Glory (8:28-30)
    2. The Believer Is Preserved for Glory (8:31-39)
      a. The foundation of this hope (8:31-32)
      b. The fullness of this hope (8:33-34)
        (1) The perfect defeat of our adversary (8:33)
        (2) The perfect defense of our Advocate (8:34)
      c. The finality of this hope (8:35-39)
        (1) No foe can daunt us (8:35-37)
        (2) No fear can haunt us (8:38-39)

PAUL HAS JUST FINISHED explaining the spiritual laws which hold the carnal Christian in bondage to sin and self. He has intimated that there is a way of escape from the constant, wearying struggle "through Jesus Christ our Lord." He will now show how that way of escape can become a practical reality in daily experience.

I. THE NEW LAW (8:1-4)

According to this new law there is complete freedom for the believer both from the penalty and power of sin.

A. *There Is No More Condemnation for Sin* (8:1)

This great eighth chapter of Romans begins with "no condemnation" and ends with "no separation." *"There is therefore now no condemnation to them which are in Christ Jesus"* (v. 1). The words, "who walk not after the flesh, but after the Spirit," are, as Sanday says, an interpolation in this verse. They seem to have been imported into verse 1 from the end of verse 4 where they are also to be found. There are no conditions attached to our freedom from condemnation; grace writes an unconditional guarantee.

The expression "in Christ" is one of Paul's favorites. It occurs in all his epistles and denotes a new sphere into which the believer is brought at conversion. The concept of being "in Christ" is not an easy one to grasp apart from an illustration; and here the Old Testament is helpful, for one of the great functions of the Old Testament is to cast light illustratively upon the New Testament. Probably by patient investigation every major teaching or concept of the New Testament could be found illustrated in the Old Testament. This concept of being secure "in Christ" is no exception.

Take, for instance, the case of Noah. When the ark was finished and a perfect way of escape from divine wrath provided, the invitation went forth, "Come thou and all thy house into the ark" (Gen. 7:1). Now, the ark was pitched "within and without with pitch" and, interestingly enough, the Hebrew word for "pitch" is the identical word used elsewhere for "atonement." Between the saved in the ark and the waters of judgment without was the hewn wood and the pitch. Once Noah and his family were safely in the ark, we read that "the LORD shut him in" (Gen. 7:16). Here was complete security. God did not say to Noah, once the ark was finished, "Now, Noah, I want you to take eight spikes and drive them into the outside timbers of the ark. So long as you and your family hang on you will be saved, but if you once let go you will be lost." No! God shut him in. What it meant for Noah to be "in the ark," it means for us to be "in Christ." In Him, God has placed us in a sphere where His wrath can never reach us and we are secure as Christ can make us. There is no more condemnation for sin.

B. *There Need Be No More Control by Sin* (8:2)

This is where the new law comes in. Paul says, "*For the law of the Spirit of life in Christ Jesus hath made me free from the law of sin and death*" (v. 2). Picture a coin falling toward the ground under the influence of the law of gravity. In itself, that coin is powerless to overcome the downward pull of this earth. It is in its very nature to fall. But before it has gone far, someone reaches out an arm, holds the coin firmly in his hand, and then lifts it higher and higher in defiance of the law of gravity. The law of the spirit of life in that person's arm overcomes the law of gravity. This does not mean that the original law has ceased to operate, but it does mean that a higher law has come into force. We sin by nature because we are victims of the fall and because it is the nature of fallen man to sin. But "in Christ Jesus" a higher law operates, "the law of the Spirit of life"; and this law sets us free from the lesser law of sin and death. The limitation of the coin illustration, of course, lies in the fact that the coin has no will of its own, whereas we do. It is possible for us to fail to enjoy release from the control of sin by disbelief or disobedience.

C. *There Should Be No More Continuance in Sin* (8:3-4)

Deliverance from the control of sin could never come through our own efforts to keep the Mosaic law. *"For what the law could not do, in that it was weak through the flesh, God sending his own Son in the likeness of sinful flesh, and for sin, condemned sin in the flesh: that the righteousness of the law might be fulfilled in us, who walk not after the flesh, but after the Spirit"* (vv. 3-4). The law was "weak through the flesh." It was not that God asked too much of man, for He can be satisfied with nothing less than absolute perfection. It was that man in the flesh simply could not and cannot live up to the claims of God's law.

But then Jesus came in flesh, just like ours, except that His flesh was sinless, untainted by the fall. For over thirty-three years He lived in a body of flesh without ever once yielding to a sinful thought, speaking a wrong word, or committing an improper act. His life was a condemnation of "sin in the flesh." People who imagine that Christ's life was given us merely as an example to follow, make a great mistake. It condemns us utterly. Like the veil in the temple, it bars us from the presence of God; and like that veil which was rent in twain, so the body of Christ had to be rent at Calvary. Essential as His immaculate life was to the completion of redemption's plan, it is not His life that saves; it is His death. The four Gospels place heavy emphasis on the death of

Christ.[1] During His life, the Lord Jesus demonstrated the possibility of God's law being fulfilled in a human life, a life lived in the flesh; that is, in the body. Through the miracle of Christ's indwelling the believer, the life that Jesus lived can now be reproduced in us by His Spirit. It is not reproduced *by* us, but *in* us if we "walk not after the flesh but after the Spirit."

II. THE NEW LORD (8:5-13)

A study of Romans 7 shows how much that chapter is dominated by the words "I," "me" and "my." In contrast, Romans 8 is dominated by the Holy Spirit, who is mentioned no less than nineteen times in the chapter. The new Lord in the believer's life is the Holy Spirit of God.

A. *The Holy Spirit Controlling the Mind of the Believer* (8:5-7)

"For they that are after the flesh do mind the things of the flesh; but they that are after the Spirit the things of the Spirit. For to be carnally minded is death; but to be spiritually minded is life and peace. Because the carnal mind is enmity against God: for it is not subject to the law of God, neither indeed can be" (vv. 5-7).

The great example of the carnal mind operating in the life of a believer is found in the story of Isaac. The *exercise* of the carnal mind is seen in Isaac's love of venison. In Genesis 27 the words "venison," "savory meat" or "eat" occur about twenty times. The clue to all this is in a preceding chapter where we are told that "Isaac loved Esau, because he did eat of his venison" (Gen. 25:28). We do not read that Isaac loved Esau because Esau was a holy man of God. That would have been something else. But no such statement is found. Esau was not a man of God; in fact, he held empire over his father by catering to his appetite, his inordinate love of food.

The *errors* of the carnal mind are illustrated in Isaac's successive mistakes recorded in Genesis 27. In the first place, he thought he was going to die (Gen. 27:2), whereas he lived for at least

[1]A survey of the four Gospels shows that about two-sevenths of Matthew's account is given to the Passion Week; about three-eighths of Mark's; almost a quarter of Luke's and nearly a half of John's. Each evangelist gives, proportionately, more space to the Passion Week than one would ordinarily expect. The Lord Jesus lived on earth about 12,060 days and His ministry lasted about 1260, yet each of the four Gospels concentrates on the last couple of weeks. The reason is, of course, that we are not redeemed by Christ's life and teaching but by His death and resurrection.

another forty years. His senses failed him one by one. He was blind, or nearly so. His sense of taste deceived him, for he mistook stewed goat for dressed venison. His hands, feeling the goat skin Jacob presented to him, wrongly told him he was feeling Esau's hairy hands. He smelled the smell of the field on Jacob and thought it was Esau. Only his hearing did not deceive him, and he couldn't trust that.

The *enmity* of the carnal mind is illustrated in Isaac's determination to give the patriarchal blessing to Esau when he knew full well that it was God's will that it go to Jacob (Gen. 25:23-26; 27:1-4, 24-33). "The carnal mind is enmity toward God."

There are countless examples in Scripture of the working and enmity of the carnal mind. Think of Abraham marrying Hagar; Lot choosing Sodom; Moses smiting the Egyptian; Joshua making a deal with the Gibeonites; Saul sparing the Amalekite cattle; Solomon's political marriages; Jonah fleeing to Tarshish; Peter smiting Malchus. These and many others illustrate the principle. There is only one way to avoid the mistakes made by the carnal mind and that is to have "the mind of Christ" (Phil. 2:5; I Cor. 2:16). The only way to have the mind of Christ is to allow the Spirit of Christ to control the mind.

B. *The Holy Spirit Controlling the Motives of the Believer* (8:8-9)

There is a great difference between being "in the flesh" and being "in the Spirit." Paul points this out next: "*So then they that are in the flesh cannot please God. But ye are not in the flesh, but in the Spirit, if so be that the Spirit of God dwell in you. Now if any man have not the Spirit of Christ, he is none of his*" (vv. 8-9). To be in the flesh is to be motivated by the desires of the flesh, but to be in the Spirit is to be motivated by the Spirit of God. This passage distinguishes between the saved and the unsaved, for the unsaved do not have the indwelling Holy Spirit.

Surrender to the Holy Spirit alone guarantees that our motives will be pleasing to God, for as Jeremiah said, "The heart is deceitful above all things, and desperately wicked: who can know it? I the LORD search the heart, I try the reins . . ." (Jer. 17:9-10). Even the best intentioned believer cannot properly evaluate his own motives except the Holy Spirit shine the light of Scripture on his conscience. We need to pray:

Search me, O God, my actions try,
    And let my life appear
As seen by Thine all-searching eye:
    To mine my ways make clear.

Search all my sense, and know my heart,
    Who only canst make known;
And let the deep, the hidden part
    To me be fully shown.

Throw light into the darkened cells,
    Where passion reigns within;
Quicken my conscience till it feels
    The loathsomeness of sin.

Search all my thoughts, the secret springs,
    The motives that control,
The chambers where polluted things
    Hold empire o'er the soul.

C. *The Holy Spirit Controlling the Members of the Believer* (8:10-13)

Paul has discussed in Romans 7 the law of the mind and the law of the members. Now he shows how the Spirit of God can raise the believer's body from the dead and, incidentally, control the very members of the believer's body and bring him victory in this realm. *"And if Christ be in you, the body is dead because of sin; but the Spirit is life because of righteousness. But if the Spirit of him that raised up Jesus from the dead dwell in you, he that raised up Christ from the dead shall also quicken your mortal bodies by his Spirit that dwelleth in you. Therefore, brethren, we are debtors, not to the flesh, to live after the flesh. For if ye live after the flesh, ye shall die: but if ye through the Spirit do mortify the deeds of the body, ye shall live"* (vv. 10-13).

The words "mortal" and "immortal" always refer to the body. It is "this mortal" which will put on immortality at the resurrection (I Cor. 15:53-54). The body is still subject to death in the ordinary course of events because of sin. The spirit has been made alive by the Holy Spirit at the time of regeneration. At the time of the resurrection these bodies of ours will be clothed with life immortal too.

The use of the name "Jesus" (v. 11) is of interest here, the only other place in the epistle where this single title is used being 3:26. The name "Jesus," of course, was Christ's human name. Paul wants to call attention to the fact that Jesus was once in the place of weakness, but God raised Him from the dead by the Spirit. The same Spirit who thus raised Jesus is dwelling in us! While these verses primarily refer to the coming resurrection, they imply also that the Holy Spirit can give us victory over the law of our members even now. Later in the epistle, Paul demands that the believer hand over his body to God as a living sacrifice (12:1). This act of surrender is one of the most important steps to a life of victory. The believer's body is the temple of the Holy Spirit (I Cor. 3:16-17; 6:19-20), and He desires complete sovereignty over His temple. Once He has control of the believer's body, the Spirit of God can then impart victory over sins which involve the use of the body's members.

III. THE NEW LIFE (8:14-39)

Granted a new law which liberates from sin; granted also a new Lord who is none other than the third Person of the Triune Godhead, it is obvious that a new life must follow. Paul's theme for the rest of this monumental chapter is this new life and the sonship and security it implies.

A. *The Emphasis on Sonship* (8:14-27)

It is a basic truth of the gospel that a person must be born again before he can be viewed as a child of God (John 1:11-13; 3:3-8; I Peter 1:23-25; I John 3:9; 4:7; 5:1, 4, 18). It is one thing, however, to be born into God's family through the miracle of regeneration, it is something else to become an adult son. Paul does not speak much about conversion in terms of a new birth, but he does speak at length on the subject of spiritual sonship and maturity.

Paul discusses first the question of our (1) *adoption into the family of God*. The idea of legal adoption into a family is more a Roman than a Jewish or Greek concept. The Romans seem to have associated adoption with full civil status. It is the Holy Spirit who places the believer as an adult son in the family of God. There are three thoughts associated with this truth. Those so adopted are *led by the Spirit*, for Paul says, "*As many as are led by the Spirit of God, they are the sons of God*" (v. 14). One evidence of sonship in the divine family is cooperation on the part of the believer with the guiding and leading ministry of the Spirit of God. There can be no doubt that God delights to guide His children. In Old Testament times He provided Israel with a fiery, cloudy pillar to lead them through the trackless wilderness. Their leading was clear, continuous and conspicuous, for even the smallest child could see when and where the cloudy pillar moved. The principles of guidance for the believer today are different, but they are nonetheless clear. Many believers lack a clear sense of divine leading in their lives. Probably the greatest hindrance to a continual sense of divine leading is a lack of a daily quiet time with God. How can God speak to us if we do not meditate on His Word? The second major hindrance is the refusal to follow once the Spirit's leading is revealed. Sons of God cooperate with the Spirit's leading.

Those adopted as sons into the family of God are not only led by the Spirit, they are *loved by the Father*. *"For ye have not received the spirit of bondage again to fear; but ye have received the Spirit of adoption, whereby we cry, Abba, Father. The Spirit itself beareth witness with our spirit, that we are the children of God"* (vv. 15-16). The cry, "Abba, Father," is very interesting. W. E. Vine tells us that " 'Abba' is the cry of an infant, the simple, helpless utterance of unreasoning trust, the effect of feeling, rather than knowledge. It is an Aramaic word (cf. English 'papa'). It was a form of address forbidden among the Jews to be used by a slave to the head of the family. 'Father' (Greek and Latin *pater*) is not a translation of 'Abba.' It is another mode of address. It is relationship intelligently realized by the one who utters it, a word of filial confidence, communion and obedience, answering to, and expressing, the enjoyment of the complacent love of God the Father. The two expressions together indicate the love and intelligent trust of the child."[2]

In Gethsemane the Lord Jesus used this identical expression, "Abba, Father" (Mark 14:36). Through the miracle of regeneration, we have been brought into the closest intimacy with our heavenly Father, the kind of intimacy Jesus Himself enjoyed. The "witness of the Spirit" in this connection is significant. This function of the Spirit of God is mentioned three times in the New Testament. He witnesses *to* us (Heb. 10:15), *in* us (I John 5:10),

[2]W. E. Vine, *The Epistle to the Romans* (Grand Rapids: Zondervan Publishing House, 1948), p. 120.

and *with* us (Rom. 8:16). Fact, faith, and feelings are succes-
sively in view in these three references. Here, of course, it is feeling, for the witness of the Spirit of God with our spirits gives
rise to the joyful cry, "Abba, Father."

Furthermore, those adopted into the family are *lifted by the
Son*. "*And if children, then heirs; heirs of God, and joint-heirs
with Christ; if so be that we suffer with him, that we may be
glorified together*" (v. 17). The "if" here is similar to the "if" in
verse 9, the hypothesis being assumed to be an actual fact, no
doubt being thrown upon the supposition. "Inasmuch" or "since"
might be a better rendering according to some authorities. Such
scriptures as II Thessalonians 1:10; I Corinthians 15:23; Colossians 3:4; and I John 3:2 confirm the truth that all believers will
be "glorified together" with Christ.

The condition for enjoying the inheritance is suffering "*with*
Christ," not mere suffering. Paul, it would seem, takes for granted
that this condition will be realized. Significantly, the only other
place in the New Testament where the expression "suffer with" is
found is in I Corinthians 12:26: "And whether one member suffer,
all the members suffer with it." The context in I Corinthians has
to do with the oneness of the body of Christ. Suffering in a body
is not a matter of choice but something necessitated by the relationship one member of a body has with every other member.
Since Christ is the head of this body, it follows that the things
that pain the head will pain the members. Adoption into the family of God, then, involves being lifted by Christ so that we can
share both His sufferings and His glory, His heartache and His
heritage, His cross and His crown.

Since adoption into the family of God is a priceless privilege,
it involves a process of discipline. God must fit us for our high
and holy calling. So Paul next discusses our (2) *adaption for the
family of God*. First there is adoption; then there is adaption. And
since adaption can be a painful process, "groaning" is mentioned
three times in the immediate context. Picture a wealthy, cultured
gentleman adopting a boy from the slums of a great city and
putting this boy into his family. After the adoption comes the
adaption. The lad would be totally unfit for his new family so
would be put into the hands of tutors to be taught how to speak
and how to behave in polite society. The process would be irk-

some to him, and it might take years before he is fitted for his
lofty destiny. But his benefactor, in the interests of the boy himself, would patiently pursue the boy's discipline and education
even though progress might at times be slow. This is exactly what
God is doing with us in this age.

Adaption for the family of God is of wide significance. Paul
speaks of *the groaning of the creation* (vv. 18-22) as being inex-
tricably bound up with the process—*"For we know that the whole
creation groaneth and travaileth in pain together until now"* (v.
22). The fall of man involved all of creation, at least so far as
this planet is concerned. The vegetable world was involved since
the temptation centered around a tree; the brute creation was
involved since the temptation was introduced by a serpent; and,
of course, the human creation was involved since the temptation
was presented to man. The curse which followed the fall involved all. Paul says, *"The creature [creation] was made subject
to vanity, not willingly, but by reason of him who hath subjected
the same in hope"* (v. 20). The word "vanity" occurs in the New
Testament only here, in Ephesians 4:17, and in II Peter 2:18. It
means "disappointing misery" in this passage in Romans. The
same Greek word is used frequently in the Septuagint to translate
the Hebrew for "vanity" in Ecclesiastes. It describes something
which does not measure up to that for which it was intended. So
creation groans.

Clearly there was a time when the whole creation neither
groaned nor travailed in pain. Dr. L. Merson Davies points out
that the third chapter of Genesis underlines three structures as
typifying the general curse upon nature. He says that these "are
all peculiarly representative of abortion and internecine strife."
The serpent, for example, is deprived of limbs and made to glide
upon its belly; thorns are aborted branches and leaves, and the
unpleasant character of thistles results from an aborted state of
the calyx.[3]

Paul tells us that *"the earnest expectation of the creature waiteth*

[3]See L. Merson Davies, "The Present Status of Teleology," *Transactions
of the Victoria Institute,* Vol. 79 (February 10, 1947), p. 72. Along these
same lines, note an interesting discussion of what makes animals fight, di-
gested from the *Audubon Magazine* in an article entitled "A Tooth and a
Claw" in *Reader's Digest,* January, 1966. Jean George, in this article, makes
this comment: "The human impulses that make a fight are precisely those
that make a masterpiece."

for the manifestation of the sons of God" (v. 19), or as Phillips renders it, "the whole creation is on tiptoe to see the wonderful sight of the sons of God coming into their own."[4] Brighter days indeed lie ahead for the whole creation (Isa. 11:6-9; 65:25; Rev. 22:3), for the time is coming when the curse will be removed and creation will be restored to its pristine splendor. As Paul says, *"I reckon that the sufferings of this present time are not worthy to be compared with the glory which shall be revealed in us"* (v. 18). He has a similar passage in his second letter to the Corinthians, "For our light affliction, which is but for a moment, worketh for us a far more exceeding and eternal weight of glory" (II Cor. 4:17). What Paul called "light affliction" would overwhelm most modern Christians (II Cor. 11:23-33). We shall have to wait to see what is involved in that "eternal weight of glory," for it is certain that it would crush us now.

Paul next speaks of *the groaning of the Christian* and points out that the Christian groans because he has not yet received his glorified body. *"And not only they, but ourselves also, which have the firstfruits of the Spirit, even we ourselves groan within ourselves, waiting for the adoption, to wit, the redemption of our body. For we are saved by hope: but hope that is seen is not hope: for what a man seeth, why doth he yet hope for? But if we hope for that we see not, then do we with patience wait for it"* (vv. 23-25).

The idea that we are saved by hope is a startling one at first glance since we normally think of salvation as being by faith rather than by hope. The reference, of course, has nothing to do with the salvation of the soul but with the redemption of the body and is linked with what Paul elsewhere calls "that blessed hope, and the glorious appearing of the great God and our Saviour Jesus Christ" (Titus 2:13). Christians tend to link "hope" with uncertainty and regard it therefore as a somewhat anemic word. It is most unsatisfactory to ask a person if he is saved and to receive the reply, "I hope so"; for in that case, hope usurps the place of faith. But hope comes into her own in its proper context. Suppose a mother were to tell her disobedient son that he would be spanked when his father arrived home from work. Suppose too, someone were to ask the boy sometime during the day, "Do you

[4] J. B. Phillips, *The New Testament in Modern English* (New York: The Macmillan Company. Copyright © by J. B. Phillips, 1958), p. 332.

think you will be punished when your father gets home?" The
boy might say, "I believe I will," but he is not likely to say, "I
hope I will!" Hope not only has to do with the future, but it has
to do with something pleasant in the future.

At this stage of our experience, we groan because of the limita-
tions of the body and temptations from the flesh. The day is
coming, however, when we shall have this body of humiliation
changed "that it may be fashioned like unto his glorious body, according to the working whereby he is able even to subdue all
things unto himself" (Phil. 3:21). This is part of our redemption;
and although we are still hoping for it, it is as certain as the
resurrection of Christ.

The groaning of creation and the groaning of the Christian, however, are comparatively easy to understand when placed alongside
the mysterious groaning Paul mentions next—*the groaning of the
Comforter.* "*Likewise the Spirit also helpeth our infirmities: for
we know not what we should pray for as we ought: but the Spirit
itself maketh intercession for us with groanings which cannot be
uttered. And he that searcheth the hearts knoweth what is the
mind of the Spirit, because he maketh intercession for the saints
according to the will of God*" (vv. 26-27). We have an Advocate
with the Father in heaven in the Person of the Lord Jesus (I John
2:1), and we have One within our hearts as well who can lay bare
before the eye of God the deepest needs of our souls.

Most of us feel particularly helpless in the matter of prayer. We
stand appalled at times before the deep antipathy of our own
hearts to prayer. Perfunctorily enough we say our prayers, but
seldom do we ever really pray. There is not much merit in saying
prayers; even an unsaved person can do that. Only a Spirit-taught
believer can really pray. It is because the ministry of prayer is a
purely spiritual ministry that we stand in such deep need of the
Holy Spirit to help our infirmities in this matter.

The word for "helpeth" in this passage occurs elsewhere in the
New Testament only in Luke 10:40 where its use is most enlightening. It is found in the story of Martha and Mary when the Lord
Jesus was the guest in their home. Mary was found at the Master's feet. But Martha could be heard banging the pots and pans
around in the kitchen. Evidently her irritation was growing. Why
should she have to slave at the sink while Mary sat on the rug in

the living room? Suddenly she burst out, "Lord, dost thou not care that my sister hath left me to serve alone? bid her therefore that she *help* me." That is the very idea behind the use of the word in Romans 8. What we need in prayer is help—the practical, down-to-earth, everyday kind of help that Martha needed in the kitchen. The very name "Comforter," used by the Lord Jesus when promising a new dispensation of the Holy Spirit, means literally, "one called alongside to help." The kind of help He gives is the help a doctor gives when he is called alongside the sick bed; the kind of help a fireman gives when he is called alongside a burning building; the kind of help a lawyer gives when he is called alongside to undertake our case. What a Helper!

This help expresses itself in "groanings which cannot be uttered" or as J. B. Phillips translates it, "his Spirit within us is actually praying for us in those agonizing longings which never find words."[5] The word for "groanings" here is *stenagmos*, found only here and in Acts 7:34 where Stephen used it in his defense before the Sanhedrin. Stephen had been describing the call of Moses and recalling the words God had used on that occasion: "I have seen, I have seen the affliction of my people which is in Egypt, and I have heard their *groaning*. . . ." How suggestive! The burden of the oppressed Israelites could only find expression in groans. The Holy Spirit, in expressing His burden for our spiritual state, groans with the same type of groans. Oh, the things in our lives which must grieve the Holy Spirit of God!

It cannot be doubted that the prayers of the Holy Spirit are effective. Paul states three very good reasons why they must be. First, God knows and searches our *hearts* as only He can. Second, He knows the Spirit's *mind*: "knoweth what is the mind of the Spirit." Third, He prays according to the *will* of God. One day this *groaning* will give place to *glory* as we, who have been adopted into the family, are finally fully adapted for that family and receive our glorified bodies and enter into God's new creation.

B. *The Emphasis on Security* (8:28-39)

The closing verses in this chapter expand more fully the great theme of the believer's eternal security. The believer is (1) *predestinated for glory* (vv. 28-30). This predestination cannot be

[5]*Ibid.*, p. 328.

altered, for it includes the present moment of time as well as the vast reaches of eternity past and future. It relates itself to *the daily concerns of men,* for Paul reminds us that *"all things work together for good to them that love God, to them who are the called according to his purpose"* (v. 28). This is a great verse, often quoted in times of distress. It needs to be looked at, however, in the light of its context. Like the cogs in an intricate piece of machinery, all things work together for good to the called of God for the simple reason that God's purposes cannot be thwarted. Although we may not see it now, everything will one day be seen to fit into God's perfect plan.

The principle is beautifully illustrated in the story of Jacob. He was reaping the harvest of his younger years. Joseph was gone; Reuben was disgraced; Judah was dishonored; Simeon and Levi had broken his heart; Dinah was defiled; Simeon even now was in prison; beloved Rachel was dead; famine threatened the family. Then came the demand from Egypt that young Benjamin must appear there before its awesome governor before any further supplies would be released. Old Jacob wept: "Me have ye bereaved of my children: Joseph is not, and Simeon is not, and ye will take Benjamin away: *all these things are against me"* (Gen. 42:36). How wrong he was! "These things" and many more were secretly working to his own good, as the end of the story proved. "All things work together for good."

The fact that we are predestinated for glory cannot be altered for another reason. Predestination relates itself not only to the daily concerns of men but also to *the eternal counsels of God. "For whom he did foreknow, he also did predestinate to be conformed to the image of his Son, that he might be the firstborn among many brethren. Moreover whom he did predestinate, them he also called: and whom he called, them he also justified: and whom he justified, them he also glorified"* (vv. 29-30). The key words in this great but admittedly difficult passage are the words "foreknow," "predestinate," "called," "justified" and "glorified." They embrace an eternity past, the present fleeting moments of time and an eternity yet to come. They bring into sharp focus the whole difficult problem of divine election versus human free will, a problem for which we have no absolute answers this side of glory.

Some have thought that the word "foreknown" is the key to the problem. All knowledge is based on fact, the argument runs; fact is not based on knowledge. A fact has to be established before it can be known. Human knowledge is largely after-knowledge of a given fact, but God is not restricted to after-knowledge. He is omniscient and therefore has foreknowledge. But whether it is after-knowledge or foreknowledge, the knowledge is based on fact. For example, John Brown accepts Christ as Saviour on a given day in his personal history and thereby establishes a fact which can be known. His friends and relatives come to know of this fact after it happens, but God can see the same fact a week, a month, a year, an eternity before it happens. Nevertheless, His knowledge, like that of John Brown's friends, is based on *the fact* of John Brown's acceptance of Christ. "Whom he did *foreknow*, he also did predestinate."

There is only one thing wrong with this line of reasoning. The text goes on to say, "Moreover whom he did predestinate, *them* he also called." Reduced to its simplest terms the problem can be stated thus: Did God choose me because I chose Him, or did I choose Him because He chose me? To say that God chose me because with His ability to foreknow the future He saw me choose Christ, robs God of His sovereignty. It would mean He has no alternative but to choose those who choose Christ—His choice is governed by ours. It throws the initiative on man. But God is sovereign and acts in accordance with His own will and, as Paul demonstrates in a later chapter, is under an obligation to nobody (9:15-23). On the other hand, to say that I chose Christ because He chose me robs me of my free will (i.e., moral responsibility) and makes me a mere puppet. Human free will then becomes a myth.

Can the will of God and the will of man be reconciled, or must we everlastingly go round and round in circles on this question? Obviously there is no pat answer. If there were, this problem would not have divided Christians for centuries. An illustration, however, might help us see that God, in the exercise of His sovereign will, does not necessarily deprive man of his free will. Imagine two men playing a game of chess; the one player is a master at the game, the other is very much an amateur. The master knows hundreds of moves for opening, pursuing, and clos-

ing the game, whereas the amateur plays blindly from one move
to the next with little skill and only limited forethought. Both
players have free will to make whatever moves they wish. But
the master of the game, without in any way violating his oppo-
nent's free will, uses every move the amateur makes to drive him
into a corner and take his king.

That is just how it is in the game of life. Each of us has a free
will and we exercise that will in a thousand ways. The choices we
make determine the way we move through life. But above and
beyond us and our choices is God. He overrules our every move
to make each one conform to His own sovereign will. When one
becomes a Christian, God says in effect, "Now, My child, it is My
will that you should win in this game of life. I will tell you which
moves to make. If you are wise, you will bring your life into line
with My will." God never violates a person's free will. Even
when at last God destines a lost soul to the caverns of the damned,
it will be in keeping with this principle. At the last God says in
effect to the Christ-rejector, "You would not have My Son to be
your Saviour; you chose to deny the Lord Jesus a place in your
life. Now I will honor your choice. You shall live forever without
Him; you shall spend eternity without God and without Christ
and without hope." Thus, man has his free will and God His
sovereignty. The illustration is not perfect perhaps, but it does
help us see how the two can be reconciled.

God brings us (a) *into the sphere of His wisdom*. He foreknew
us—all the bad and all the good; all that would please Him and all
that would cause Him pain. Then He brings us (b) *under the
sovereignty of His will*. He predestinates us for glory, to be conformed to the image of His Son. He brings us (c) *under the
sound of His Word*. He calls us. He brings us then (d) *under
the shadow of His wing*. He justifies us, gives us a standing before Himself so impeccable, so immaculate, so pure and spotless
that no power in earth or hell or heaven can bring any accusation
against us. Finally, He brings us (e) *into the splendor of His
world*. He glorifies us. Actually the verb is in the past tense. It
says that whom He called "them he also justified: and whom he
justified, them he also glorified." We do not have to wait until
we die to see whether or not we are going to heaven. In God's
eternal counsels we are already glorified! The believer is predestinated for glory.

But what about all the years between the believer's conversion and his consummation? Is there not a possibility that during these years of testing and trial something might go wrong which will cause him to forfeit his salvation? No! For the believer is not only predestinated for glory, he is also (2) *preserved for glory* (vv. 31-39). The closing verses of this magnificent chapter explore all possible avenues of departure from the salvation which is in Christ Jesus only to find every one blocked and guarded by the grace of God. Paul considers in these verses (a) *the foundation of our hope of glory* and finds it unshakable. "*What shall we then say to these things? If God be for us, who can be against us? He that spared not his own Son, but delivered him up for us all, how shall he not with him also freely give us all things?*" (vv. 31-32). The foundation of our hope is the grace of God and the gift of God. "If God be for us, who can be against us?" The "if" in this statement in no way implies a doubt. There is no question as to whether or not God is for us. The word means "*since* God is for us, who can be against us?" The strength of any possible adversary is utter weakness compared with the omnipotence of God.

Our hope of glory rests on the fact that God is graciously for us and has given us His Son. He spared not His Son! Horatius Bonar, the Scottish Presbyterian poet-preacher and author of many of our best loved hymns has caught the spirit of Romans 8:32:

> Blessed be God, our God,
> Who gave for us His well beloved Son,
> The gift of gifts, all other gifts in one;
> Blessed be God, our God!
>
> What will He not bestow!
> Who freely gave this mighty gift unbought,
> Unmerited, unheeded and unsought,
> What will He not bestow?
>
> He spared not His Son!
> 'Tis this that silences each rising fear,
> 'Tis this that bids the hard thought disappear;
> He spared not His Son!
>
> 'Tis God that justifies!
> Who shall repeal His pardon or His grace?
> Or who the broken chain of guilt replace?
> 'Tis God that justifies!

Mount Moriah was the high point in Abraham's experience (Gen. 22) as this pilgrim patriarch who began his walk with God by giving up his *father* ended it by giving up his *son*. Between these two crisis points in his experience he gave up the well-watered plains of Jordan; the offered gifts of the king of Sodom; Hagar, the Egyptian; and even his beloved Ishmael. The giving up of Isaac, however, was the greatest single act in his life as God Himself acknowledged. "Lay not thine hand upon the lad," said God, "neither do thou anything unto him: for now I know that thou fearest God, seeing thou hast not withheld thy son, thine only son from me" (Gen. 22:12). In the Septuagint the word "withheld" is rendered by the same Greek word translated "spared" in Romans 8:32. Just as Abraham spared not Isaac, so God spared not Jesus. Paul may well have been drawing a deliberate parallel. It is difficult to believe that Abraham could ever have held back anything from God after sparing not his son. It is difficult to see how God could hold back anything from us after giving up His Son for us. Whatever is necessary for our justification, sanctification and glorification is given in the gift of God's Son.

A wealthy Roman had a son who broke his heart and a slave who commanded his admiration. He decided on his deathbed to disinherit his son and leave everything to his slave, Marcellus. He drew up the papers and called in his son to tell him what he had done. "I have deeded everything to the slave Marcellus," he said. "However, you may choose one item from my estate for yourself." "I'll take Marcellus!" was the son's reply. When we take Christ, we take all. Charles Wesley captured the idea and expressed it in his well-known hymn, "Jesus, Lover of My Soul."

> Thou, O Christ, art all I want;
> More than all in Thee I find.

Then Paul considers (*b*) *the fullness of our hope of glory*. There is no possibility of any charge being brought against us. Paul emphasizes in this connection *the perfect defeat of our adversary*. *"Who shall lay anything to the charge of God's elect? It is God that justifieth"* (v. 33).

There is a dramatic incident recorded in Zechariah 3 that well illustrates this. There we see Joshua the high priest standing before the angel of the Lord with Satan standing at his right hand to accuse him. Joshua was arrayed in filthy garments, a most expressive figure of his own personal unfitness for the presence of God. What Satan's arguments were we are not told, but the context seems to imply that he was urging on God Joshua's evident vileness and disgrace. Satan is a liar and a deceiver, but sad to say, when he appears as the accuser of the brethren (Rev. 12:10), he does not have to use falsehoods. There is plenty of ground for his telling the truth about us. Joshua had no word to use in his own defense. But before he could even speak, God took up his case. "And the LORD said unto Satan, The LORD rebuke thee, O Satan; even the LORD that hath chosen Jerusalem rebuke thee: is not this a brand plucked out of the fire . . . and he answered and spake unto those that stood before him, saying, Take away the filthy garments from him. And unto him he said, Behold, I have caused thine iniquity to pass from thee, and I will clothe thee with change of raiment. And I said, Let them set a fair mitre upon his head. So they set a fair mitre upon his head, and clothed him with garments. And the angel of the LORD stood by" (Zech. 3:1-5). "Who shall lay anything to the charge of God's elect? It is God that justifieth."

The fullness of our hope of glory rests not only on the perfect defeat of our adversary but also on *the perfect defense of our Advocate. "Who is he that condemneth? It is Christ that died, yea rather, that is risen again, who is even at the right hand of God, who also maketh intercession for us"* (v. 34). Even if a charge is made, who will condemn? The Judge is none other than the Lord Jesus, the very One who makes condemnation impossible (8:1). He died; He arose; He ascended; He intercedes—and all for us! Let the adversary make any charge he will; the perfect answer is the upraised, pierced hand of our Intercessor. That is all that is needed. The believer is preserved for glory.

In concluding his argument, Paul shows (c) *the finality of our hope for glory* and declares that nothing, absolutely nothing, can shake the believer's security. *"Who shall separate us from the love of Christ? shall tribulation, or distress, or persecution, or famine, or nakedness, or peril, or sword? As it is written, For thy sake we are killed all the day long; we are accounted as sheep for the slaughter. Nay, in all these things we are more than con-*

querors through him that loved us" (vv. 35-37). In other words, no foe can *daunt* us! These seven enemies have been the common foe, more or less, of Christians from the earliest days of the church. Paul himself had faced them all and knew from personal experience that none of them had power to sever a soul from Christ. On the contrary, they but drew the believing heart closer to the Lord. That they are allowed by God is no proof that He has ceased to love us, "for whom the Lord loveth he chasteneth" (Heb. 12:6).

Communists have been described as "dead men on furlough." Long before the disciples of Marx and Lenin took such a view of their relationship to the world, Christians had been accounting themselves "as sheep for the slaughter." In these things we can not only be conquerors but "more than conquerors through him that loved us." Peter illustrates what this means. He had been arrested by Herod and the sentence of death had been passed upon him. On the morrow he was to die. James had already died at Herod's hands, and Peter knew that the Herods knew no mercy. If looking into his cell that night we had seen him bravely resolving to die nobly and unflinchingly for Christ, we would have seen a conqueror. Instead, we see him rolled up in his blanket, sleeping peacefully with fine contempt for the plans of Herod (Acts 12:1-10). He was *more* than conqueror!

"*For*," says Paul, "*I am persuaded, that neither death, nor life, nor angels, nor principalities, nor powers, nor things present, nor things to come, nor height, nor depth, nor any other creature, shall be able to separate us from the love of God, which is in Christ Jesus our Lord*" (vv. 38-39). In other words, no fear can *haunt* us! Can *death* separate us from the love of God? Of course not! Death ushers the believer into glory itself. Death but renders the service of making us "absent from the body" and consequently "present with the Lord" (II Cor. 5:8). Can *life* separate us from that love? No indeed, for Jesus said, "Lo, I am with you alway, even unto the end of the world" (Matt. 28:20). This was David Livingstone's text. Again and again, at the crisis points in his life, says F. W. Boreham, "Livingstone would enter Matthew 28:20 into his diary with the words, 'It is the word of a Gentleman of the most strict and sacred honor, so there's an end of it.' "[6]

[6]F. W. Boreham, *A Bunch of Everlastings* (London: The Epworth Press, 1920), p. 118.

Can *angels* separate us from God's love? No! "Are they not all ministering spirits, sent forth to minister for them who shall be heirs of salvation?" (Heb. 1:14). They crowd the unseen world to aid us in our journey home. Can *principalities* or *powers?* No, for arrayed in the whole armor of God, we can put them to flight (Eph. 6:12-17); and this for the simple reason that Christ has already "exposed them, shattered, empty and defeated" at the cross of Calvary (Col. 2:15, Phillips).

Can *things present* separate us from the love of God? Of course not, for He is the I AM, the One who dwells eternally in the present (Exodus 3:14; John 8:58). Then what about *things to come;* can they come between us and God's love? No, because the Lord Jesus is the coming One, and of all things to come, the supreme and vital future advent is His (John 14:1-3; Rev. 22:20). Can *height* or *depth* separate us from the love of God which is in Christ Jesus? No, because He has plumbed the deepest depth for us and scaled the highest height and is enthroned yonder on the highest pinnacle of glory.

No foe can daunt us; no fear can haunt us! Can any other creature come between us and God? No, for after all, a creature is but a creature and He who has enveloped us in His love is the Creator "over all, God blessed for ever" (9:5). So then, whether it be things from experience or beings from the realm of spirits; whether it be matters of time or matters of space, nothing can separate us from God's love. The love that took the initiative in lifting us from the miry clay will lift us to the halls of heaven. What more could we ask for than that?

II. THE PROBLEMS OF THE GOSPEL

9:1–11:36

GOD'S PAST DEALINGS WITH ISRAEL
9:1-33

I. Paul's Anguish for the Jewish People (9:1-3)
  A. How Solemnly It Is Avowed (9:1*a*)
  B. How Significantly It Is Attested (9:1*b*)
  C. How Soberly It Is Assessed (9:2-3)

II. Paul's Analysis of the Jewish Problem (9:4-33)
  A. How He Sees the Problem (9:4-29)
    1. God's Gracious Dealings with Israel (9:4-5)
    2. God's Governmental Dealings with Israel (9:6-29)
      a. Based on His superlative wisdom (9:6-13)
      b. Based on His sovereign will (9:14-24)
      c. Based on His spoken word (9:25-29)
  B. How He Summarizes the Problem (9:30-33)
    1. The Gentiles Have Attained Righteousness—by Faith (9:30)
    2. The Jews Have Attempted Righteousness—but Failed (9:31-33)
      a. Explained specifically (9:31-32)
      b. Explained scripturally (9:33)

Paul has now come to an end of the first major portion of his epistle. He has discussed the *principles* of the gospel, drawing together the various threads that make up the tapestry picture of man's sin, salvation and sanctification. In the next three chapters he discusses the *problems* of the gospel, particularly as these problems relate to the Jewish people.

God had made many exceeding great and precious promises to Abraham, Isaac and Jacob, to Moses, David and Solomon. Many of these promises centered in the person of the Messiah, the Lord Jesus Christ, murdered by the Jews at Calvary. In His love, God gave the nation a second chance, an opportunity to reverse its terrible verdict and, by repentance and faith, to accept Christ as Saviour. The book of Acts, in the history of which Paul himself plays a prominent part, records this second chance. The Jews, however, were obdurate. First the Jews of the homeland and then the Jews of the Diaspora endorsed the original verdict concerning Jesus of Nazareth and rejected Him again.

When Paul wrote the letter to the Romans, the temple was still standing in Jerusalem; the sacrifices were still being offered; the elaborate ritual of Judaism, now meaningless, was still being continued. The shadow of the nation's fate had not yet begun to darken the horizon. Paul knew, however, that Christianity was the death knell of Judaism. Even before his conversion, he knew the two systems could not coexist, hence his bitter hatred of Christianity in those days and his zeal to stamp it out. As a mature believer and the very apostle of the Gentiles, he knew he must come to grips with the problems of the gospel as they related to the Jew. What about all those ancient promises? Were they cancelled now? Where does the Jew stand in relation to God in this new dispensation? No thoroughgoing exposition of the gospel could evade questions like these. That is why this great parenthesis appears at this point in the epistle.

In these chapters Paul looks first at the past, then at the present, and finally at the future. He shows in each successive chapter that the key to all of God's *past* dealings with Israel is the *sovereignty* of God; that the key to all God's *present* dealings with Israel is the *salvation* of God; and that the key to all God's *promised* dealings with Israel is the *sincerity* of God. In Romans 9, then, he weighs carefully God's past dealings with Israel and finds that all those dealings are based on the simple principle of divine sovereignty.

I. PAUL'S ANGUISH FOR THE JEWISH PEOPLE (9:1-3)

The problem with which Paul grapples in these chapters is not merely one of academic interest to him. It is one in which he is deeply and emotionally involved, one which wrung out his heart in deepest, bitterest agony.

A. *How Solemnly This Is Avowed* (9:1a)

Paul affirms his love and anguish for his own nation in the words, *"I say the truth in Christ, I lie not."* The Jews had beaten him, imprisoned him, cursed and castigated him. Wherever he went, they stirred up the populace against him. Despite the emancipating verdict of the Jerusalem conference (Acts 15), even Christian Jews added to his burdens by subverting his converts to a lower form of Christianity in which Judaistic rules and rituals undermined the gospel. Paul perhaps expected that his avowal of love would be denied, so he states it in language hedged about with solemn affirmations.

Such a love is not of nature; it is supernatural and a fruit of the Spirit (Gal. 5:22). This same supernatural love today sends missionaries to labor in leper colonies; to unlovely, primitive, dangerous tribes; and into the vile slums of the world's great cities. It is this kind of love which writes the glowing pages of the church's history. It sends a Paton to the cannibals of the New Hebrides; a Livingstone to blaze a trail through the wilds of Africa; and a Judson to the jungles of Burma. It is the love which many waters cannot quench, the love which is stronger than death, the love of I Corinthians 13. It is the love of Christ shed abroad in our hearts by the Holy Ghost. It is love which drew God's Son down from the highest heaven to die in agony, blood and shame upon the cross of Calvary. "I say the truth in Christ, I lie not!" says Paul as he affirms his love for his Jewish kin.

B. *How Significantly This Is Attested* (9:1b)

What Paul is about to say concerning his love for his people is so startling, so abounding in superlatives, so revolutionary that he feels he must call in a witness extraordinary to attest to his honesty in the statement he is about to make. *"I say the truth in Christ, I lie not, my conscience bearing me witness in the Holy Ghost."* His conscience, strengthened by the Holy Spirit, attests to the truth of what he is going to say. A person's conscience cannot always be trusted as reliable, but a conscience quickened and made sensitive by the Holy Spirit can. Paul's conscience was not left to itself, but it was informed and enlightened by the Holy Spirit and was therefore able to bear reliable witness to the truth of Paul's confession.

C. *How Soberly This Is Assessed* (9:2-3)

Now comes the statement concerning Paul's anguish. "*I have great heaviness and continual sorrow in my heart. For I could wish that myself were accursed from Christ for my brethren, my kinsmen according to the flesh.*" Alford points out that this word "accursed" is "anathema," and says, "It never denotes simply an exclusion or excommunication, but always a devotion to perdition —a curse. Attempts have been made to explain away the meaning here, by understanding *excommunication*; or even *natural death* only; but excommunication included cursing and delivering over to Satan: and the mere wish for natural death would, as Chrysostom eloquently remarks, be altogether beneath the dignity of the passage."[1] Paul's soul-winning passion for men, especially for his own countrymen, was such that he could actually, soberly, honestly say that he would be willing to go to hell and be eternally damned, if that were possible, if by so doing it would lead his kinsmen to a saving knowledge of their Messiah, the Lord Jesus Christ. It is no wonder that Paul was such a successful soul winner!

II. PAUL'S ANALYSIS OF THE JEWISH PROBLEM (9:4-33)

Paul's analysis of the problem of the Jew is clear and comprehensive. It is not only completely satisfying to the intellect but also sobering and challenging as well. First, he tells how he sees the problem, and then he summarizes his findings.

A. *How Paul Sees the Problem* (9:4-29)

The first thing Paul sees, as he thinks through the problem of the Jewish rejection of the Messiah and the consequent question mark this raised as to the future of the special status the Jew had in the economy of God, is (1) *God's gracious dealings with Israel in the past*. There can be no doubt that the Jewish people were marked off by God for special treatment. Paul says of them

[1] Henry Alford, *The New Testament for English Readers* (Chicago: Moody Press, n.d.), p. 918.

that they "*are Israelites; to whom pertaineth the adoption, and the glory, and the covenants, and the giving of the law, and the service of God, and the promises; whose are the fathers, and of whom as concerning the flesh Christ came, who is over all, God blessed for ever. Amen*" (vv. 4-5).

This is a most remarkable list of privileges. The name *Israelites* was not only the national name, it was a name of honor as well (Gen. 32:28; Hosea 12:3; John 1:47; II Cor. 11:22; Phil. 3:5). The word *adoption* may refer to Exodus 4:22 and Hosea 11:1 where God spoke of Israel as a son and indicated that the nation had a special relationship to Himself in contrast to other nations. The *glory* was the Shekinah cloud of fire which rested on the tabernacle and later on the temple (Exodus 40:34-35; I Kings 8:10-11; II Chron. 5:13). The *covenants* included the Abrahamic covenant (Gen. 12:1-3; 15:1-7; 17:1-8); the renewals of this covenant with Isaac and Jacob (Gen. 26:2-5; 28:1-3, 12-15); the Mosaic covenant concerning the law (Exodus 20-21) and the land (Deut. 29-30); the Davidic covenant (II Sam. 7:16; I Chron. 17:7-15; Ps. 89:27); and the new covenant (Jer. 31:33; Ezek. 34). The *law*, of course, was the Mosaic law, the greatest legislative code ever given and the foundation of all true legal codes ever since. The *service* was the ceremonial ritual of worship associated with the law and given in Exodus and Leviticus. The *promises* were the great Messianic and millennial promises woven into the warp and woof of the Old Testament. The *fathers* were the patriarchs and the other great worthies whose illustrious stories are the national heritage of the Jewish people and the living fiber of the Old Testament.

Great as all these privileges were, there was one that eclipsed them all. Paul, as it were, saves the best wine until last. "And of whom as concerning the flesh Christ came, who is over all, God blessed for ever" (v. 5). What more could be said than that? God's gracious dealings with Israel were crowned with the highest and noblest honor which could conceivably be bestowed upon any people. To them Christ came. He was born of a Jewish mother and reared in a Hebrew home. He attended a Jewish synagogue and was given a Jewish education. He lived and labored in the promised land, ministering to "the lost sheep of the house of Israel" (Matt. 15:24). "He came unto his own, and his own received him not" (John 1:11). He sang to His beloved the song of the vineyard, but the grapes of Israel were wild (Isa. 5:1-7).

Paul was impressed by God's gracious dealings with Israel in the past. He was just as impressed with (2) *God's governmental dealings with Israel in the past.* He saw clearly that grace is never administered at the expense of government and that God's past dealings with Israel were always in keeping with His wisdom, His will and His Word. There is nothing capricious about God's ways; they follow fixed and righteous principles.

God's past dealings with Israel were based on *His superlative wisdom.* God knows them that are His. *"Not as though the word of God hath taken none effect,"* says Paul. *"For they are not all Israel, which are of Israel: neither, because they are the seed of Abraham, are they all children"* (vv. 6-7a). The rejection by God of the majority of the Jews does not mean that God's promises have failed, because in the wisdom of God the rejected Jews were never included in the promises at all. The number of those who are "of Israel" is not determined by natural descent but by God's wisdom.

Paul gives two examples of what he means, both taken from early patriarchal history and both intended to show that birth into the patriarchal family did not of itself automatically confer spiritual privilege. First, he takes the case of Ishmael and Isaac. Both were born into the same family, but one was chosen—the other rejected. Then he takes the case of Esau and Jacob. These too were born into the same family, but again, one was chosen— the other rejected. Here is Paul's summary of the two cases: *"In Isaac shall thy seed be called. That is, They which are the children of the flesh, these are not the children of God: but the children of the promise are counted for the seed. For this is the word of promise, At this time I will come, and Sarah shall have a son. And not only this: but when Rebecca had also conceived by one, even by our father Isaac; (for the children being not yet born, neither having done any good or evil, that the purpose of God according to election might stand, not of works, but of him that calleth;) it was said unto her, The elder shall serve the younger. As it is written, Jacob have I loved, but Esau have I hated"* (vv. 7b-13).

The wisdom of God chose Isaac and rejected Ishmael, and the wisdom of God chose Jacob and rejected Esau. In both instances the outworking of history has demonstrated the farseeing wisdom of God's choice. From Ishmael have come the Arab nations, bitter foes of Israel to this day, and for long centuries passionate adherents of Islam. From Esau came Edom, bitterest and most vengeful of all Israel's ancient neighbors. As time went by, both Ishmael and Esau personally manifested hostility to the things of God, whereas Isaac and Jacob personally manifested love for the things of God.

God's choice is based upon His superlative wisdom, not upon the merit of a given individual. In the two cases cited by Paul, both the rejected men had been born into the patriarchal family and in each case the parent wished to see the rejected one inherit the promise. Abraham pleaded with God for Ishmael (Gen. 17:18), and Isaac did his best to pass on the patriarchal blessing to Esau (Gen. 27:1-4, 30-33). Paul's point is that in His dealings with Israel, God dealt with them on governmental lines in accordance with His wisdom and His sovereignty, never intending that all the natural descendants of Abraham, Isaac and Jacob should be counted as children of the promise.

God's past dealings with Israel, moreover, were based not only on His superlative wisdom but also on *His sovereign will*. God is under no obligation to explain His ways to men. He is sovereign and does whatever He pleases. Since He is God, what He does is always right and cannot legitimately be questioned by men who are limited in intelligence and in knowledge and whose moral and spiritual capacities are impaired by sin. This next section of Romans is one of the greatest passages in the Bible on the subject of the sovereignty of God. Paul goes back again into Jewish history and shows God in His sovereignty *pardoning* erring Israel (vv. 14-15) and *punishing* erring Pharaoh (vv. 16-18). Both illustrations are most enlightening.

The first illustration is drawn from Israel's rebellions in the wilderness. The law had scarcely been given to Moses on the tables of stone when, coming down from Sinai, he found that Israel had apostatized against the Lord by making a golden calf (Exodus 32). In a deeply significant act he smashed the tables of stone, ground the golden calf to powder, mingled the cursed gold with their water supply, and forced the rebellious nation to drink it. Then he issued his great challenge, "Who is on the LORD's side?" Only the tribe of Levi responded. Moses commanded the Levites to put the rebels to the sword. Then he went in to intercede with God for the remainder in a way that is hauntingly like Paul's impassioned, agonizing cry in Romans 9 (see Exodus 32:31-33). The Lord's anger, however, was very fierce, and He informed Moses that henceforth He would no longer lead the nation but would assign an angel to do so in His place. Once again Moses pleaded with God in words of majesty and power, and by way of answer God spoke words to Moses that Paul now quotes to illustrate the sovereignty of the divine will in pardoning His people. *"What shall we say then? Is there unrighteousness with God? God forbid. For he saith to Moses, I will have mercy on whom I will have mercy, and I will have compassion on whom I will have compassion. So then it is not of him that willeth, nor of him that runneth, but of God that sheweth mercy"* (vv. 14-16). What is Paul's conclusion? That God showed mercy on Israel. The nation had forfeited all right to blessing, yet God showed mercy. Thus, God's sovereignty does not exclude His mercy. That any come into blessing at all is of His mercy alone. This incident of mercy softens somewhat Paul's next illustration, the hardening and punishing of Pharaoh.

"For the scripture saith unto Pharaoh, Even for this same purpose have I raised thee up, that I might shew my power in thee, and that my name might be declared throughout all the earth. Therefore hath he mercy on whom he will have mercy, and whom he will he hardeneth" (vv. 17-18). There are two extremes we must always avoid. The one extreme is to overemphasize the mercy of God and conclude that God is too kind to condemn a person to an eternity of woe. The other extreme is to overemphasize the severity of God and make God (in this instance, for example) the author of Pharaoh's stubbornness. Since no scripture is of "private interpretation" (II Peter 1:20), no scripture should be isolated from its context and from other parts of God's Word which illuminate the subject. It is especially important, therefore, in a difficult portion such as this to get the full biblical picture. The historical account of God's dealings with Pharaoh is in Exodus 1-14.

Alfred Edersheim is most helpful in explaining what actually happened when God hardened Pharaoh's heart. "Twice ten times in the course of this history does the expression *hardening* occur in connection with Pharaoh. Although in our English version only the word 'harden' is used, in the Hebrew original three different terms are employed, of which one (as in Exodus 7:3) literally means *to make hard* or *insensible*; the other (as in 10:1) *to make heavy*, that is, unimpressionable; and the third (as in 14:4), *to make firm or stiff*, so as to be immovable. Now it is remarkable, that of the twenty passages which speak of Pharaoh's hardening, exactly ten ascribe it to Pharaoh himself, and ten to God, and that in both cases the same three terms are used. Thus, the making 'hard,' 'heavy,' and 'firm' of the heart is exactly as often and in precisely the same terms traced to the agency of Pharaoh himself as to that of God. . . .

"Proceeding further, we find that, with the exception of the two passages in which the divine agency in hardening is beforehand announced to Moses for his instruction, the hardening process is during the outworking of the actual history, in the first place, traced to Pharaoh himself. Thus, before the ten plagues, and when Aaron first proved his divine mission by converting the rod into a serpent, 'the heart of Pharaoh was hardened,' that is, by himself (7:13-14). Similarly, after each of the first five plagues (7:22; 8:15, 19, 32; 9:7) the hardening is also expressly attributed to Pharaoh himself. Only when still resisting after the sixth plague do we read for the first time that 'the Lord made firm the heart of Pharaoh' (9:12). But even so, space for repentance must have been left, for after the seventh plague we read again (9:34) that 'Pharaoh made heavy his heart'; and it is only after the eighth plague that the agency is exclusively ascribed to God.

"Moreover, we have to consider the *progress* of his hardening on the part of Pharaoh, by which at last his sin became ripe for judgment. It was not only that he resisted the demand of Moses, even in view of the miraculous signs by which his mission was attested; but that, step by step, the hand of God became more clearly manifest, till at last he was, by his own confession 'inexcusable.' If the first sign of converting the rod into a serpent could in a certain manner be counterfeited by the Egyptian magicians, yet Aaron's rod swallowed up theirs (7:12). But after the third plague, the magicians themselves confessed their inability to carry on the contest, declaring; 'This is the finger of God' (8:19). If any doubt had still been in his mind, it must have been removed by the evidence presented after the fifth plague (9:7), when 'Pharaoh sent, and, behold, there was not one of the cattle of the Israelites dead.' Some of the Egyptians, at least, had profited by this lesson, and on the announcement of the seventh plague housed their cattle from the predicted hail and fire (9:20-21).

"Lastly, after the seventh plague, Pharaoh himself acknowledged his sin and wrong (9:27), and promised to let Israel go (v. 28). Yet, after all, on its removal, he once more hardened his heart (v. 35). Can we wonder that such high-handed and inexcusable rebellion should have been ripe for the judgment which appeared in the divine hardening of his heart? Assuredly in such a contest between the pride and daring of the creature and the might of the Lord God, the truth of this divine declaration had to be publicly manifested: 'Even for this purpose have I raised thee up, that I might show My power in thee, and that My name might be declared throughout all the earth' (Exodus 9:16)."[2]

Having given *examples* of the sovereignty of God's will, Paul next gives an *explanation* of that sovereign will. God does not have to answer to man because being God He is both infinite and independent (vv. 19-24). *"Thou wilt say then unto me, Why doth he find fault? For who hath resisted his will?"* (v. 19). There seems to be some irritation on the part of the objector. The question may be rephrased, "If it be God's will to harden the sinner, and the sinner goes on in his sin, he does not resist, but goes with the will of God."[3] Such an attitude is wrong on at least two counts. In the first place, it supposes that man, a mere creature, is wise enough to question God, the Creator; and in the second place, it ignores the fact that God's sovereignty is always expressed righteously and ever tempered with mercy.

How foolish it is for man to set himself up against the Creator. Paul illustrates this by referring to the potter (vv. 20-24). Just as the potter must be granted absolute sovereignty over the clay, so

[2]Alfred Edersheim, *The Bible History, Old Testament, Vol. I* (reprint; Grand Rapids: Wm. B. Eerdmans Publishing Co., 1956), pp. 59-61. Used by permission.
[3]Alford, *op. cit.,* p. 924.

God must be granted absolute sovereignty over men. *"Nay but, O man, who art thou that repliest against God? Shall the thing formed say to him that formed it, Why hast thou made me thus? Hath not the potter power over the clay, of the same lump to make one vessel unto honour, and another unto dishonour? What if God, willing to shew his wrath, and to make his power known, endured with much longsuffering the vessels of wrath fitted to destruction: and that he might make known the riches of his glory on the vessels of mercy, which he had afore prepared unto glory, even us, whom he hath called, not of the Jews only, but also of the Gentiles?"* (vv. 20-24).

There is a remarkable change in the form of expression used to describe those destined for destruction and those destined for glory. Those marked for destruction are "fitted to destruction," but it is not stated that God so fitted them, as if God had prepared those vessels for wrath in contrast with those He prepared for mercy.[4]

God does not create people in order to damn them. However, when people behave like Pharaoh, God so deals with them that the inbred wickedness reveals itself in such a way that they become fit objects for His punishment.

Paul concludes the whole argument of this section by stressing the fact that the Gentiles are as much an object of God's mercy as are the Jews—an important fact to bear in mind. The salvation of Gentiles is not an afterthought with God. (Indeed, someone has well said that all the saved are not God's afterthoughts, but His forethoughts!) Paul is now going to demonstrate from the Old Testament that God's governmental dealings with Israel have never been at the expense of His love to all men.

God's past dealings with Israel, then, were based on His superlative wisdom and on His sovereign will. They were also based on *His spoken word.* The Word of God predicted very clearly the ultimate blessing of God in a great Gentile revival. *"As he saith in Osee, I will call them my people, which were not my people; and her beloved, which was not beloved. And it shall come to pass, that in the place where it was said unto them, Ye are not my people; there shall they be called the children of the living*

[4]See W. E. Vine, *The Epistle to the Romans* (Grand Rapids: Zondervan Publishing House, 1948), pp. 147-148.

God" (vv. 25-26). The words originally spoken by the broken-hearted Hosea to the adulterous nation of Israel are adapted by the apostle to his purpose. No Gentile peoples were ever called the people of God. The Lord Himself once referred to the Gentiles as "dogs" (an expression which needs to be studied in its context, Mark 7:24-30);[5] but now both Jews and Gentiles in Him are lifted far higher than anything the nation of Israel will ever know. We are sons of the living God!

The same Old Testament which predicted the ultimate blessing of God on the Gentiles, also spoke clearly of the blessing of God on a small Jewish remnant. *"Esaias also crieth concerning Israel, Though the number of the children of Israel be as the sand of the sea, a remnant shall be saved: for he will finish the work, and cut it short in righteousness: because a short work will the Lord make upon the earth. And as Esaias said before, Except the Lord of Sabaoth had left us a seed, we had been as Sodoma, and been made like unto Gomorrha"* (vv. 27-29). God's ways are perfectly consistent. Historically, not all the descendants of the patriarchs were counted as Israelites. God's true people have ever been a mere remnant, and for the rest, sooner or later God acts toward them in righteous judgment.

A study of the Old Testament clearly brings to light God's ways with men. For a long time He waits in long-suffering patience; then suddenly He acts, making a short work of judgment. The flood, the judgment of Sodom and Gomorrah, the cutting off of the rebels in the wilderness, the Assyrian and later the Babylonian invasions, all illustrate the point. After Calvary, God waited for forty years, and then suddenly the armies of Vespasian and Titus swept through the land like a flood, bringing to an awful end the nationhood of Israel. God acts in accordance with His spoken word and in judgment remembers mercy, always reserving to Himself a faithful remnant, the true Israel. The wisdom, the will, and the Word of God all agree that God deals in both mercy and in judgment according to righteous principles with clear foresight, with compelling force, and with consistent fairness. That is how Paul sees the problem.

[5]The Greek word used means "little" or "domestic dogs." It occurs only in Mark 7:27-28 and Matthew 15:26-27. These were not the pariah dogs of the street, but domestic pets.

B. *How Paul Summarizes the Problem* (9:30-33)

Clearly and concisely, Paul draws the various threads together. The Jews have no claim to salvation as a national right. The way of salvation was plain but they refused to go that way. They ran indeed, but down the wrong path, whereas the Gentiles, hearing the gospel, gladly responded and so attained the salvation vainly sought by the Jews. Paul emphasizes that (1) *the Gentiles have attained righteousness—by faith. "What shall we say then? That the Gentiles, which followed not after righteousness, have attained to righteousness, even the righteousness which is of faith"* (v. 30). Actually, the Gentiles were not pursuing after righteousness when the glad tidings of the gospel broke upon them. Gentile cities were centers of superstition, vice and idolatry. Yet again and again, no sooner did they hear the gospel than in hundreds and thousands they "turned to God from idols to serve the living and true God; and to wait for his Son from heaven" (I Thess. 1:9-10).

While the Gentiles so gladly embraced the gospel, the Jews in those same cities, except for a believing remnant, turned in hatred, anger, and bitterness on the missionaries, stoning them, cursing them, raising insurrection and riot against them, and pursuing them from city to city. Paul emphasizes that (2) *the Jews have attempted righteousness—but failed. "But Israel, which followed after the law of righteousness, hath not attained to the law of righteousness. Wherefore? Because they sought it not by faith, but as it were by the works of the law. For they stumbled at that stumblingstone; as it is written, Behold, I lay in Sion a stumblingstone and rock of offence: and whosoever believeth on him shall not be ashamed"* (vv. 31-33). Every Israelite believed that possession of the law of Moses was all that was required so long as he tried to live up to it. It was an unattainable goal at which he aimed. And to add to the tragedy of Jewish perversity, when the Messiah came, the One of whom the law and the prophets all spoke, the Jew stumbled over Him. The Jew wanted a militant Messiah, a Lion; God sent a Lamb. The Jew wanted a throne; God gave a cross.

So far, then, as God's past dealings with Israel are concerned, God has dealt with them in accordance with His sovereignty.

GOD'S PRESENT DEALINGS WITH ISRAEL
10:1-21

I. CHRIST REVEALED AS SAVIOUR (10:1-4)
   A. Paul Declares That the Jew Is Lost (10:1)
   B. Paul Describes Why the Jew Is Lost (10:2-4)
      1. By His Misguided Religious Exercise (10:2)
      2. By His Misguided Religious Enterprise (10:3-4)

II. CHRIST RECEIVED AS SAVIOUR (10:5-15)
   A. Considering Christ As Saviour (10:5-9)
      1. The Problem Inherent in Acquiring Righteousness by
         the Law (10:5)
      2. The Principles Inherent in Accepting Righteousness
         Through the Lord (10:6-9)
         a. The sensible prohibitions (10:6-7)
            (1) Don't try to bring Christ down,
                i.e., to repeat the incarnation (10:6)
            (2) Don't try to bring Christ up,
                i.e., to repeat the resurrection (10:7)
         b. The simple provisions (10:8-9)
            (1) The Scripture is most accessible (10:8)
            (2) The Saviour is most accessible (10:9)
   B. Confessing Christ As Saviour (10:10-15)
      1. The Evidential Value of Confessing Christ (10:10-13)
         a. It gives personal expression to the lordship of Christ
            (10:10-11)
            (1) It is a revealing of faith (10:10)
            (2) It is a reassuring of faith (10:11)
         b. It gives public exposure to the lordship of Christ
            (10:12-13)
            (1) He is Lord of all (10:12)
            (2) He is Lord for all (10:13)
      2. The Evangelistic Value of Confessing Christ (10:14-15)

III. CHRIST REJECTED AS SAVIOUR (10:16-21)
   A. Jewish Unbelief Is Unreasonable (10:16-20)
      1. They Could Believe (10:16-18)
      2. They Should Believe (10:19-20)
   B. Jewish Unbelief Is Unrelenting (10:21)

THE KEY TO GOD'S PAST DEALINGS with Israel is His sovereignty. The key to His present dealings is His salvation. Today God is offering salvation to the Jew on exactly the same terms as to the Gentile, and He makes no national difference at all. In this dispensation it is not the Jew nor the Gentile but the church which is God's channel of blessing for mankind. The special privileges and prerogatives of the Jew are in abeyance. If a Jew today wants to come into God's favor, he must come to Calvary as a lost sinner and accept his Messiah as Saviour and Lord. This is the theme of Romans 10.

I. CHRIST REVEALED AS SAVIOUR (10:1-4)

Nationally the Jew has rejected Jesus of Nazareth and invoked the curse of God upon the nation (Matt. 27:25). Individually, the Jew needs to recognize his lost condition the same as anyone else and join the remnant, the true Israel of God, by a personal acceptance of Christ.

A. *Paul Declares That the Jew Is Lost* (10:1)

Paul wastes no words in coming to grips with the problem which faces every Jew in this dispensation. *"Brethren,"* he says, *"my heart's desire and prayer to God for Israel is, that they might be saved"* (v. 1). The tender word "brethren" softens both what has preceded and what follows. Paul may use a gentle tone of voice, but not for one moment will he water down the truth. The Jew needs to be saved.

B. *Paul Describes Why the Jew Is Lost* (10:2-4)

He spells out two basic reasons why the Jew is lost, reasons which apply in a general sense to many Gentiles also. The Jew is lost because of (1) *his misguided religious exercise. "For I bear them record that they have a zeal of God, but not according to knowledge"* (v. 2). "A zeal of God" is a great thing so long as it is rightly directed; but it is a tragic thing if it drives a person along a wrong religious road. Paul knew what he was talking about here. Speaking to King Agrippa in later years he could testify, "I verily thought with myself, that I ought to do many things contrary to the name of Jesus of Nazareth. Which thing I also did in Jerusalem: and many of the saints did I shut up in prison, having received authority from the chief priests; and when they were put to death, I gave my voice against them. And I punished them oft in every synagogue, and compelled them to blaspheme; and being exceeding mad against them, I persecuted them even unto strange cities" (Acts 26:9-11). Then too, when he himself was imprisoned in Rome for the cause of Christ, he could write back to his friends at Philippi and reminisce about his unconverted days. "If any other man thinketh he hath where-of he might trust in the flesh, I more: circumcised the eighth day, of the stock of Israel, of the tribe of Benjamin, an Hebrew of the Hebrews; as touching the law, a Pharisee; concerning zeal, perse-cuting the church; touching the righteousness which is in the law, blameless. But what things were gain to me, those I counted loss for Christ" (Phil. 3:4-7).

Paul himself had come to the place where at last he realized that all his supposed religious assets were actually liabilities. He must take all of them from the profit side of the balance sheet and put them on the loss side. He must write them off as worthless and put Christ in their place. Before his conversion, he had "a zeal of God, but not according to knowledge" even though he had received the finest religious Bible-centered education possible in his day.

Nothing can be worse than misguided religious exercise. A certain town in Canada has four roads leading from it. One goes north until it joins the Alaska Highway. One runs south toward the American border. One leads east to the foothills of the Rockies where it comes to an abrupt end. The other goes west to the Pacific coast. Suppose a motorist wants to drive south to the American border but instead of obtaining specific directions, he decides to take the road which most appeals to him. The road north looks the best, so he blithely starts off along this road at top speed. This would be a case of misguided zeal. The faster and the farther he drives along that road, the farther and farther he gets away from his desired destination. Just so, many people plunge into zealous religious activity, careless of the fact that their zeal is misguided and is actually hurrying them along a totally false path. "There is a way which seemeth right unto a man, but the end thereof are the ways of death" (Prov. 14:12).

The Jew is lost not only because of his misguided religious

exercise but also because of (2) *his misguided religious enter-prise*. *"For they being ignorant of God's righteousness, and going about to establish their own righteousness, have not submitted themselves unto the righteousness of God. For Christ is the end of the law for righteousness to every one that believeth"* (vv. 3-4). The great enterprise of the Jew was to build for himself an edi-fice of righteousness in his own strength based on the edicts of Sinai—an utterly impossible task. Righteousness is to be found not at Sinai but at Calvary; it lies not in the acceptance of a precept but of a Person; not in servitude to commandments but in sub-mission to Christ. To submit to God's righteousness means to lay aside one's own "righteousness" and acknowledge complete fail-ure. This is something the Jew and all "religious" persons gen-erally refuse to do. But without such submission a person is not only lost but inexcusably lost since Christ has been revealed as Saviour.

II. CHRIST RECEIVED AS SAVIOUR (10:5-15)

Paul next shows that there is something that precedes an ac-ceptance of Christ and something that follows it. An acceptance of Christ is preceded by a fair consideration of Him, and it is followed by a frank confession of Him.

A. *Considering Christ As Saviour* (10:5-9)

Before pointing us away to Calvary, Paul would have us take one last look at Sinai and consider afresh (1) *the problem in-herent in acquiring righteousness by the law*. *"For Moses de-scribeth the righteousness which is of the law, That the man which doeth those things shall live by them"* (10:5). The quota-tion is from Leviticus 18:5 and points out that in order to be saved by the law a person must live according to all the precepts of the law without violating a single one. Should a person be able to do this, he would have earned his title to heaven. This underlines the inherent problem in the law because nobody can live such a perfect life. "This do and thou shalt live" is cold comfort for the person who realizes his impotence to live according to the divine decree. It is not the *law* that you must appeal to for right-eousness, says Paul to the Jew, it is the *Lord*. It is not Moses, it is Christ—the very One you have rejected.

To emphasize the contrast he spells out (2) *the principles inherent in accepting righteousness through the Lord.* Notice (*a*) *the sensible prohibitions he underlines.* "*The righteousness which is of faith speaketh on this wise, Say not in thine heart, Who shall ascend into heaven? (that is, to bring Christ down from above:) or, Who shall descend into the deep? (that is, to bring up Christ again from the dead)*" (vv. 6-7). The quotation is from Deuteronomy 30:11-14 and is not without its difficulties. Some have contended that Moses' words concerning the law are taken by Paul and twisted to apply to the gospel. However, the contrast is not between the law and faith but between the righteousness which stems from the two. Moreover, Paul enters into the spirit of the original passage. Just as Moses had said that there was no need for anyone to go up to heaven to bring down the law, so it is true that no one needs to go up to heaven to bring the Messiah down. Just as Moses had said that there was no need for anyone to go "across the sea" to find the law, so no one need search the depths to find the Messiah.

Notice also (*b*) *the simple provisions he underlines.* "*But what saith it? The word is nigh thee, even in thy mouth, and in thy heart: that is, the word of faith, which we preach*" (v. 8). Just as in Moses' day the Word was most accessible, so now the Lord is most accessible. The Christian message stipulates no impossibilities to mock the sinner such as bringing Christ down from heaven or up from the abyss. The "word of faith" includes the whole message of the gospel with its glorious tidings that Christ *has* come down from heaven; He *has* ascended from the regions of the dead. The two greatest miracles of the Christian faith are the *incarnation* which tells us that Christ has come down from heaven, and the *resurrection* which tells us that He has come up from the grave. They only have to be believed in the heart. The Scripture, "the word of faith," is most accessible.

But then the Saviour is most accessible too. Paul says, "*If thou shalt confess with thy mouth the Lord Jesus [Jesus as Lord], and shalt believe in thine heart that God hath raised him from the dead, thou shalt be saved*" (v. 9). The emphasis is on Jesus as *Lord,* that is, on His deity. The emphasis is also on righteousness by faith in contrast to righteousness by works. At the heart of the gospel message is the resounding, victorious assertion concerning the Lord Jesus, "God hath raised him from the dead." The resurrection of Christ from the dead is one of the best proved facts in history. No theory ever propounded can explain it away. It was the mighty shout of the infant church, and the fact was so well attested that none could deny it. "He was seen! He was seen!" cried the early Christians, and everyone knew it was so (I Cor. 15:5-8).

"Believe in thine heart that God hath raised him from the dead," says Paul. The gospel appeal is primarily to the heart rather than to the head. God does not ask merely for intellectual assent to dogma but for personal committal to Jesus as Lord. In Hebrew thought "the heart" comprised the whole man. It is interesting to compare Romans 10:9 with II Conrinthians 4:4, 6. Satan blinds the *mind* but God enlightens the *heart*.

The Saviour is most accessible. He must be believed on in the heart and confessed with the mouth. "Confess with thy mouth Jesus as Lord," says Paul. This was the one thing the Jews refused to do, and refuse to do to this day. They will not confess the deity of Jesus. Such a confession is one lasting evidence that conversion has taken place in the soul. The confession seems to be both Godward and manward. Paul has more to say about this in the verses that follow.

B. *Confessing Christ As Saviour* (10:10-15)

The value of confessing Christ is (1) *evidential*. In the first place, it gives (a) *personal expression to the lordship of Christ*. Two values are here: one is that there is a revealing of personal faith, and the other is that there is a reassuring of personal faith. *"For with the heart man believeth unto righteousness; and with the mouth confession is made unto salvation"* (v. 10). There is a change in the order of "heart" and "mouth" here because in verse 9 Paul is following Moses' order and in verse 10 the order of experience. Believing comes before confessing. The "confessing" here is not a legalistic requirement. It is not something which must be done in order to be saved. It is a natural consequence of true faith. Jesus said, "Out of the abundance of the heart the mouth speaketh" (Matt. 12:34).

Stifler says, "If one believes with the heart, that belief brings him into righteousness, right standing before God; and if now he confesses openly in his life his adherence to Jesus, that confession leads on to final salvation. Thus salvation is resolved into its two elements, a heart trust that provokes a true confession. And yet the two are one; for confession without belief is either self-deception or hypocrisy, while trust without confession may be cowardice (John 19:38)."[1] W. E. Vine takes a similar position: "The actual order is now given: faith first, then confession. In order to be saved righteousness must be reckoned, and this depends on faith; but faith necessarily leads to confession. Absence of confession betokens lack of faith."[2] Sanday's comment is similar: "The beginning of the Christian life has two sides: internally it is the change of heart which faith implies; this leads to righteousness, the position of acceptance before God: externally it implies the 'confession of Christ crucified. . . .' "[3] Sanday goes too far when he says that this confession is made in baptism.

The first value then in giving personal expression to the lordship of Christ lies in the fact that it is a revealing of faith. Doubtless this takes place Godward first, in the heart, but numerous commentators are agreed that it is also outward and manward. The second value lies in the fact that it is a reassuring of faith. *"For the scripture saith, Whosoever believeth on him shall not be ashamed"* (v. 11). This does not mean, as the Authorized Version implies, that the believer will not be ashamed of confessing Christ before men. It means rather that whoever believes on the Lord Jesus will "not be put to shame" or, as J. B. Phillips renders it, "will not be disappointed." The quotation is from Isaiah 28:16.

The value of confessing Christ is evidential not only because it gives personal expression to the lordship of Christ but also because it gives (*b*) *public exposure to the lordship of Christ.* Paul's emphasis here seems to be twofold. He draws attention to the fact that Christ is Lord *of* all: *"For there is no difference between the Jew and the Greek: for the same Lord over all is rich unto all that call upon him"* (v. 12). Earlier in the epistle Paul had proved

[1]James M. Stifler, *The Epistle to the Romans* (Chicago: Moody Press, 1960), p. 177.
[2]W. E. Vine, *The Epistle to the Romans* (Grand Rapids: Zondervan Publishing House, 1948), p. 157.
[3]William Sanday and A. C. Headlam, *A Critical and Exegetical Commentary on the Epistle to the Romans* (Edinburgh: T. & T. Clark, 1911), p. 290.

that "all have sinned." Now he shows that all can be saved. There is no difference or distinction between Jew and Gentile either in the matter of sin or in the manner of salvation. The lordship of Christ in this matter of salvation is equally applicable to both.

Then Paul points out that Jesus is Lord *for* all: *"For whosoever shall call upon the name of the Lord shall be saved"* (v. 13). Could the gospel message ever be reduced to simpler terms than that? Where, within the compass of one short verse, can be found a better statement of the scope ("whosoever"), the simplicity ("call upon the name of the Lord") and the substance ("shall be saved") of the gospel? Anyone can call. Jew or Gentile can call. The young and the old, the bond and the free, the rich and the poor, the cultured and the crude—anyone can call. Confessing the name, confessing Jesus as Lord gives personal expression and public exposure to the fact that Jesus saves. Here is its evidential value.

This leads on, quite naturally, to the fact that the value of confessing Christ is (2) *evangelistic*. Since salvation through Christ has been provided for all men, it must be proclaimed to all men. *"How then shall they call on him in whom they have not believed? and how shall they believe in him of whom they have not heard? and how shall they hear without a preacher? and how shall they preach except they be sent? as it is written, How beautiful are the feet of them that preach the gospel of peace, and bring glad tidings of good things!"* (vv. 14-15).

III. Christ Rejected As Saviour (10:16-21)

Paul now returns to the sad fact that occupies his mind all through these chapters. The Jew has rejected Christ as Saviour. Before drawing to a close the section which treats of God's present dealings with Israel, Paul shows how unreasonable and how unrelenting Jewish disbelief in the Lord Jesus really is.

A. *Jewish Unbelief in Christ Is Unreasonable* (10:16-20)

Paul maintains that Jewish unbelief in Christ is unreasonable on two counts. (1) *They could believe.* Note (*a*) that the *unique power* of God's Word makes belief in Christ possible. *"But they have not all obeyed the gospel. For Esaias saith, Lord, who hath believed our report? So then faith cometh by hearing, and hearing by the word of God* [lit. *the word of Christ*]*"* (vv. 16-17).

Paul mourns with Isaiah (Isa. 53:1) over the unreasonable unbelief of his people, for the gospel is not some new thing; it is rooted and grounded firmly in the Old Testament.

Faith cometh by *hearing*. It is only as the message is proclaimed that a response can be kindled. The supreme tragedy is that people refuse to hear. Israel refused to hear. The Lord Jesus again and again cried, "He that hath ears to hear, let him hear" (Matt. 11:15; 13:9, 43). Often, too, those who consent to *listen* fail to *hear*. The energizing power of the Word guarantees, however, that those who hear and respond have their faith quickened. Peter emphasizes a similar truth when he speaks of "being born again, not of corruptible seed, but of incorruptible, by the word of God, which liveth and abideth for ever" (I Peter 1:23). So then, because there is power in the word of Christ for those who hear, Jewish unbelief is unreasonable.

Not only does the unique power of the Word make belief possible, but (*b*) the *universal proclamation* of the Word makes belief possible. Paul says, *"But I say, Have they not heard? Yea verily, their sound went into all the earth, and their words unto the ends of the world"* (v. 18).

Jewish unbelief is unreasonable not only because they could believe but because (2) *they should believe*. The Gentiles have embraced the gospel, Paul argues, and this fact alone should arouse the Jewish conscience. *"But I say, Did not Israel know? First Moses saith, I will provoke you to jealousy by them that are no people, and by a foolish nation I will anger you. But Esaias is very bold, and saith, I was found of them that sought me not; I was made manifest unto them that asked not after me"* (vv. 19-20). Paul cites Moses and Isaiah as witnesses that the Hebrew Scriptures themselves foretold the conversion of the Gentiles. The Jews should believe, if for no other reason, out of sheer jealousy of the fact that the Gentiles have stolen a march, so to speak, on them.

B. *Jewish Unbelief in Christ Is Unrelenting* (10:21)

In spite of God's privileges to the nation of Israel, in spite of His long-suffering and in spite of His repeated invitations and warnings, Israel has persisted in rebellion and remonstrance. As the Lord says through Isaiah, *"All day long have I stretched forth my hands unto a disobedient and gainsaying people"* (v. 21). The word "disobedient" means "to refuse to be persuaded," emphasizing the unrelenting character of Jewish unbelief.

So far then as God's present dealings with Israel are concerned, God is speaking to the individual Jew. He is offering him salvation on the same basis as the Gentile. Gentiles are pressing into the kingdom but only comparatively few Jews pay any heed to the gospel call.

GOD'S PROMISED DEALINGS WITH ISRAEL
11:1-36

I. THE FAIRNESS OF GOD'S DEALINGS WITH ISRAEL (11:1-10)
  A. Paul Cites Himself As an Example (11:1)
  B. Paul Cites History As an Example (11:2-10)
    1. God's Dealings with the Believing Minority (11:2-6)
    2. God's Dealings with the Blinded Majority (11:7-10)

II. THE FARSIGHTEDNESS OF GOD'S DEALINGS WITH ISRAEL
    (11:11-29)
  A. God Acts Disapprovingly (11:11-22)
    1. But with the Prospective Restoration of Israel in Mind
       (11:11-16)
    2. And with the Present Redemption of the Gentiles in
       Mind (11:17-22)
  B. God Acts Dispensationally (11:23-29)
    1. It Is Within the Power of God to Restore Israel
       (11:23-24)
    2. It Is Within the Purpose of God to Restore Israel
       (11:25-29)
      a. His constitutional guarantee (11:25)
      b. His Christological guarantee (11:26)
      c. His contractual guarantee (11:27-29)

III. THE FAITHFULNESS OF GOD'S DEALINGS WITH ISRAEL
     (11:30-36)
  A. The Mercy of God's Ways (11:30-32)
    1. His Mercy to the Gentiles (11:30)
    2. His Mercy to the Jew (11:31)
    3. His Mercy to the World (11:32)

B. The Majesty of God's Ways (11:33-36)
  1. Beyond All Human Inferences (11:33-35)
  2. Beyond All Human Interferences (11:36)

THE KEY TO GOD'S PROMISED DEALINGS with Israel is His sincerity.
The solemn promises made to Abraham and his seed concerning
the Hebrew *racial* family and to David and his seed concerning
the Hebrew *royal* family have not been cancelled—only postponed. They are centered in Christ, and until His return they are
in abeyance. Their ultimate fulfillment awaits His coming again
when the nation which rejected Him will hail Him at last as
Messiah and Kinsman-Redeemer. During the present age, as we
have seen, God is offering salvation to Jew and Gentile alike on
an individual basis. Those who accept Jesus as Saviour become
members of the church and heirs of the privileges and prerogatives set forth in the New Testament. Mistakes in interpreting
Romans 11 can be avoided by observing that its theme is *not* the
church. It is the Jewish nation, and also the Gentile nations which
occupy, for this dispensation, the place of religious privilege tem-
porarily forfeited by the unbelieving Jew.

In chapter 11 Paul shows that although the Jew has forfeited
his national religious privileges for the time being, the day will
come when God will reactivate the promises and bring them to
fulfillment. The Christian is not heir to the distinctively Jewish
promises but is rather the *heavenly* seed of Abraham (Gen. 15:5-
6; Gal. 3:8, 29) and a partaker of the spiritual blessings of the
Abrahamic covenant (Gen. 15:18). The Jew is God's *earthly*
people and the great promises woven into the fabric of the Old
Testament concerning a literal, earthly kingdom will yet be fulfilled. "For the gifts and calling of God are without repentance"
(Rom. 11:29). God does not change His mind. In this chapter
Paul sets forth the fairness, the farsightedness and the faithfulness
of God in His dealings with His ancient people Israel.

I. THE FAIRNESS OF GOD'S DEALINGS WITH ISRAEL (11:1-10)

Paul begins by showing that God deals with peoples on fixed
principles. Moreover, His overruling government is ever mingled
with grace.

A. *He Cites Himself As an Example* (11:1)

That God has not given up His ancient people entirely is evidenced by the conversion of Saul of Tarsus, once one of the bitterest enemies of the gospel and an archpersecutor of the church. *"I say then, Hath God cast away his people? God forbid. For I also am an Israelite, of the seed of Abraham, of the tribe of Benjamin"* (v. 1).

B. *He Cites History As an Example* (11:2-10)

Paul next divides Jews into two classes, a believing minority and a blinded or hardened majority. He wants his brethren to see that God's dealings with the Jews have been fair and perfectly consistent. Look first at (1) *the believing minority.* God's dealings with this believing remnant is based upon His fathomless wisdom (vv. 2-4) and His finished work (vv. 5-6). *"God hath not cast away his people which he foreknew. Wot ye not what the scripture saith of Elias? how he maketh intercession to God against Israel, saying, Lord, they have killed thy prophets, and digged down thine altars; and I am left alone, and they seek my life. But what saith the answer of God unto him? I have reserved to myself seven thousand men, who have not bowed the knee to the image of Baal"* (vv. 2-4). Elijah's complaint against Israel was wrung from his lips in the darkest hour of personal depression and in the midst of fearful national apostasy. The story is found in I Kings 18–19.

The mighty victory on Carmel, to which Paul refers, had dealt a devastating blow to Jezebel's power structure and to the Satanic cult of Baal on which it was based. But that victory had been incomplete. The wiley Jezebel had not sent all her prophets to the Carmel duel but had kept in reserve the four hundred prophets of the groves. Thus she was ready to counter Elijah's victory, which she did with energy and resolve, shaking even that fiery prophet's iron nerve. He fled! When he finally pulled himself up exhausted, it was to find himself far from the scene of conflict and beneath the historic crags of Horeb. Ashamed and disappointed, the prophet flung himself down. Then, tenderly the voice of God came to the man of God: "What doest thou here, Elijah?" (I Kings 19:9).

In reply the prophet interceded, as Paul so pointedly puts it, against Israel. Then came the tempest, the earthquake and the fire, each suited to the prophet's mood; the very weapons he would have liked to have had at his command in his anger against Israel. But God was in none of these things. Instead, there came a still small voice, and in that tender voice God dwelt and with it spoke: "What doest thou here, Elijah?" It was a lesson of grace; but Elijah's wrath kindled now against Israel was not to be pacified thus. In answer to the question he gave the same answer word for word. "I have been very jealous for the LORD God of hosts: because the children of Israel have forsaken thy covenant, thrown down thine altars, and slain thy prophets with the sword; and I, even I only, am left; and they seek my life, to take it away" (I Kings 19:14). Suddenly there came a new command from Him who would not be denied. "Anoint Hazael to be king over Syria . . . Jehu the son of Nimshi . . . to be king over Israel: and Elisha the son of Shaphat . . . *to be prophet in thy room*" (vv. 15-16).

Why was not God in the tempest, the earthquake, or the fire? Why were not these effective instruments placed into the hands of Elijah? Why did God not send His servant back with a fresh commission against the prophets of the groves? By the time he had brooded all the way to Horeb, Elijah's anger had been kindled, now not against Jezebel's prophets but against Israel. Unlike Moses who had interceded *for* Israel, Elijah interceded *against* them. Hence, he was not to be trusted with such mighty weapons of war, for sprinkled among the godless majority of Israel, unknown to Elijah but known to God, was a believing minority. "I only am left," complained the prophet. "I have reserved to myself seven thousand men, who have not bowed the knee to Baal," said God.

As it was in Elijah's day, so it was in Paul's and ever has been. God never leaves Himself without a remnant. There have been times in the history of the church, as it was with Israel, when the lamp of testimony has burned dim, but it has never gone out.

God's dealings with Israel were based not only on a fathomless wisdom, but also on a finished work. *"Even so then at this present time also there is a remnant according to the election of grace. And if by grace, then is it no more of works: otherwise grace is no more grace. But if it be of works, then is it no more grace: other-*

wise work is no more work" (vv. 5-6). God's remnant has always been those who have accepted the principles of salvation by faith through grace. For example, "The first followers of Christ were at one and the same time the last believing remnant of the old community and the first nucleus of the new."[1]

In contrast with the believing minority is (2) *the blinded majority.* While God ever had His "Gulf Stream" of believers in Israel, there was also the ocean of the nation, the unbelieving majority. The picture Paul gives of the nation as a whole is sad. He speaks of *the search,* the unavailing search of the nation. *"What then? Israel hath not obtained that which he seeketh for; but the election hath obtained it, and the rest were blinded"* (v. 7). The word "blinded" is "hardened" or "calloused." It is used in the Gospels to describe Pharisees who were angered at the Lord Jesus for healing a man in the synagogue on the sabbath day (Mark 3:5). It is used later by Paul to describe unconverted Gentiles who "walk in the vanity of their mind, having the understanding darkened, being alienated from the life of God through the ignorance that is in them, because of the blindness of their heart" (Eph. 4:17-18). The great business of the Jewish nation was its search after righteousness. The passion of the Greek was for knowledge; the passion of the Roman was for power; but the passion of the Jew was for righteousness. They missed their national goal by missing Christ and so were hardened, except for the elect remnant.

Paul speaks of *the stupor* of the nation. *"According as it is written, God hath given them the spirit of slumber, eyes that they should not see, and ears that they should not hear; unto this day"* (v. 8). The nation became so insensible to spiritual realities that it became the subject of judicial hardening. Paul has already cited God's dealings with Pharaoh as an example of judicial hardening. Isaiah speaks very solemnly of a similar doom for Israel (Isa. 29:10). In a coming day, God will deal with apostate Christendom in the same way (II Thess. 2:11-12). As leprosy renders the flesh insensitive, so the soul of the Jewish nation has been rendered insensitive to Christ.

Paul speaks of *the snare* of the nation. *"And David saith, Let their table be made a snare, and a trap, and a stumblingblock,*

[1]F. F. Bruce, *The Books and the Parchments* (Westwood, N.J.: Fleming H. Revell Co., 1963), p. 84.

and a recompence unto them" (v. 9). In the holy place of the
tabernacle of Israel was a table. Israel's high and holy privilege
was to eat with Jehovah at His table, a privilege not reserved for
the priests alone, but in their peace offerings for the people as
well (Exodus 24:11; Lev. 6:16; 7:18, 20). In their feast days also
Israel sat at table, so to speak, with Jehovah (Lev. 23:6; Num.
15:17-21; 18:26-31; Deut. 12:7, 18; 14:23; 27:7). This, the highest,
holiest, and happiest of all national privileges, became a snare to
the nation in its unbelief. They became more occupied with the
outward ceremonial than with the spiritual reality.

Paul speaks of *the servitude* of the nation. "*Let their eyes be
darkened, that they may not see, and bow down their back alway*"
(v. 10). The bowing of the back, the loosening of the loins, is a
vivid picture of servitude and fear. From generation to generation
the Jew has fled from land to land, ever pursued by the vicious
curse of anti-Semitism. The national rejection of Christ has
brought in its train untold miseries from age to age. Hitler's death
camps have been but one more high tide mark in the sorrows of
the wandering Jew. From what is written on the prophetic page
of Scripture we know those horrors will not be the last; for still
ahead of the nation are the horrors of the great tribulation. After
that final agony, however, God "will pour upon the house of David,
and upon the inhabitants of Jerusalem, the spirit of grace and of
supplications: and they shall look upon me whom they have
pierced, and they shall mourn for him, as one mourneth for his
only son, and shall be in bitterness for him, as one that is in
bitterness for his firstborn. In that day shall there be a great
mourning in Jerusalem, as the mourning of Hadadrimmon in the
valley of Megiddon. And the land shall mourn, every family
apart" (Zech. 12:10-12).

So then, we have the fairness of God's dealings with Israel. The
believing minority have found favor in the sight of God and have
been added to the church. The blinded majority have tasted that
judicial hardening and blindness of which the nation was forewarned in the prophets.

II. THE FARSIGHTEDNESS OF GOD'S DEALINGS WITH ISRAEL
    (11:11-29)

The setting aside of Israel as a nation for the time being is in

keeping with God's long-range goals for the Jewish people. It
also has some immediate benefits for the Gentile nations. Japheth
has come to dwell in the tents of Shem (Gen. 9:27). The setting
aside of Israel is not a permanent move on God's part, for that
would involve the cancellation of promises secured to Abraham
and his seed by solemn and unconditional guarantees. That the
promises have not been cancelled but their fulfillment merely
postponed is Paul's theme in the second part of this chapter.

A. *Today God Is Dealing with Israel Disapprovingly* (11:11-22)

This subject is dealt with mainly from the Gentile standpoint.
Paul is afraid that the Gentiles will become proud of their present
position of privilege and fall into the same error as Israel of old.
As in olden times the Jew regarded himself as heaven's special
favorite and despised the Gentile, so in this dispensation there is
danger of the Gentile regarding himself as heaven's favorite and
despising the Jew. The section is filled with warnings against
such religious pride, as Paul explains the relative positions of
Jew and Gentile in this present age and highlights some of God's
plans for the nation of Israel in the future.

In this age, although God is dealing with Israel disapprovingly,
it is (1) *with the prospect of Israel's restoration in mind.* First,
Paul *explains* this fact. *"I say then, Have they stumbled that they
should fall? God forbid: but rather through their fall salvation is
come unto the Gentiles, for to provoke them to jealousy. Now if
the fall of them be the riches of the world, and the diminishing of
them the riches of the Gentiles; how much more their fulness?"*
(vv. 11-12). Paul had seen this principle work in city after city
of the Roman Empire, where invariably his turning to the Gentiles
was followed by deep resentment and jealousy on the part of the
Jewish community. These experiences would be very fresh in his
mind, for at Corinth, where he was residing as he wrote this
epistle to Rome, the Jews had manifested their usual opposition
to the gospel. They had in this case, however, been divinely
restrained from a personal attack on Paul although vehemently
blaspheming the Lord (Acts 18). Later, when Paul was giving
his testimony to the Jerusalem mob, the Jews heard him patiently
until he told how God had said to him, "I will send thee far hence
unto the Gentiles." Then they "lifted up their voices, and said,

Away with such a fellow from the earth: for it is not fit that he should live. And as they cried out, and cast off their clothes, and threw dust into the air, the chief captain commanded him to be brought into the castle" (Acts 22:21-24). It enraged the Jews to think that the Gentiles should have even that which they themselves despised.

They were bitterly jealous of the Gentiles and resented any extension of religious privilege to them. Theirs, however, was strictly a dog-in-the-manger attitude. They did not want the gospel and they did not want the Gentiles to have it either.

Despite the present attitude of Israel toward the gospel, Paul looks forward to the day when the nation will be converted. What a day that will be! If through their stubbornness, jealousy and rebellion the Gentiles have fallen heir to such blessings, what riches are in store for the world when Israel is restored to its rightful position! God has not lost sight of His ultimate goal.

Paul not only explains what God is doing, he *exploits* what God is doing. *"For I speak to you Gentiles, inasmuch as I am the apostle of the Gentiles, I magnify mine office: if by any means I may provoke to emulation them which are my flesh, and might save some of them. For if the casting away of them be the reconciling of the world, what shall the receiving of them be, but life from the dead? For if the firstfruits be holy, the lump is also holy: and if the root be holy, so are the branches"* (vv. 13-16). Paul hoped that by throwing himself into his great life's work of Gentile world evangelism, some of his Jewish brethren would be saved even if jealousy were the motive.

Again Paul anticipates the day when the nation of Israel will embrace the Lord Jesus. He likens the resulting world revival to "life from the dead." In that day "the earth shall be full of the knowledge of the LORD, as the waters cover the sea" (Isa. 11:9). Paul's reference to the root and the branches introduces what follows. Abraham seems to be the *root* since he was the depository of the promises. (Some see Christ as the root here since He is described in this same epistle as "the root of Jesse" [Isa. 11:10; Rom. 15:12] and is ultimately the root of every blessing, earthly and heavenly). The *tree* is the race of Abraham. In the next paragraph Paul will define the tree as an olive tree, reminding us of Jeremiah 11:16 where the prophet says to Israel, "The

172

LORD called thy name, A green olive tree." The *natural branches* are the Jews, those who first partook of the tree's root and fatness. As we shall see a few verses further on, many of the Jews were broken off from the place of divine blessing in Abraham because of unbelief. A remnant will be grafted in again after the tribulation, and once more blessings will flow to men through Israel. The *ingrafted branches* are the Gentiles, placed upon the root, not the trunk or branches. The Gentile does not become a Jew nor does he become "of Israel" but enters directly into the blessing promised by God to the Gentiles through Abraham (Gen. 12:3). This is the theme Paul develops next.

While God is acting disapprovingly with Israel but with the prospective restoration of Israel in mind, He is also acting (2) *with the present redemption of the Gentiles in mind.* It is in this section (vv. 17-22) that Paul develops his famous parable of the olive tree. *"And if some of the branches be broken off, and thou, being a wild olive tree, wert graffed in among them, and with them partakest of the root and fatness of the olive tree; boast not against the branches. But if thou boast, thou bearest not the root, but the root thee. Thou wilt say then, The branches were broken, that I might be graffed in. Well; because of unbelief they were broken off, and thou standest by faith. Be not highminded, but fear: for if God spared not the natural branches, take heed lest he also spare not thee. Behold therefore the goodness and severity of God: on them which fell, severity; but toward thee, goodness, if thou continue in his goodness: otherwise thou also shalt be cut off"* (vv. 17-22). There are several important lessons here. The first is that the Gentiles are represented as being a wild olive tree grafted into the root of a good tree. Later on Paul will remind us that this process is "contrary to nature," so comment will be reserved until we come to verse 24.

This section raises a problem. It seems to contradict the teaching of Romans 8 regarding the eternal security of the believer. Paul's reference here to branches being broken off, intended as a clear warning to his Gentile readers, has led some to think that Christians can lose their salvation. We need to proceed with caution at this point. What does Paul mean when he says, "If God spared not the natural branches, take heed lest he also spare not thee"? God says in chapter 8 that nothing can separate the child of God from His love, yet here God speaks of the danger of being "cut off."

It is important to observe the context here with care. The subject matter of Romans 8 was the *church;* here in chapter 11 it is the *Jew* and the *Gentile.* The three classes must be dealt with separately in sound exposition because God does not deal with each alike. In Romans 9 and 10, as we have seen, Paul has been discussing the Jews. Now he distinctly says, "I speak to you Gentiles" (11:13). The warnings of this section, then, are not addressed to the church at all.

Next, we need to observe the symbolism used. The olive tree was one of three to which Israel is compared in the Old Testament. The fig tree symbolizes Israel's *national* privileges; the vine, Israel's *spiritual* privileges; and the olive, Israel's *religious* privileges.[2] This gives us the clue to Paul's warning. The Jew has lost his religious privileges for the time being. In the Old Testament some twenty-five passages threatened the Israelite with the penalty of being "cut off from his people," judicial death (not necessarily eternal death) being meant. Those so cut off, of course, lost all privileges connected with the covenant of Abraham. Except for the believing remnant, this was happening to Israel on a national scale in the time of Paul. This judicial breaking off was the result of unbelief on the part of the Jews.[3]

Gentiles, through faith in Christ, were being grafted in to replace the broken branches. Since Gentiles now have all the religious privileges once proudly displayed by the Jews, they must beware of religious pride. They have come into the system of blessing initiated by God with Abraham; but, like the Jews, they can be cut off from those privileges which are so graphically pictured by the olive tree. God does not play favorites. The question of eternal salvation, however, does not arise since it is not the subject matter of the chapter. Religious privilege is the theme,

[2] Dispensationally, the vine pictures Israel up to the time when the nation rejected Christ; the fig, Israel in this age until the second coming of Christ; the olive, Israel in a coming age when the national and religious privileges of Israel will be restored.

[3] See G. H. Lang, *Pictures and Parables* (London: Paternoster Press, 1955), pp. 366-372.

not eternal life in Christ. The subjects of the chapter are Jews
and Gentiles, not the church. It is perfectly true that we can
make an *application* to the individual believer underlining the
dangers of abusing privileges enjoyed in Christ; but the true
interpretation belongs not to the church, but to Gentile and Jew.

B. *Today God Is Dealing With Israel Dispensationally* (11:23-29)

Paul has not finished with the theme introduced in the above
section. He continues with the same symbolism to show that God
has every intention of ultimately restoring Israel to all her former
privileges. He shows (1) *it is within the power of God to restore
Israel.* "*And they also, if they abide not still in unbelief, shall be
graffed in: for God is able to graff them in again. For if thou wert
cut out of the olive tree which is wild by nature, and wert graffed
contrary to nature into a good olive tree: how much more shall
these, which be the natural branches, be graffed into their own
olive tree?*" (vv. 23-24). The restoration of Israel is well within
God's power. The ingrafting of the Gentiles was "contrary to
nature."

Thomson gives some interesting comments on the olive and the
grafting process. "The olive, in its natural wild state, bears no
berries, or but few and these small and destitute of oil. The olive
. . . is wild by nature and must be grafted by the *good* before it
will bear fruit; but here the Apostle speaks of grafting the wild
into the good, not the good *upon* the wild. . . . Observe, he expressly says that this is *contrary* to nature, as it really is. I have
made particular inquiries on this point, and find that in the *kingdom of nature* generally, certainly in the case of the olive, the
process referred to by the Apostle never succeeds. Graft the good
upon the wild and, as the Arabs say, it will *conquer* the wild; but
you cannot reverse the process with success. If you insert a *wild*
graft into a good tree, *it will conquer the good.* It is only in the
kingdom of grace that a process thus contrary to nature can be
successful; and it is this circumstance which the Apostle has seized
upon with admirable tact, to magnify the mercy shown to the
Gentiles by grafting them, a wild race, *contrary to the nature* of
such operations, into the good olive tree. . . . The Apostle lived in
the land of the olive, and was in no danger of falling into a blun-

der in founding his argument upon such a circumstance in its cultivation."[4]

What a fitting picture the olive is to portray God's dealings with Jew and Gentile alike! If, Paul says, the grafting in, *contrary to nature,* of the Gentiles has been so fruitful, what will it be when Israel, the natural branches, come back into their own!

Having shown that it is within the power of God to restore Israel, Paul next shows (2) *it is within the purpose of God to restore Israel.* There is indeed a threefold guarantee that God will ultimately do just that. The first of these is (a) the *constitutional* guarantee. *"For I would not, brethren, that ye should be ignorant of this mystery, lest ye should be wise in your own conceits; that blindness in part is happened to Israel, until the fulness of the Gentiles be come in"* (v. 25). There are two great expressions in the New Testament concerning the Gentiles which repay careful study. The first is "the times of the Gentiles" (Luke 21:24) and the other is "the fulness of the Gentiles" mentioned in this passage. The two expressions are similar but not the same. The "times of the Gentiles" have to do with the period during which Jerusalem is under Gentile power. This period began with Nebuchadnezzar and will continue until the return of Christ when the throne rights will be visibly assumed by Him whose right it is

---

[4]W. M. Thomson, *The Land and the Book* (Grand Rapids: Baker Book House, 1954 ed.), pp. 53-55. Thomson goes on to say:

"The Apostle speaks of the *root* of the good olive, implying that, by some means or other, it had been changed. You observe certain knobs, or large warts, so to speak, on the body of this tree. Cut off one of these which has a branch growing out of it, *above* the place where it has been grafted; plant it in good soil, water it carefully, and it will strike out roots and grow. It is now a good tree from the root, and all scions taken from it are also 'good by nature.' But if the knob or branch be taken below the grafting, your tree becomes wild again. . . . I am told by olive growers that there is a tendency to degenerate, and that it is often a great improvement to graft even a good tree with one that is still better. . . .

"This tree is of slow growth, and the husbandman must have long patience. Except under circumstances peculiarly favorable, it bears no berries until the seventh year; but then 'the labor of the olive' is extremely profitable, and it will continue to yield its fruit to extreme old age, like the excellent of the earth. So long as there is a fragment remaining, though externally the tree looks dry as a post, yet does it continue to yield its load of olive berries, and for twenty generations the owners gather fruit from the faithful old patriarch. This tree also requires but little labor or care of any kind, and, if long neglected, will revive again when the ground is dug or ploughed, and begin afresh to yield as before. Vineyards forsaken die out almost immediately, and mulberry orchards neglected run rapidly to ruin; but not so the olive. . . . Large trees, in a good season, will yield from ten to fifteen gallons of oil."

to reign. It is noteworthy that when the exiles returned to the promised land during the days of Zerubbabel and Ezra, they went not to found an independent kingdom but a dependency; not to build a palace but a temple; not to set up a throne but an altar. The expression "the times of the Gentiles," then, has to do with the *political* ascendency of the Gentiles, Nebuchadnezzar being the first Gentile sovereign to reign by divine right (Dan. 2:37).

In contrast with this, the "fullness of the Gentiles" has to do with the *spiritual* ascendency of the Gentiles. When Israel crowned all its former rebellions with the crucifixion of the Messiah and then endorsed that act by resisting the Holy Spirit as recorded in the book of Acts, God took away from the nation its spiritual privileges too. Increasingly in the book of Acts the emphasis is on the Gentiles. It was not long before Antioch, Corinth, Ephesus and Rome eclipsed Jerusalem as centers of spiritual influence; and when in A.D. 70 Titus razed Jerusalem to the ground, all semblance of Jewish authority in the church collapsed.

"The fullness of the Gentiles," then, refers to the spiritual blessing of the Gentile described by Peter in the words, "God at the first did visit the Gentiles, to take out of them a people for his name" (Acts 15:14). The fullness of the Gentiles will be complete at the rapture, at which time God will once more bless men through Israel. The world will then see the Jew evangelizing the Gentile. "But in the meantime one glance will tell us that the light and energy and blessing of the gospel lie in Gentile hands, and not in Jewish. That the Gentiles should form missionary societies to the Jew is proof enough of the state of things."[5] This state of affairs is only to continue "until" (v. 25). There is a constitutional guarantee that the Jew will again come into prominence spiritually when the moment covered by that word "until" arrives.

There is not only the constitutional guarantee that God will restore Israel; there is (b) the *Christological* guarantee. *"And so all Israel shall be saved: as it is written, There shall come out of Sion the Deliverer, and shall turn away ungodliness from Jacob"* (v. 26). This Deliverer, of course, is the Lord Jesus, the Kinsman-Redeemer-Avenger as the Hebrew word *Goel* implies. The greater

[5]Algernon J. Pollock, *Things Which Must Shortly Come to Pass* (London: The Central Bible Truth Depot, n.d.), p. 45.

part of the nation of Israel will perish during the judgments of the great tribulation (Jer. 30:5–31:40; Dan. 12:1; Rev. 7), but at the return of the Lord Jesus the surviving remnant will all be converted (Zech. 12:10-14), and "so all Israel shall be saved." Paul appeals to two passages in Isaiah to support this (Isa. 59:20-21; 27:9). "All Israel," of course, does not refer to all the Jews who have ever lived, but to all those alive at the end of the great tribulation. Paul sees in the return of Christ a Christological guarantee that God will restore Israel.

In addition, there is (c) the *contractual* guarantee. *"For this is my covenant unto them, when I shall take away their sins. As concerning the gospel, they are enemies for your sakes: but as touching the election, they are beloved for the fathers' sakes. For the gifts and calling of God are without repentance"* (vv. 27-29). Paul looks here to the new covenant mentioned in Jeremiah 31. God does not change His mind, nor is He shortsighted. He does not begin to build a tower without first counting the cost (Luke 14:28-29), nor does He underestimate the opposition He will encounter in the pursuit of His ultimate objectives (Luke 14:31-32). No contingency can arise which He has not already taken fully into account and for which He has not made provision. His contractual agreements with the fathers (unconditional as so many of them were) are not to be thwarted by human failure. The glory of God's great name and the honor of His throne are involved, as Moses so pertinently, yet humbly, reminded the Lord on two notable occasions (Exodus 32:7-14; Num. 14:11-20).

So then, in speaking of God's promised dealings with Israel Paul explains both the fairness and the farsightedness of God's dealings. He has but one more point to make and then he will come back to the main theme of the epistle.

III. THE FAITHFULNESS OF GOD'S DEALINGS WITH ISRAEL (11:30-36)

The closing verses of the chapter summarize the argument and break into a mighty doxology of worship to God for the marvel and mystery of God's dealings with men.

A. *The Mercy of God's Ways* (11:30-32)

Four times in these verses Paul points to God's mercy. First, there is His mercy to (1) *the Gentiles. "For as ye in times past*

*have not believed God, yet have now obtained mercy through
their unbelief"* (v. 30). He reemphasizes the fact that God's dealings in government with Israel have been a means of His extend-
ing His grace to the Gentiles. Mercy is the brightest light that
plays upon the throne of God. Then there is His mercy to (2)
*the Jews. "Even so have these also now not believed, that through
your mercy they also may obtain mercy"* (v. 31). Paul is drawing
here an exact parallel. Once the Gentiles were the unbelievers,
but through disobedience of the Jews have found mercy. Now
the Jews are unbelievers, but by the mercy of the Gentiles they
too may find mercy. This statement should stimulate Jewish evangelism. Finally, there is His mercy to (3) *the world. "For God
hath concluded them all in unbelief, that he might have mercy
upon all"* (v. 32). Or, as some have rendered it, "God has shut
up all unto disobedience, that He might have mercy upon all."
In other words, God has overruled the disobedience of men, Jew
and Gentile alike, that He might offer to all His mercy. The argument takes us back to chapter 3.

Well might Shakespeare put into the lips of Portia the words:

> The quality of mercy is not strained;
> It droppeth as the gentle rain of heaven
> Upon the place beneath: it is twice blest;
> It blesseth him that gives and him that takes:
> 'Tis mightiest in the mightiest; it becomes
> The throned monarch better than his crown;
> His sceptre shows the force of temporal power,
> The attribute of awe and majesty,
> Wherein doth sit the dread and fear of kings;
> But mercy is above this sceptered sway;
> It is enthroned in the heart of kings,
> It is an attribute of God himself;
> And earthly power doth then show likest God's
> When mercy seasons justice. Therefore, Jew,
> Though justice be thy plea, consider this—
> That in the course of justice none of us
> Should see salvation: we do pray for mercy.[6]

B. *The Majesty of God's Ways* (11:33-36)

Paul concludes with one of the greatest doxologies in the Bible
celebrating the majesty of God's ways. Those ways are (1) *be-*

---

[6]William Shakespeare, *The Merchant of Venice,* Act IV, Scene I.

yond all human inferences. "O the depth of the riches both of the wisdom and knowledge of God! how unsearchable are his judgments, and his ways past finding out! For who hath known the mind of the Lord? or who hath been his counsellor? Or who hath first given to him, and it shall be recompensed unto him again?" (vv. 33-35). Man is a great thinker! The world's libraries attest to that. His restless intellect probes the heights above and the depths beneath as it inquires into the nature of the universe and seeks the reason why. But God's ways and dealings are beyond all human inferences. "For my thoughts are not your thoughts, neither are your ways my ways, saith the LORD. For as the heavens are higher than the earth, so are my ways higher than your ways, and my thoughts than your thoughts" (Isa. 55:8-9). When those ways are revealed to us, all we can do is to bow and worship.

Those ways, likewise, are (2) *beyond all human interferences.* "For of him, and through him, and to him, are all things: to whom be glory for ever. Amen" (v. 36). He is the Creator and Sustainer of the universe. He pursues His plans and purposes from age to age. No act of human rebellion can thwart the ultimate fulfillment of His will. His goals will all be reached at last. When the people rage and "the kings of the earth set themselves, and the rulers take counsel together, against the LORD, and against his anointed, saying, Let us break their bands asunder, and cast away their cords from us. He that sitteth in the heavens shall laugh: the LORD shall have them in derision" (Ps. 2:1-4).

His dealings with Israel are beyond all human interferences. His fairness, His farsightedness, His faithfulness guarantee beyond all question that His promised dealings with Israel shall come to pass.

III. THE PRACTICE OF THE GOSPEL

12:1–16:24

THE CHRISTIAN AS A BELIEVER
12:1-2

I. How the Christian Is Challenged As a Believer (12:1)
   A. To Give an Unbridled Sacrifice
      1. The Proper Thing to Do
      2. The Practical Thing to Do
   B. To Give an Unblemished Sacrifice
   C. To Give an Unbiased Sacrifice

II. How the Christian Is Changed As a Believer (12:2)
   A. Morally
   B. Mentally
   C. Motivationally

PAUL HAS COMPLETED HIS DIGRESSION and now returns to the main stream of his thesis. Having discussed the *principles* of the gospel and the *problems* of the gospel, he now begins to deal with the *practice* of the gospel, and this is his theme throughout the remainder of the epistle. It is typical of the teaching of the epistles that belief is followed by behavior; doctrine, by deeds.

This last section of Romans is in two parts. First, Paul discusses *the laws of Christian life* (12:1–13:7), and then he discusses *the laws of Christian love* (13:8–16:24). The first of these sections is in three parts and deals respectively with the believer's spiritual, social and secular relationships of life. The reader is referred to the overall analysis of the epistle on page 7-8 to get the general perspective.

The discussion of the spiritual life of the Christian is in two parts. First, Paul deals with the Christian as a *believer* (12:1-2), and then with the Christian as a *brother* (12:3-13).)

I. How the Christian Is Challenged As a Believer (12:1)

The challenge has to do with the believer's body, which Paul now reveals to be the ultimate key to the practice of the victorious Christian life. It is of little avail to know theoretically the truths of Romans 6–8 if the body is not surrendered so that the life of Christ can be expressed in the everyday affairs of life.

A. *The Body As an Unbridled Sacrifice* (12:1)

God does not compel and coerce the believer into presenting his body. He does not corral him and bridle him like a horse and force him to obey. He beseeches him. He wants an unbridled sacrifice. He makes it clear that to present the body to God is, for the believer, (1) *the proper thing to do.* "*I beseech you therefore, brethren, by the mercies of God, that ye present your bodies a living sacrifice, holy, acceptable unto God, which is your reasonable service*" (v. 1).

It is an axiom of Bible study that when we come across the word "therefore" we should pause and see what it's *there for!* In this case it links God's demand for the believer's body with those "mercies" Paul has been describing in both the doctrinal and dispensational sections of the epistle. God has saved us from sin, from its penalty and its power. He has saved us from self in all its features and all its forms. He has overruled the destinies of nations. He has triumphed in His grace and multiplied His mercies. He has, as it were, besieged us with His mercies, brought them up against us in countless number, built the bulwarks of His grace against our souls, poured a ceaseless cannonade of kindness in upon the breaches in our hearts. He has overwhelmed us with unmerited favor and carried all before Him on the resistless arms of love. "I beseech you therefore," says Paul, "by the mercies of God, that ye present your bodies." It is the proper thing to do. It is the only possible thing to do. It is the only fitting answer we can give to "love so amazing, so divine."

It is not only the proper thing to do, it is (2) *the practical thing to do.* It makes possible the translation of the principles of Romans 1–8 into the practice of Romans 12–16. It is all very well to have our heads in the theological clouds and enjoy the great truths of positional sanctification. God wants us to live a holy life in the home and on the highway, at the bench, the counter or the desk. The link between the two is the presented body. There is a very real sense in which to present our bodies to God is the most strategic thing we can do as Christians.

It is possible for us, as believers, to live lives on one of three levels. We can live lives that are sensual, soulish or spiritual. A person, for example, who is ruled by the physical is *sensual*. To be sensual does not necessarily mean that we live in the constant indulgence of the worst forms of carnality. It simply means that we are ruled by the senses.

Think of each of the following expressions: "I don't like the smell." "It's too hot." "I'm too tired." "Does it taste good?" "What does it feel like?" "Don't do that, it hurts." "Isn't it ugly?" "Let me tell you what Betty said." Each one of these statements reflects a physical reaction. People who are ruled by such considerations are ruled by the senses—by what they see, feel, hear, taste or smell. The motivation from this source may be very subtle, very well disguised, very genteel; but, nevertheless, people motivated by such considerations are sensual. It is possible for a Christian to be sensual. He will not go to prayer meeting because it is too hot. He will not work in the slums because they are too smelly. He doesn't like John Jones because he uses bad grammar. In other words, he is a sensual Christian. He may be saved, but he is living his life on the lowest possible plane.

On the other hand, it is possible for us to be *soulish* in our expression of the faith, to be ruled from the intellect, the emotions or the will. This is a far more subtle possibility. A life so lived can come so close to genuine spirituality that it can be very difficult to detect the flaw. For example, a believer may give himself over to *intellectual* pursuits in his practice of Christianity. He studies his Bible and becomes a walking Bible encyclopedia. He becomes a great theologian, a great controversialist for the faith. People admire and respect him for his great grasp of truth. He is not necessarily spiritual, however. This grasp of truth all too often is merely intellectual. It may be soulish.

Or he may be strongly given to *emotion*. At the Lord's Supper, the thought of Calvary brings tears to his eyes and he weeps. At the prayer meeting he gets so worked up he shouts his hallelujahs. He is so deeply moved at the thought of the poverty of Korean orphans or the masses of India that he will empty his pocketbook into the offering when an appeal is made. He is not necessarily spiritual, however. All too often such displays are mere excesses of emotion. An unsaved man might do as much.

On the other hand, a believer might have an iron *will*. When he is saved he learns he should give up smoking, shall we say, so he immediately throws his cigarettes into the fire and never smokes again. That may not be a spiritual victory, it may simply be the assertion of a strong will. Indeed, there may be a combination of two, or even all three factors—intellect, emotions and will, so that a person appears as an exemplary Christian without being truly spiritual at all. It is a very subtle trap.

Now, of course, this is not to say that the intellect, emotions and will play no part in the life of a spiritual Christian, because they do. But just to be intellectual, emotional or determined does not constitute the essence of spirituality. If the sensual side of a man is controlled by the soulish side, the person is indeed a fine specimen of humanity. But he is not spiritual and may not even be saved at all.

For me to be *spiritual* the Holy Spirit must have complete control of me, and the key to this lies in the surrender of the body. For it is through the members of the body that all impressions are received and all impulses expressed. If, therefore, the Holy Spirit has control of the body He can control the whole man. To be truly spiritual a believer needs to hand over his body to God for Him to fill and use. Then, not only are the senses controlled, but the intellect, emotions and will are controlled, and the person is a spiritual Christian expressing in all his ways the beauties of the Lord Jesus.

How then can we decide whether or not a given act is to be traced back to the soul or to the spirit? Surely the line drawn here is very fine. In fact, there is only one instrument which can cleave between the two and that is God's Word. "For the word of God is quick, and powerful, and sharper than any twoedged sword, piercing even to the dividing asunder of soul and spirit, and of the joints and marrow, and is a discerner of the thoughts and intents of the heart" (Heb. 4:12). It is only as, in our daily waiting upon God, we allow Him to bring His Word to bear upon our motives that we can discern, through the Spirit's enlightenment, the true reasons for our conduct and conversation. The word translated "discerner" is especially significant. It is the word *kritikos*. "Once, and only once, has God used *kritikos;* thus confining it to His own Word as a 'critic.' . . . 'Dividing asunder' of soul and spirit means not only differentiating between that which is begotten of the flesh and that which is begotten of the Spirit (John 3:6) in the individual, but also between the natural (Gr. *psuchikos*) man and the spiritual (Gr. *pneumatikos*) man."[1]

B. *The Body As an Unblemished Sacrifice* (12:1)

When the Holy Spirit has control of the body, He can express through the believer's members the fruits of Christ's sacrifice. The offering of the believer's body is therefore a living sacrifice in contrast with the sacrifices of the Old Testament. In the Old Testament, when a body was offered the animal was slain. Now, when the believer offers his body, he begins to really live.

Paul tells us that the offering is to be (1) a *living* sacrifice in contrast with the Old Testament sacrifices which were all dead ones, for when the Spirit controls the believer's body the *victory* resulting from Calvary is made good in our experience. All deadness is displaced as the triumphant life of the Lord Jesus is expressed through the members of the believer's body. It is to be (2) a *holy* sacrifice, for when the Spirit has His way with the believer's body the *virtue* resulting from Calvary is made good in our experience. All defilement is displaced by the perfect and unblemished purity and piety of Christ. It is to be (3) an *acceptable* sacrifice, for when the Holy Spirit has His way in the believer's body all the *value* of Christ's sacrifice is experienced by the believer. He is not only "accepted in the Beloved" but his life becomes a living, holy sacrifice, pleasing and acceptable to God. Nothing less will do.

C. *The Body As an Unbiased Sacrifice* (12:1)

Paul says that such a sacrifice is our *"reasonable service"* or, as some render it, our reasonable worship. There is no coercion here, no high pressure, no forcing of the will, no bending or biasing of

[1] *The Companion Bible* (London: The Lamp Press, n.d.), p. 1828.

the personality to make it conform to the divine will. God takes it that we are reasonable people, that the reasonableness of this demand will be so evident that there will be an immediate and prompt response.

> When I survey the wondrous cross,
>   On which the Prince of glory died,
> My richest gain I count but loss,
>   And pour contempt on all my pride.

> Were the whole realm of nature mine
>   That were an offering far too small;
> Love so amazing, so divine,
>   Shall have my heart, my life, my all.

This, then, is how the Christian is challenged as a believer. Beseeched and besieged by the mercies of God he capitulates to the winsome logic of Calvary. God asks for nothing more and nothing less than that. All other faiths make sacrifice the root, Christianity makes it the flower.

II. How the Christian Is Changed As a Believer (12:2)

The presentation of the body results in a transformed life. The body of the believer is the vehicle through which the new life is expressed. We do not *cultivate* the body like the ancient Greeks, who worshiped its beauty and its strength and glorified their worship in sculptured works of art and in their Olympic games, which were far more than mere athletic contests, partaking indeed of the nature of a sacred celebration. We do not *crucify* the body like the ascetics who considered it evil and starved and mutilated it. Simeon Stylites, for example, is said to have sat for thirty years on top of a column. Others wore hair skirts and scourged themselves with cruel whips. We simply *consecrate* the body that the Holy Spirit, who has made it His temple, might have free access to all its courts and free control over all its activities. The believer who thus presents his body is changed.

A. *He Is Changed Morally* (12:2)

"*Be not conformed to this world,*" says Paul. The word "conformed" is *suschēmatizō*, which "refers to the act of an individual assuming an outward expression that does not come from within him, nor is it representative of his inner heart life."[2] It lays stress on that which is external. We are not to be fashioned by the world. J. B. Phillips expressively renders the sentence, "Don't let the world around you squeeze you into its own mold." The word for "world" here "signifies the condition of humanity, which, since the fall, is in spiritual darkness, with a nature, tendencies, and influences controlled by the powers of darkness in opposition to God, and now under the prince of this world."[3] The world has its fads and fashions and they change with each generation. Its mold exerts pressure on us all, not only in such relatively minor matters as dress and diet, but in such far more serious areas of life as morals, ethical standards and religious beliefs. The world is the devil's *lair* for sinners and his *lure* for saints. It is human life and society with God left out.

The believer whose body has been laid on the altar for God will not be conformed to the world. He is morally changed. His life is not molded from without but from within. Jesus provided us with a picturesque illustration when speaking of Solomon He pointed to the flowers of the field and said, "Solomon in all his glory was not arrayed like one of these" (Matt. 6:29). Solomon's splendor was put on from without, the glory of the lily grows from within. The believer has an inward power to overcome the pressures of the world, and his presented body makes it possible for that power to be unleashed. He is not molded by the world's morals; he sets the standard for the world.

B. *He Is Changed Mentally* (12:2)

"Be ye transformed by the renewing of your mind," says Paul. This is a call for a transfigured life. The Greek word translated "transformed" in this passage occurs in only three other places in the New Testament. It is used to describe the transfiguration of the Lord Jesus (Matt. 17:2; Mark 9:2) and it is used to describe the glorious change wrought in the believer when he steadfastly contemplates the Lord Jesus (II Cor. 3:18).

The Greek word is *metamorphoomai* from which our word "metamorphosis" is derived. The dictionary defines metamor-

---

[2]Kenneth S. Wuest, *Romans in the Greek New Testament* (Grand Rapids: Wm. B. Eerdmans Publishing Co., 1955), p. 206. Used by permission.
[3]W. E. Vine, *The Epistle to the Romans* (Grand Rapids: Zondervan Publishing House, 1948), p. 177.

phosis as "change of form or change of character." An example is the caterpillar which undergoes metamorphosis in its chrysalis and emerges a glorious butterfly. The same creature which enters the filmy tomb eventually emerges, but the change is so remarkable that it cannot be recognized as the same. It is this kind of change the Holy Spirit wishes to work in the life of the believer, but to do it He must have control of the body and free access to the mind.

On two notable occasions recorded in Scripture, the metamorphosis in the life of a believer was so complete as to be evident to all to see. It left its imprint on the face. When Moses came down from the mount after forty days and nights alone with God, he "wist not that the skin of his face shone" (Exodus 34:29). Likewise Stephen, filled with the Holy Spirit, faced his enemies in the Sanhedrin and they "looking stedfastly on him, saw his face as it had been the face of an angel" (Acts 6:15). Every believer will experience a change like this when he comes face to face with the Lord Jesus. "Beloved, now are we the sons of God, and it doth not yet appear what we shall be: but we know that, when he shall appear, we shall be like him; for we shall see him as he is" (I John 3:2).

The Holy Spirit desires to etch this likeness to the Lord Jesus into our characters now, so that it might be reflected to some degree in our faces here below. We have all met Christians whose saintly lives have left an indelible mark of serenity and peace upon their brow and in their eyes and even in the set of their mouth. The face, after all, is "the index of the soul." When asked to appoint a certain man to a high post in his government, Abraham Lincoln once said, "I don't like his face!" "But surely," said the petitioner, "the man isn't responsible for his face." Said Lincoln, "Every man over forty *is* responsible for his face."

The Holy Spirit does not apply a mere cosmetic to the skin to bring about this nobility of countenance. He works within. He renews the mind and transforms the soul.

C. *He Is Changed Motivationally* (12:2)

"That ye may prove what is that good, and acceptable, and perfect will of God." Every Christian is responsible to discover for himself what God's will is for his life. When through the proc-

ess of his daily communion with the Lord he discovers some aspect of the revealed will of God, he will embrace it, because it is *good*. God cannot ask us to do anything that is not for our eternal good. The demand may cut right across our opinions, our ambitions, our tastes, as it did Peter's when God commanded him to go to the house of the Gentile Cornelius (Acts 10). What God plans for us will be the very best that omniscient wisdom and divine love can conceive. "God meant it unto good" was Joseph's testimony when the dark clouds of uncertainty had finally rolled away and he could look back and see how marvelous were God's leadings and providential overrulings in his life (Gen. 50:20). It is Satan who suggests that God is not to be trusted; that He plans for us some unpleasant experience; that He will let us down and leads us into anguish, pain and loss. Satan ever seeks to frighten us into a lack of trust of God. But God's will is good.

It is also *acceptable*. God will not ask us to do that which we cannot accept. He brings us along life's path, maturing us as we go, so that when we come to Canaan and its giants, we are ready for them, or at least, we should be. This was Israel's experience. A glance at the map will show that when the nation left Egypt the shortest route to Canaan lay due east. But God led them far to the south, all along the rim of the Sinai peninsula, bringing experience after experience into their lives that these children of His might learn to trust Him more. He decided indeed that the longest way around was the shortest way home. Well He knew what a pall of fear the giants of Canaan would cast upon the stoutest heart and how unacceptable His will would seem to the majority when at last, at Kadesh-barnea, the time came to move forward into Canaan. Of the adult population only Joshua and Caleb seemed to have learned the lessons of the wilderness. To these two alone was the will of God acceptable. When the bulk of the nation decided that God's will was unacceptable, their decision was inexcusable and was met with summary judgment from God (Num. 13–14).

In Abraham also we find an example of how acceptable God's will is, even when it confronts us with the humanly impossible. In Genesis 22 Abraham discovered that God's will for his life meant taking Isaac to a certain place and offering him up as a burnt offering. Hard as the demand was, Abraham considered the will of God to be acceptable. He did not know why God demanded this sacrifice, nor did he know how God would make good His promises which were all centered in Isaac. But he did believe that God could raise Isaac from the dead (Heb. 11:19) even though he had no actual guarantee that He would. He accepted God's will without question.

We have previously noted that at the beginning of his pilgrimage God told Abraham to surrender his father, and at the end of his pilgrimage God told him to surrender his son. It is far harder, of course, to give up one's only son than it is to give up one's father, but between the two surrenders were years of maturing experiences in Abraham's life. God always sees to it that "His commandments are not grievous" (I John 5:3). His will is always acceptable. If for any reason God's will seems unacceptable to us, it must be because we are blindly overlooking something He is showing us, for God never asks us to take a step for which we are not ready. Here again, Satan tries to deceive us into believing that God makes impossible demands upon us. However, God's will is acceptable, and those who have presented their bodies in living sacrifice will prove it so.

Finally, God's will is *perfect*. No plan of ours can improve on the plan of God. We only see bits and pieces; He sees the whole. We see only fragments of the past. We measure things by the narrow horizon of our present vision. He sees past, present and future in its total context as related to eternity. He sees when, where and why we touch the lives of others. He weighs all actions. He controls all circumstances. His will is perfect.

So then, the Christian is both challenged and changed as a believer. He presents his body to God and takes on a whole new, higher, greater dimension of living. How this new quality of life touches on all human relationships is the subject of the rest of the book.

THE CHRISTIAN AS A BROTHER
12:3-13

I. His Relationship to Other Brethren (12:3-5)

    A. It Is to Be an Intelligent Relationship (12:3)

    B. It Is to Be an Intimate Relationship (12:4-5)

II. HIS RESPONSIBILITIES TO OTHER BRETHREN (12:6-13)
   A. In the Exercise of Gift (12:6-8)
      1. Those Gifted to Expound the Word of God (12:6-8*a*)
         a. The inspiration of truth (prophesy)
         b. The incarnation of truth (minister)
         c. The interpretation of truth (teach)
         d. The intention of truth (exhort)
      2. Those Gifted to Expand the Work of God (12:8*b*)
         a. By giving
         b. By guiding
         c. By going
   B. In the Exercise of Grace (12:9-13)
      1. His Character (12:9)
      2. His Contacts (12:10)
      3. His Conduct (12:11)
      4. His Convictions (12:12)
      5. His Concern (12:13)

PAUL IS STILL DISCUSSING the spiritual life of the Christian. As an individual *believer,* he is to present his body to God as a living sacrifice that the life of Jesus may be expressed in daily living. As a *brother,* related to other believers in the Lord Jesus, he is to express the abundant life in all the varying relationships and responsibilities of the local church.

I. THE CHRISTIAN'S RELATIONSHIP TO OTHER BRETHREN (12:3-5)

When a person becomes a Christian he enters into a new relationship with God and into a new relationship with God's people. Both these new relationships call for major adjustments in the new believer's thinking and attitudes. His relationship to God is adjusted by the believer's consecration of his own body to God. His relationship to other believers is adjusted by the believer's consideration for the new body (the mystical body, the church) into which he has been introduced. His relationship to the body of believers is to be both intelligent and intimate.

A. *It Is to Be an Intelligent Relationship* (12:3)

The Christian is to understand exactly how he relates to others in the church. *"For I say, through the grace given unto me, to*

*every man that is among you, not to think of himself more highly
than he ought to think; but to think soberly, according as God
hath dealt to every man the measure of faith"* (v. 3). In other
words, the believer, introduced into a local fellowship of Christians, is to have a proper opinion of himself and others. There are
two dangers here. He may either overestimate his own importance, or he may go to the other extreme and depreciate himself
to the point of false humility. C. S. Lewis describes both these
extremes in his interesting and penetrating book *Screwtape Letters*. The book contains a series of imaginary letters from a senior
devil to a junior devil in which the junior is instructed in the art
of temptation. Wormwood, the junior devil, has a client who,
much to Screwtape's indignation, has just become a Christian.
Having castigated Wormwood, Screwtape instructs his under-
study in ways to make the most out of the new Christian's first
contacts with the church.

"One of our great allies at present," he says, "is the Church itself. Do not misunderstand me. I do not mean the Church as we
see her spread out through all time and space and rooted in eternity, terrible as an army with banners. That, I confess, is a spec-
tacle which makes our boldest tempters uneasy. But fortunately
it is quite invisible to these humans. All your patient sees is the
half-finished, sham Gothic erection on the new building estate.
When he goes inside, he sees the local grocer with rather an oily
expression on his face bustling up to offer him one shiny little
book containing a liturgy which neither of them understands, and
one shabby little book containing corrupt texts of a number of
religious lyrics, mostly bad, and in very small print. When he
gets to his pew and looks round him he sees just that selection of
his neighbours whom he has hitherto avoided. You want to lean
pretty heavily on those neighbours. Make his mind flit to and fro
between expressions like 'the body of Christ' and the actual faces
in the next pew. It matters very little, of course, what kind of
people that next pew really contains. You may know one of them
to be a great warrior on the Enemy's side. No matter. Your patient, thanks to Our Father Below, is a fool. Provided that any of
those neighbours sing out of tune, or have boots that squeak, or
double chins, or odd clothes, the patient will quite easily believe
that their religion must therefore be somehow ridiculous. At his

present stage, you see, he has an idea of 'Christians' in his mind which he supposes to be spiritual but which, in fact, is largely pictorial."[1]

This graphic piece of prose from the pen of C. S. Lewis describes one extreme to which the believer can go in his relationship with other brethren. He can imagine himself to be superior to them. He may "think of himself more highly than he ought to think." He can become snobbish and proud, put on all kinds of airs and graces and picture himself to be a cut above other believers. But there is also the opposite possibility. He may develop an inferiority complex, and, because he cannot preach with passion and with power or hold people spellbound with penetrating and persuasive private conversation, he may think he has no gift or is lacking in full measure of faith. Worse still, he may be so convinced of the necessity of being humble that he dons a mask of false humility or assumes a pose of humility without any idea as to what true humility is. In *The Screwtape Letters* C. S. Lewis has Screwtape tell Wormwood how to develop this kind of warp in the human personality. "I see only one thing to do at the moment. Your patient has become humble; have you drawn his attention to the fact? All virtues are less formidable to us once the man is aware that he has them, but this is specially true of humility. . . .

"You must therefore conceal from the patient the true end of Humility. Let him think of it, not as self-forgetfulness but as a certain kind of opinion (namely, a low opinion) of his own talents and character. Some talents, I gather, he really has. Fix in his mind the idea that humility consists in trying to believe those talents to be less valuable than he believes them to be. No doubt they *are* less valuable than he believes, but that is not the point. The great thing is to make him value an opinion for some quality other than truth, thus introducing an element of dishonesty and make-believe into the heart of what otherwise threatens to become a virtue. By this method thousands of humans have been brought to think that humility means pretty women trying to believe that they are ugly and clever men trying to believe they are fools. . . . The Enemy wants to bring the man to a state of mind

[1]From *The Screwtape Letters* by C. S. Lewis. Copyright © 1961 by C. S. Lewis. Reprinted by permission of The Macmillan Company, New York, from Macmillan Paperback Edition, tenth printing, 1968, p. 12.

in which he could design the best cathedral in the world, and know it to be the best, and rejoice in the fact, without being any more (or less) or otherwise glad at having done it than he would be if it had been done by another. The Enemy wants him, in the end, to be so free from any bias in his own favour that he can rejoice in his own talents as frankly and gratefully as in his neighbour's talents. . . ."[2]

B. *It Is to Be an Intimate Relationship* (12:4-5)

Paul here introduces one of his favorite illustrations. *"For as we have many members in one body, and all members have not the same office: so we, being many, are one body in Christ, and every one members one of another"* (vv. 4-5). Nothing could be more beautifully coordinated than a body with each member fitted to its proper place and carrying out its rightful function. There is no rivalry between the members of a body, only mutual respect and harmony. There is also the closest intimacy between members of a body, each one depending for certain things upon every other member. Then, too, each member is controlled by the head and seeks no independent action. All this illustrates the relationship the believer must have to his brethren in the church, the mystical body of Christ.

II. THE CHRISTIAN'S RESPONSIBILITIES TO OTHER BRETHREN (12:6-13)

The Christian's responsibilities to his brethren are twofold. He has a responsibility in the exercise of gift and a responsibility in the exercise of grace.

A. *In the Exercise of Gift* (12:6-8)

Generally speaking the gifts enumerated by Paul in this section of Romans have to do with expounding the Word of God and with expanding the work of God. The two are intimately related. Every believer has a gift, some have several, and every believer is responsible before God to find out what his gift is, develop it through exercise and use it in the work of the kingdom. There are (1) *those gifted to expound the Word of God. "Having then gifts differing according to the grace that is given us, whether prophecy, let us prophesy according to the proportion of faith; or*

[2]*Ibid.,* pp. 62-64.

ministry, let us wait on our ministering: or he that teacheth, on teaching; or he that exhorteth, on exhortation" (vv. 6-8a).

There are four specific gifts mentioned here. The first deals with the *inspiration* of truth—the gift of prophecy. In the early church prophets were inspired teachers. "The foretelling of future events was not the usual form which their inspiration took, but that of an *exalted and superhuman teaching,* ranked by St. Paul 'above speaking with tongues,' *being the utterance of their conscious intellect informed by the Holy Spirit."*[3] This gift of being able to utter God's will under direct impulse of the Holy Spirit was necessary in the infant church when as yet the New Testament was incomplete. Like the apostolic gift, it was associated with the foundation of the church (Eph. 2:20) and with the revelation of the mystery of Christ (Eph. 3:5). It was a transitional gift and was exercised in proportion to a man's faith. Prophets in this sense are no longer in the church, although in a lesser degree preachers occupy their role. The modern preaching gift has the element of *illumination* rather than the element of prophetic inspiration.

The second gift in the list illustrates the *incarnation* of truth, the gift of ministry. Ministry is service of all kinds. It is the practical application of the Word of God to daily living. It is voluntary service in contrast with bondservice. In Mark 10:45 we are told that "the Son of man came not to be ministered unto, but to minister, and to give his life a ransom for many." This verse not only sets before us the twofold division of that gospel (the Son of man giving His life in service and the Son of man giving His life in sacrifice), but it perfectly illustrates what is meant by ministering. Just as the Lord Jesus incarnated His teaching in daily living for others, so should we. This is one gift within the reach of every believer.

The third gift in the list emphasizes the *interpretation* of truth, the gift of teaching. The teacher is the man who studies the Bible diligently, comparing scripture with scripture, using sound methods of exegesis, hermeneutics, homiletics, analysis and synthesis, and who edifies others with the fruits of his efforts. The gift of teaching is listed high in the enumeration of gifts (I Cor. 12:28).

---

[3]Henry Alford, *The New Testament for English Readers* (Chicago: Moody Press, n.d.), p. 729.

The teacher's task is to set forth the fundamental truths of the Bible for the building up and edification of the saints.

The fourth gift in the list emphasizes the *intention* of truth, the gift of exhorting. Exhortation is most frequently addressed to the conscience and the heart, whereas teaching is more often addressed to the mind. In many European homes, rooms are heated by small open fireplaces. Standard equipment with such a fireplace is a poker, a piece of metal used from time to time to stir up the smoldering embers so that they burst back into flame. This is the work of the exhorter. He must stir up the consciences of God's people so that truth does not become merely abstract theology but is worked out in practical, down-to-earth living.

Besides those gifted to expound the Word there are (2) *those gifted to expand the work of God.* "*He that giveth, let him do it with simplicity; he that ruleth, with diligence; he that sheweth mercy, with cheerfulness*" (v. 8*b*). The three gifts mentioned here have to do with the forward outreach of the gospel and the work of God. The work of God can be extended by our *giving.* Giving must be done with singleness of heart and not from mixed or doubtful motives, as was the case with Ananias and Sapphira (Acts 5). The true Christian attitude toward material goods is not "how much of my money shall I give to God" but rather, "how much of God's money shall I keep for myself" (I Cor. 6:20; 7:23). Love is ever measured by its gift.[4]

The work of God can be extended by our *guiding.* There are some who have special gifts of leadership and are able to oversee the work of God. God's work needs well-taught elders, able to preside over the work in a given church and guide it into scriptural and fruitful paths. It is said of the men of Issachar in Old Testament times that they "had understanding of the times, to know what Israel ought to do" (I Chron. 12:32). There is a great need for such men in the church today. The elders of Antioch had an understanding of the Spirit's leading and of the times in which they lived when they laid hands on Barnabas and Saul and sent them forth to evangelize the western world for God (Acts 13:1-3).

---

[4]Compare, for example, "For God so loved the world that he *gave* . . ." (John 3:16); "Christ also loved the church and *gave* . . ." (Eph. 5:25); "He loved me, and *gave* . . ." (Gal. 2:20); "And Jonathan loved him as his own soul . . . and *gave* . . ." (I Sam. 18:1, 4).

The work of God can be extended by our *going*. There are some who have a special gift for going after those in distress and showing them the kindness of God. David did this for Mephibosheth in his day (II Sam. 9) and the Good Samaritan did it for the man who fell among thieves (Luke 10:30-37). Some feel that this gift is given especially to those who are called of God to do visitation work among the sick and afflicted. It is not to be done with a long face but with "cheerfulness" or, as some have rendered it, with "hilarity"! Solomon well said, "A merry heart doeth good like a medicine" (Prov. 17:22).

B. *In the Exercise of Grace* (12:9-13)

Our responsibilities to other brethren extend to the exercise of grace as well as to the exercise of gift. This exercise affects all aspects of the Christian's life. (1) It affects our *character*. "*Let love be without dissimulation. Abhor that which is evil; cleave to that which is good*" (v. 9). J. B. Phillips renders that, "Let us have no imitation Christian love. Let us have a genuine break with evil and real devotion to good." Counterfeit love is worthless coin in the kingdom of God. The thought behind the word "dissimulation" is that of hypocrisy. In olden times the "hypocrite" was a man who played a part on a stage. When we assume a character we do not have, we play the hypocrite.

True Christian character is founded on true Christian love and is expressed in a hatred of evil and a love for good. An outstanding example is that of George Müller. His early life was one of gross wickedness, and although well educated, confirmed and in the communion of the church, he was not a Christian. Living deep in sin, he had spent time in jail when, at about the age of twenty, he visited a Moravian mission and was soundly saved. Eventually, Müller moved from Germany to England where he took up his residence in Bristol and was led of God to found the famous orphan homes that bear his name. He believed that through faith and prayer alone God would supply temporal as well as spiritual needs. During his life of service for the destitute, George Müller handled some eight million dollars, and at his death, so consistent was he to his passion for doing good, his personal possessions totaled less than a thousand dollars. More than ten thousand orphans had been cared for in his orphan homes, which remain to this day as a testimony to the power of faith and the passion of love.[5]

Another example comes from Harold Begbie's chronicles of the early days of the Salvation Army in London. He begins his series of case histories with the story of "the Puncher." The Puncher started out on his career of wildness and daring as a boy by getting into trouble at school and with the police. He was wild and ungovernable. He took to fighting as a career, fought sixteen famous fights and won them all. Many times he entered the ring so drunk that the referees objected but although blind drunk he never lost a fight to anyone his own weight. With money to burn, the Puncher married, bought a business and lived in high style.

As his fighting days drew to a close he started a racing business, traded on his famous name, and tricked and cheated in a hundred ways. At last he was exposed and lost his fame, his popularity and his good name. He fell from wealth to poverty, dragging his family with him into the gutter and earning their scorn and contempt. His wife left him time and time again. To obtain drink he simply walked into a tavern and demanded liquor. It was given to him without question so long as he would go away. Food had no attraction to him, only drink; he was a blazing mass of alcohol, living now in common lodgings occupied by the lowest of the low. No one dared to interfere with him. Murder shone in his eyes, the man had become a demon. One day the Puncher's eldest son, wearing the uniform of the Salvation Army, sought him out in his low haunts, and pleaded with him to become a Christian. The Puncher laughed him to scorn.

The next day was Sunday. The Puncher was spending it in jail, tortured by thirst, mad with the rage of a caged beast, cursing God and furious at his imprisonment. He spent the time reviewing his life, loathing it but also loathing his intention to reform it. He decided to commit suicide. He would murder his wife and end his life by dying gamely on the scaffold. So fixed did the idea become that it destroyed his craving for drink. One demon went out and another came in.

He left the prison, drank himself drunk with some friends because they pressed him, borrowed some money and bought a

[5]See Elgin S. Moyer, *Who Was Who in Church History* (Chicago: Moody Press, 1962), p. 297. Also, the five volumes by Müller, *The Narration of Some of the Lord's Dealings with George Müller.*

butcher's knife. He went to his wife, proposed a reconciliation
and suggested a visit to a local music hall. She accepted the pro-
posal, apparently out of fear of his fists, and together they left
the house and went down the street. A Salvationist who knew
both the Puncher and his son joined them. To get rid of this un-
welcome company, the Puncher struck across the street and entered a tavern, leaving his wife at the door to await her would-be
murderer. While sitting at the bar, the Puncher had a sudden and
shaking vision. He saw the dreadful deed done, himself hanged
for murder, and the world pointing the finger of scorn at his son,
who in reality he really loved. He walked out of the bar, deeply
smitten by shame and horror, and although drunk went straight
to the Salvation Army. His wife went with him. Together they
knelt at the penitent's bench and accepted Christ as Saviour.

The past dropped clean away. He became a shining Christian
and a clear testimony to his old companions. He joined the Salvation Army and his home became comfortable and happy. He
gave himself to the task of winning to Christ his friends and neighbors in the London slums. The years passed by with only one
brief relapse followed by swift and lasting restoration. But his
wife's interest in the things of God waned. "The shadows," says
Begbie, "have deepened for him. His wife's lack of sympathy is
an increasing distress and discomfort in the house. His children
do not care about their father's religion. He has to earn his living
among men who are not Christians and who do not show him
sympathy. But in spite of this the Puncher remains in the neigh-
borhood, perhaps the greatest force for personal religion among
the sad, the sorrowful, the broken, and the lost who cram its
shabby streets."[6]

"Let love be without dissimulation. Abhor that which is evil;
cleave to that which is good." The exercise of grace transforms
the believer's character.

The exercise of grace does more. (2) It affects our *contacts*.
"*Be kindly affectioned one to another with brotherly love; in
honour preferring one another*" (v. 10). In his contacts with his
brethren, the believer has a responsibility to show grace. He is
to show brotherly love. Love for the brethren is a proof of spir-

[6]Harold Begbie, *Twice-Born Men* (Chicago: Moody Press, n.d.), pp. 9-28.

itual life (I John 3:14), but to be really kindly affectioned to the brethren is a rare grace. Someone has put it this way:

> To dwell above, with saints in love,
>   That will indeed be glory;
> To dwell below with saints we know,
>   Well, that's a different story!

But it can be done. When it became obvious to Jonathan that David was preferred before him and that David, not Jonathan, was God's heir-apparent to the throne, Jonathan showed brotherly love to David and in honor preferred him. He was glad for David's sake. Then when David came to the throne he forgot and forgave for Jonathan's sake the bitter hatred of the house of Saul, sought out Jonathan's unfortunate son Mephibosheth and showed to him the very kindness of God (II Sam. 9).

The exercise of grace (3) affects our *conduct*. *"Not slothful in business; fervent in spirit; serving the Lord"* (v. 11). The first eleven chapters of Romans emphasize justification by faith; here we have "justification" by works. "Not slothful in business," that's the *outward look;* "fervent in spirit," that's the *inward look;* "serving the Lord," that's the *upward look.*

The expression "not slothful in business" has nothing to do primarily with secular work. It has to do, as the context reveals, with the exercise of the gifts God has given for the furtherance of *His* work. The word "business" is the word translated "diligence" in verse 8. Spiritual activity rather than secular activity is in Paul's mind. Other translations bring this out very clearly. The New American Standard Version renders the verse, "Not lagging behind in diligence, fervent in spirit, serving the Lord." Williams translates it, "Never slack in earnestness, always on fire with the Spirit, always serving the Lord." The New English Bible renders it, "With unflagging energy, in ardour of spirit, serve the Lord." The word "fervent" reminds us of water brought to the boil. The inner springs of the believer's life must be so fired by the Spirit that he continually boils over with enthusiasm in his service for the Lord.

The exercise of grace (4) affects our *convictions*. *"Rejoicing in hope; patient in tribulation; continuing instant in prayer"* (v. 12). Praise! Patience! Prayer! The Christian has an anchor for the future; he has hope. Not just a vague and sentimental optimism, but hope as bright as the promises of God. The Christian does not rebel in tribulation nor rashly accuse God. He is patient, knowing that God is too wise to make any mistakes, too loving to be unkind and too powerful to be thwarted in His ultimate aims.

Nowhere in the New Testament is the church promised freedom from tribulation. On the contrary, such freedom is far from the norm (John 16:33; Acts 14:22; I Thess. 3:4). The church was born in tribulation and for three hundred years passed through fire and flood, writing with martyr blood some of its noblest chapters. It is going through tribulation today; indeed, it is claimed by some that more people have been martyred for the cause of Christ in this generation than in all the previous generations of the church. This is not hard to believe when one studies the history of the church in Korea, China, Russia and many of the emerging nations of Africa.[7] It is, then, a very practical and pertinent word of the apostle—"patient in tribulation."

The Christian is also "instant in prayer." That is, he is persevering in prayer, and probably nothing adds more passion and importunity to his prayer than tribulation. Tribulation makes the believer's hope more real, and it makes his prayers more real as well. It adds a whole new dimension to his convictions.

Finally, the exercise of grace (5) affects our *concern*. "*Distributing to the necessity of saints; given to hospitality*" (v. 13). The thought here is of actually pursuing opportunities for hospitality, not just passively waiting for them to come. A lavish generosity with one's worldly goods is a mark of true discipleship.

"There (in the temple court in Jerusalem) stood thirteen chests, each with a brazen, trumpet-shaped receiver into which the worshippers dropped their offerings; nine of them were marked 'for Jehovah,' and four of them were marked 'for the poor.' The widow would fain manifest her love to the Lord and to her neighbour as well. If she casts the mite into His chest it will be known in heaven that one of the Lord's lovers has been in the treasury that day; if she casts it into the box marked 'for the poor' it will show her care for her fellows, but will it not seem to place human need above divine worship? The solution she adopts is

---

[7]See, for example, *Come Wind, Come Weather* (Chicago: Moody Press) for the tragic story of the modern church in China.

both simple and costly; she will balance the claims of heaven and earth, and drop two mites into separate chests. With eager joy the Lord called the attention of the twelve to her actions, and offers them a problem in the arithmetic of heaven. She loved God and her neighbour."[8]

Abraham pressed his hospitality upon the wayfarers that were journeying past his door (Gen. 18) and thereby entertained angels unawares (Heb. 13:2), not to mention the One whom the angels worship! "Ye took me in" will be the Lord's commendation to the righteous in that coming day. "I was an hungered, and ye gave me meat: I was thirsty, and ye gave me drink: I was a stranger, and ye took me in. . . . Then shall the righteous answer him, saying, When . . . when . . . when . . .? And the King shall answer and say unto them, Verily I say unto you, Inasmuch as ye have done it unto one of the least of these my brethren, ye have done it unto me" (Matt. 25:35-40).

Nobody can lose who follows God's pattern for giving. A farmer, known for his prosperity and his lavish giving to the cause of Christ, explained it this way: "I keep shoveling into God's bin, and God keeps shoveling back into mine, and God has the bigger shovel!"

Here then is Paul's portrait of the Christian as a brother. He enjoys his relationship to his brethren and he shoulders his responsibilities to other brethren. In so doing he exercises both gift and grace, and as a consequence becomes increasingly like his Lord.

THE SOCIAL LIFE OF THE CHRISTIAN
12:14-21

When dealing with non-Christians we are to

I. MATCH THEIR MOODS (12:14-15)
   A. Disarming Opposition (12:14)
   B. Discovering Opportunity (12:15)

II. MIND OUR MANNERS (12:16)
   A. Don't Be Partial
   B. Don't Be Proud

[8]Harold St. John. Quoted by A. Naismith, *1200 Notes, Quotes and Anecdotes* (Chicago: Moody Press, 1962), p. 80.

III. MARK THESE METHODS (12:17-21)
   A. Live Passively (12:17*a*)
   B. Live Peerlessly (12:17*b*)
   C. Live Peaceably (12:18)
   D. Live Positively (12:19-21)
      1. The Prerogative of Vengeance Is God's
      2. The Principle of Vengeance Is God's

THE LAWS OF CHRISTIAN LIFE deal not only with the *spiritual* life
of the Christian but with his *social* life as well. The believer
sustains a relationship to the world as well as to the church.
Paul has three things to say about our daily contacts with those
outside of Christ. We are to show the unbeliever sympathy and
understanding, we are to take good heed to our attitude, and we
are to live before men unimpeachable and exemplary lives.

I. MATCH THEIR MOODS (12:14-15)

Consciously or unconsciously, many Christians assume airs and
graces which are highly objectionable to their unsaved neighbors.
The believer must be careful that, while maintaining absolute
loyalty to the Lord Jesus, he does nothing to unnecessarily
antagonize his nonchristian associates. This cannot be done merely by being negative. We must seek points of contact with unbelievers and form "redemptive friendships" with them. Paul
Little has some very excellent comments on this.

"We are all rather amused," he says, "by Simple Simon, who
sets up his barrel, drops in his little line, and is very saddened
because he doesn't catch any fish. And we think, 'How stupid
can you be? Fish don't come and jump in barrels: you have to
go where the fish are.' But what do we do in evangelism? We set
up barrels and we invite the fish to come and jump in, and we
are very sad when they bypass us in droves. As Harold Wildish
said one time, 'The Holy Spirit cannot save saints or seats. There
have to be some non-Christians.' . . .

"There is a place for evangelistic meetings to which we invite
people, of course, but basically the method of evangelism that our
Lord taught was to go where the people are. Now this has several implications. One is that we must realize that separation
from the world is not the same thing as isolation from the world.

. . . I have had people come up to me with pride in their voices to tell me, waiting to be congratulated, that they had not one single non-Christian friend. I have had to shake my head in amazement as to how they could have missed the plain teaching of the New Testament.

"There is a second implication. Sometimes in all good faith and generosity, the non-Christian says, 'Come with me to do such and such,' or 'Here, have such and such.' And we respond almost instinctively, 'No thanks, I don't do such and such. I am a Christian.' Bang, you can hear the iron curtain clang down. Some think to themselves, 'My, I had a tremendous opportunity to witness.' But in my opinion we have done two very serious things. One, we have condemned the person out of hand as a pagan in a way he doesn't really understand. Secondly, we have garbled the gospel of the Lord Jesus Christ because we have suggested that inherent in being a Christian is not doing whatever it happened to be at the moment he asked us to do. . . .

"With non-Christians we must look for that which we can honestly commend, and if we are alert, we can find it. And when a person invites us to do something, you might say, 'No thanks, but let me know when you are going to do such and such.' Immediately make an alternative suggestion so that you do not seem to reject him or his friendship. We do not need to be apologetic about it. If you invite a non-Christian to play chess, he doesn't hem and haw around about it and say, 'Well, no thanks, I don't play chess, I am a non-Christian.' He just says, 'No thanks, chess leaves me cold, but when you are going to play ping-pong let me know.'"[1]

First, then, we have to learn to match their moods, and this brings with it a twofold challenge, that of disarming opposition and that of discovering opportunity.

A. The Challenge of Disarming Opposition (12:14)

Many of the noblest concepts of the Sermon on the Mount are repeated in the epistles. Here is one of them, *"Bless them which persecute you: bless, and curse not"* (v. 14). The word for

[1]Paul E. Little, "You Can Win Men," *Moody Monthly*, May, 1966, pp. 20-36. Adapted from one of five messages delivered at Moody Bible Institute Founder's Week Conference, 1966. See also his book, *How to Give Away Your Faith* (Chicago: Inter-Varsity Press, 1966).

"bless" here is the same word from which we get "eulogize." When we eulogize a person we speak well of him. Paul commands that this should be our habitual attitude toward those who ill-treat us. The Arabs have a custom (not always sincere) of touching the head, the lips and the heart in turn when paying a compliment. The gesture means, "I think highly of you, I speak well of you, my heart beats for you." This is to be the attitude we should bear toward those opposed to us. We must disarm opposition by opposing his black piece on the chessboard of life with our white piece. Hatred is to be countered with love. Some maintain that Christianity has failed. It would be more correct to say that it has very rarely been tried.

D. L. Moody, in one of his sermons, pictures the Lord Jesus after His resurrection giving directions to Peter. "Go, find the man," He says, "who thrust his spear into My side and tell him there's a much quicker way to My heart. Find the man who crowned Me with thorns and tell him I should like to give him a crown of life." It is a dramatic way of depicting the true spirit of Christianity. Did not Jesus practice what He preached? On the cross He prayed for them that despitefully used Him. He opened the gates of paradise for that thief who moments before had been pouring curses on His head. It was this that won completely the centurion in charge of the crucifixion. "This was the Son of God," he cried (Matt. 27:54). Thus we see the challenge of disarming opposition exemplified and gloriously successful on that skull-shaped hill of shame. Christ's policy of blessing those that cursed Him won to Himself that day a Gentile and a Jew, blessed firstfruits of His cross.

Can we hope to live like that? The annals of the church are filled with illustrations. Take, for instance, the case of Adoniram Judson. Judson was converted from agnosticism and called by God to serve the cause of Christ in Burma. He and his wife were to pay a terrible price in opposition before their first convert was won. On one occasion Judson, reduced to a mere skeleton, was driven beneath a lash across a burning desert until he prayed for death. On another occasion, he was imprisoned for nearly two years and subjected to every conceivable barbarity and cruelty. In the meantime his wife was giving birth to a child. Soon after the birth the mission house was burned down, leaving the young mother bereft of every comfort and with not even a chair or seat to sit on. Added to this the eldest child developed smallpox and the distracted mother was driven to the verge of despair.

Then Judson's execution was announced. The young couple prepared for the worst, but in the meantime Judson was smuggled away and his wife was unable to discover where he was. By the time they were reunited, the cost in suffering was terrible. The husband was scarred and maimed and worn down by suffering; the wife's glossy black curls had been shaved from her head and she was dressed in rags and reduced to utter destitution.

Yet through it all the Judsons never lost sight of their goal—to love their enemies into the kingdom of God. In all their sufferings they were sustained by the matchless Calvary love of the Lord Jesus. Judson's two ambitions were to translate the Bible into the native tongue and to see a church of one hundred members established before his death. He more than realized both these goals. By blessing them that persecuted, by blessing and cursing not, Adoniram Judson disarmed opposition and came through more than conqueror.

B. *The Challenge of Discovering Opportunity* (12:15)

There are many experiences we share in common with all men, and these can often be made legitimate points of contact by which we can build bridges into the hearts, lives and homes of our unsaved neighbors, associates and friends. *"Rejoice with them that do rejoice, and weep with them that weep,"* says Paul (v. 15). It is significant, surely, that the first of John's "signs" in his gospel was performed by the Lord at a wedding, the last at a funeral. The one was performed in life's gladdest hour, the other in life's saddest hour. In the one Jesus rejoiced with those that rejoiced, and in the other He wept with those that wept.

The principle is illustrated by the game of dominoes. "It occurred to me whilst we were playing," says F. W. Boreham, "that life itself is but a game of dominoes. Its highest art lies in matching your companion's pieces. Is he glad? It is a great thing to be able to rejoice with those who do rejoice. Is he sad? It is a great thing to be able to weep with those that weep. It means, of course, that if you answer the challenge every time, your pieces will soon be gone. But, as against that, it is worth remembering that victory lies not in accumulation, but in exhaustion. The player who is left with empty hands wins everything. . . .

"The beauty is that anyone can play the game. You have but to grasp two essential principles. You must clearly understand in the first place that, at every turn, you must match your companion's play, laying a six beside his six, a three beside his three, and so on. And you must clearly understand in the second place that the whole success lies, not in hoarding, but in spending. Victory lies in paying out the little ivory tablets with as prodigal a hand as possible. It is better in dominoes to give than to keep. It is better to play a domino with twelve black dots on it than a domino with only two. Dominoes teaches me to 'measure my life by loss instead of gain, not by the wine drunk, but by the wine poured out'. . . .

"And what about Paul? Was not Paul a past master at both the principles that govern a game of dominoes? He knew that the secret of success was not to save your pieces but to get rid of them. 'Most gladly, therefore,' says he, 'will I spend and be spent for you.' And was there ever one as clever at matching his companion's play? 'I made myself a slave,' he says, 'that I might win slaves; unto the Jews I became as a Jew, that I might gain Jews; to them that are under the law, as under the law, that I might gain them that are under the law; to them that are without law, I became as without law, that I might gain them that are without law. To the weak became I as weak, that I might gain the weak; I am made all things to all men, that I might by any means save some.' That was the greatest game of dominoes ever played!"[2]

II. MIND OUR MANNERS (12:16)

Not only are we to show sympathy, understanding and friendship to the unsaved, we are to take good heed to our attitude, avoiding both partiality and pride.

A. *Don't Be Partial* (12:16a)

Says Paul, "*Be of the same mind one toward another.*" Paul is not asking for uniformity but for unanimity. We are to make allowances for each other. The Lord Jesus treated the woman

[2]F. W. Boreham, *The Silver Shadow* (London: The Epworth Press, 1918), pp. 12, 16, 19. Used by permission.

at the well (John 4) with the same consideration, courtesy and compassion as He treated the knightly and polished Nicodemus (John 3). He was as charitable to the dying thief as He was to His own mother. He was as patient with Judas as He was with John.

C. Don't Be Proud (12:16b)

Pride has no place in the Christian life. *"Mind not high things, but condescend to men of low estate. Be not wise in your own conceits."* We have in the New Testament the example of Diotrephes "who loveth to have the preeminence" (II John 9). Such a spirit is foreign to true Christianity.

The word "condescend" in modern English bears the stigma of patronage. Nothing could be further from Paul's mind. We are not to court humble people with a patronizing air; on the contrary, we are to get "carried away" with them, for that is what the original suggests. (Compare Gal. 2:13 and II Peter 3:17, the only other places in the New Testament where the word occurs.) It is not clear whether Paul means that we are to be carried away with humble men or with lowly things. Whichever is the case, it is clear he is advocating the opposite of pride. In a world where everyone is scrambling for position, prominence and recognition, it is rare, even in the ranks of the redeemed, to find those who are deliberately courting the lowly and the meek.

The way to learn this grace is to sit at the feet of Jesus. He said, "Learn of me; for I am meek and lowly in heart" (Matt. 11:29). It has been well said of the Lord Jesus that His life and death are "a standing rebuke to every form of pride to which men are liable. Pride of birth and rank—'Is not this the carpenter's son?' (Matt. 13:55); pride of wealth—'The Son of man hath not where to lay his head' (Luke 9:58); pride of respectability—'Can any good thing come out of Nazareth?' (John 1:46); pride of personal appearance—'He hath no form nor comeliness' (Isa. 53:2); pride of reputation—'A friend of publicans and sinners' (Luke 7:34); pride of learning—'How knoweth this man letters, having never learned?' (John 7:15); pride of superiority—'I am among you as he that serveth' (Luke 22:27); pride of success— 'He is despised and rejected of men' (Isa. 53:3); pride of ability— 'I can of mine own self do nothing' (John 5:30); pride of self-will—'I seek not mine own will, but the will of the Father which hath sent me' (John 5:30); pride of intellect—'As my Father hath taught me, I speak' (John 8:28)."[3]

So then, the Christian is to shun pride. "Be not wise in your own conceits," says Paul. This expression occurs seven times in Scripture: Romans 11:25; 12:16; Proverbs 3:7; 26:5, 12, 16; 28:11. Solomon says there is more hope for a fool than for such a man. He says such a man is a sluggard. This sin is a snare for the rich. Only green corn stands upright, ripe corn bends low.

III. MARK THESE METHODS (12:17-21)

The Christian in his social contacts is to follow along the highway marked out by the Sermon on the Mount. Four principles are highlighted by the apostle.

A. *Live Passively* (12:17a)

"Recompense to no man evil for evil" is the first of these rules. It takes for granted the fact that some will do evil to the child of God. To retaliate in kind is natural. To turn the other cheek and to go further and reward good for evil is divine. It was exactly in this way that Joseph treated his brothers. They persecuted him, ridiculed him and sold him into slavery. He provided for them, protected them, pardoned them and promoted them. This was David's attitude toward Saul and his house. Saul, murder-bent, persistently sought to corner David and assassinate him. David held back his hand from Saul, even when he was in his power, and then sought out refugees from Saul's fallen house to show "the kindness of God" to them. Thus, too, Paul himself treated his own people. They sought to slay him, did their best to undermine his work, sowed discord and heresy in the churches he had planted and never ceased to turn even his converts against him. He prayed passionately for their conversion and never ceased trying to win them to Christ.

B. *Live Peerlessly* (12:17b)

The second rule is *"provide things honest in the sight of all men."* In all his social dealings the Christian is to live beyond reproach. He is to be scrupulously honest in all his dealings with

---

[3]A. Naismith, *1200 Notes, Quotes, and Anecdotes* (Chicago: Moody Press, 1962), p. 159.

his fellowmen. His word must be his bond no matter how inconvenient it may be later to make it good. He is not to profess one thing and practice another.

It is instructive to trace how Paul practiced the principles he preached. Think of his financial dealings as they are mentioned here and there throughout the New Testament. He was careful to associate others with him in the handling of public funds so that there should be no hint of misappropriation (I Cor. 16:3-4). He worked with his own hands (I Cor. 4:11-12; 9:9-12, 18-19), even supporting other members of the missionary team (Acts 20:34), so that new believers and infant churches might not feel he was making merchandise of them in the things of God (II Cor. 12:14-18). He laid down careful rules so that high-pressure methods might be avoided in church collections (I Cor. 16:1-2). He did not want his personality and presence to stimulate giving. He could challenge church elders to show one thing wrong in his conduct (Acts 20:33-35). He gladly welcomed a public accounting of his dealings. He was beyond reproach. Even when a bribe to a corrupt official would have secured his release from prison, he scorned such misconduct (Acts 24:26). In this matter he lived peerlessly.

C. *Live Peaceably* (12:18)

The third rule is, *"If it be possible, as much as lieth in you, live peaceably with all men."* Paul was a realist and he knew full well from personal experience that the gospel would be resisted with great violence wherever it was preached with power.[4] He himself was looked upon as a disturber of the peace. Indeed some have argued that Luke's reason for writing the book of Acts was

[4]On Cyprus Paul had to contend with Elymas the sorcerer (Acts 13:8); at Antioch in Pisidia he was driven from the city by persecution (Acts 13:50); in Iconium a general assault was made on him (Acts 14:2, 5); at Lystra the mob stoned him and left him for dead (Acts 14:19); at Antioch in Syria he was opposed by legalists in the church (Acts 15:2); at Philippi he was scourged and imprisoned (Acts 16:22-23); at Thessalonica he was forced out of the city (Acts 17:6-9); at Berea opposition forced him to leave (Acts 17:13-14); at Athens he was publicly mocked (Acts 17:32); at Corinth his presence led to insurrection (Acts 18:12); at Ephesus the whole city was in a tumult because of him (Acts 19:23-41); and at Jerusalem he was repeatedly the center of violent opposition (Acts 21-23). Jesus said, "Think not that I am come to send peace on earth: I came not to send peace, but a sword" (Matt. 10:34). Although the most conciliatory of men where no vital spiritual issue was concerned, Paul certainly proved this statement true.

to provide Paul with a brief to prove his innocence when he appeared before Caesar. Whether or not this is true, the apologetic
motive in Acts is very evident. Luke takes pains to prove the
law-abiding character of Christianity and to demonstrate the fact
that all disturbances were instigated by its enemies. He shows
repeatedly how Roman officials discharged cases brought before
them in which Paul was accused of disorderly conduct. It is not
always possible to live peaceably with all men, but the initiative
in disturbing the peace should never lie with the Christian.

D. *Live Positively* (12:19-21)

Opposition, hatred and persecution are to be repaid positively
with good. On no account is a Christian to seek revenge for in-
juries done to him. He is to recognize that (1) *the prerogative
of vengeance is God's.* Paul says, *"Dearly beloved, avenge not
yourselves, but rather give place unto wrath: for it is written,
Vengeance is mine; I will repay, saith the Lord"* (v. 19).

Geoffrey Farnol makes this the theme of one of his great tales
of adventure. Martin Conisby, heir to a landed estate, was the
victim of a feud which had dragged on for centuries between his
family and the neighboring Brandons. Sir Richard Brandon had
killed Conisby's father and sold Martin to a living death as an
oar-slave on a Spanish galleon. "O God of justice," cried the
wretched man as he toiled at the heavy oar, "for the agony I
needs must now endure, for the bloody stripes and bitter anguish
give me vengeance—vengeance, O God, on mine enemy!"

The story tells how Martin escaped and went seeking his vengeance. It tells how he found his enemy at last in the dungeons
of the Spanish inquisition in Nombre de Dios. In his blind hate
Martin Conisby had himself arrested by officers of the inquisition
in the hope that he might find himself in the same cell as his foe.
He was taken to a dark cell, choked with foul air. In a corner
of this cell he found an old, withered creature crouched on feeble
knees. Upon him the tormentors had done their worst. His body
bore "many grievous scars of wounds old and new, the marks of
hot and searing iron, of biting steel and cruel lash, and in joints
swollen and inflamed, he read the oft-repeated torture of the
rack." It was his enemy, Richard Brandon! He had come seeking
a man hale and strong on whom he could wreak his hate and

slake his thirst for retribution. Instead he found a man broken in body and ennobled by his sufferings.

Farnol tells how his hero helped his foe escape from the clutches of the inquisition and how together they fled across the wild wastes of Darien. And all the time Martin grew to love and honor his one-time foe, while Brandon came to love the man he once had wronged as he would love an only son. When Sir Richard died on the weary journey to the sea, Martin Conisby wept for the only man he had ever truly loved and honored.[5] It is a great tale and is skillfully woven around the theme that vengeance is God's prerogative. Those who take revenge into their own hands are apt to pierce themselves through with many sorrows and find at last that vengeance is a bitter fruit. When God avenges a wrong He does so with perfect equity and justice, never in that spirit of retaliation which so characterizes human schemes of vengeance.

The Christian is not only to recognize that the prerogative of vengeance is God's, he is to recognize (2) *the principle of vengeance that is God's.* Paul says, *"Therefore if thine enemy hunger, feed him; if he thirst, give him drink: for in so doing thou shalt heap coals of fire on his head. Be not overcome of evil, but overcome evil with good"* (vv. 20-21). It was in this very way that God reacted to Calvary. The cross represents the very highest manifestation of the hatred in the heart of man toward God. At the same time it represents the very highest manifestation of the love in the heart of God toward man. That very spear which pierced the Saviour's side drew forth the blood that saves.

THE SECULAR LIFE OF THE CHRISTIAN
13:1-7

The believer is to recognize

I. THE RESPONSIBILITIES OF A NATION'S LEADERS (13:1-6)

   A. Their Godward Responsibilities (13:1-2)

      1. Governments Are Appointed by God (13:1)

      2. Governments Are Approved by God (13:2)

   B. Their Governmental Responsibilities (13:3-6)

      1. They Are Responsible for National Safety (13:3-5)

---

[5]See Geoffrey Farnol, *Black Bartley's Treasure* and *Martin Conisby's Vengeance.*

       a. To Protect the Community (13:3-4*a*)
          (1) By Resisting Outlawed Members of the Community (13:3*a*)
          (2) By Recognizing Outstanding Members of the Community (13:3*b*-4*a*)
       b. To Punish the Criminal (13:4*b*-5)
    2. They Are Responsible for National Solvency (13:6)

II. THE RIGHTS OF A NATION'S LEADERS (13:7)
    A. Their Right to Our Monetary Support
      1. To Our Tribute
      2. To Our Custom
    B. Their Right to Our Moral Support
      1. Fear—Rendered to Bad Rulers
      2. Honor—Rendered to Good Rulers

HAVING SHOWN that the laws of the Christian life regulate the believer's spiritual and social relationships, Paul next shows that they control his secular relationships as well. The believer's relationship to human government is as much a matter of divine revelation as his relationship to elders in the church. Paul's viewpoint in this section of his epistle places the emphasis on the leaders of a nation and from this perspective shows how a Christian is to act.

I. THE RESPONSIBILITIES OF A NATION'S LEADERS (13:1-6)

The responsibilities of a nation's leaders are both Godward and manward. Since it is the Christian's duty to "render unto Caesar the things which are Caesar's," Paul emphasizes how Caesar is to behave. They are clearly rare occasions when a Christian must respectfully decline to obey a governmental order (Acts 5:29). The Bible frowns on civil disobedience. God is on the side of constituted authority.

A. *The Godward Responsibilities of Rulers* (13:1-2)

Human government derives its authority from God. Paul shows that governments are (1) *appointed by God.* He says, "*Let every soul be subject unto the higher powers. For there is no power but of God: the powers that be are ordained of God*" (v. 1). Human government was inaugurated by God after the flood when He placed into Noah's hand the sword of the magistrate. "Whoso sheddeth man's blood, by man shall his blood be shed" (Gen. 9:6) were the words which launched man on the road to self-government under God. The highest function of government is the judicial taking of life, the one thing emphasized in the divine decree. All other functions of government are implied in that.

Like everything else entrusted to man, human government soon failed. The sword of the magistrate became the sword of the conqueror. The right to legislate and govern man proved to be a heady wine for a fallen race. The story of the tower of Babel shows how man used his new-found authority to plan organized rebellion against the very throne of God itself. Up until this time rebellion had been on an individual basis, now it had become federated. The world's first "united nations" with headquarters at Babylon symbolizes the last one. Genesis 11 and 12 foreshadow Revelation 13, 17–18.

Despite the abuses of governmental power, human government is still a divine institution. "The powers that be are ordained of God." The word "powers" here means "delegated authorities" and the word "ordained" means "appointed." Evil men may be elected to power or may seize power. They may have no thought of God at all, but the very fact that He permits them to seize the reigns of government means that He has a purpose to fulfill even through their misrule. It is a saying well worth considering that "people get the kind of government they deserve." Governments may be weak or strong, just or oppressive, benevolent or cruel, wise or foolish, but in each case God has His way and moves His own plans forward. Democracies and dictatorships alike are under His control. God balances one nation off against another. He uses one nation to chastise another. Nations come and go, kingdoms rise and fall, empires wax and wane, but behind them all is God, overruling in the affairs of men. Wars and rumors of war, famines and pestilences, depressions and disasters—all are woven into the fabric of history. From our viewpoint the strands may seem tangled, meaningless, hopelessly knotted, unequal and wrong. But the tapestry He is weaving is perfect, and all the pressures of Satanic force and human sin are gloriously overruled

by a God who is both omnipotent and omniscient. What James
Russell Lowell said of individuals is just as true of nations:

> Careless seems the great Avenger; history's pages but
>   record
> One death-grapple in the darkness 'twixt old systems and
>   the Word.
> Truth forever on the scaffold, Wrong forever on the
>   throne—
> Yet that scaffold sways the future and, behind the dim
>   unknown,
> Standeth God within the shadow, keeping watch above
>   His own."

One of the great lessons of the book of Daniel is that God keeps
a firm hand on history. Nebuchadnezzar, mighty king of Babylon,
had to learn that "the heavens do rule" (Dan. 4:26). When after
a terrible experience this truth was brought home to him, he
issued a formal state document in which he asserted: "I blessed
the most High, and I praised and honoured him that liveth for
ever, whose dominion is an everlasting dominion, and his kingdom is from generation to generation: and all the inhabitants of
the earth are reputed as nothing: and he doeth according to his
will in the army of heaven, and among the inhabitants of the
earth: and none can stay his hand, or say unto him, What doest
thou?" (Dan. 4:34-35). The whole of Bible history is intended to
reinforce the truth that "the powers that be are ordained of God."

Paul goes on to show that governments are (2) *approved by
God*. He says, "*Whosoever therefore resisteth the power, resisteth
the ordinance of God: and they that resist shall receive to themselves damnation*" (v. 2). Disobedience to governmental authority is disobedience to God and will be judged. The rule of
law militates against the right of an individual to decide which
laws are right and which laws are wrong, and to take it upon himself either to obey or disobey just as he pleases. Such a philosophy
leads to anarchy, riot and national disintegration. If a law is unjust it must be repealed through legal channels not just disobeyed.

Since governments are appointed by God they must be obeyed.
On the other hand, those in positions of government must recognize the fact that their authority is derived from God. They are
not appointed to public office in order to promote their own selfish interests. They are there to represent God's rule on the earth.

Therefore they must acknowledge God in the administration of national affairs. They must uphold divine principles of righteousness and they must refrain from legislation which would undermine the individual's right to worship God according to the dictates of his conscience. It is significant that the divine ideal of an Old Testament king was a shepherd.

B. *The Governmental Responsibilities of Rulers* (13:3-6)

A government's prime responsibilities are twofold—to secure the nation against all forms of lawlessness and to keep the nation financially solvent. Paul discusses these two functions of government next.

Governments are (1) *responsible for national safety.* This means they must (*a*) *protect the community.* There are two ways in which this can be done, one negative in character and the other positive. The negative method is to *resist* the criminal elements in the community; the positive method is to *reward* the conscientious members of the community. Paul sets forth the first of these by asserting that "*rulers are not a terror to good works, but to the evil. Wilt thou then be afraid of the power?*" (v. 3*a*). The only people who should live in fear of the representatives of the law are those who break the law.

We are living in days when God's Word has been largely set aside so far as government goes, even in lands nominally Christian. It is all the more important, therefore, that we give heed to what these and other scriptures have to say regarding lawlessness and law enforcement.

The Bible teaches that the last days will be marked by increasing lawlessness. Jesus, in His great prophetic discourse, said, "Iniquity [lawlessness] shall abound [increase]" (Matt. 24:12). Dr. Wilbur M. Smith points out that there are four words in the Greek New Testament which are used to describe outbursts of passion and lawlessness.[1] A study of these will help us realize how imperative it is that nations have strong governments dedicated to protecting the community from the free expression of man's criminal passions.

The first word is *kōmos* (translated "revellings" in Gal. 5:19-

[1]See Wilbur M. Smith, "Deep Roots of Lawlessness," "In the Study," *Moody Monthly,* December, 1965, pp. 45-48.

21). According to Archbishop Trench, *kōmos* is used to describe "a troop of intoxicated revelers who at the close of an orgy, with garlands on their heads and torches in their hands, with shouts and songs, wander through the streets with insult and wanton outrage for everyone they meet." What a vivid picture!

Every generation has had its oddballs on the fringe of decent society just as we today have our beatniks, hippies and LSD "acid heads." But Paul does not reserve the use of *kōmos* for such. He uses it to describe the lawless nature of the heart of man in general. All men have a bent toward these "revellings." It is not surprising, therefore, to find that millions of "decent" citizens are looking for an escape from the fearful pressures and problems of the age in illicit forms of pleasure.[2]

The second word for lawlessness mentioned by Dr. Smith is the Greek word *echthra* which is generally translated "hatred" or, more accurately, "enmity." According to one authority quoted by Dr. Smith the ancient world knew of three kinds of enmity. There was enmity between class and class, the haves and the have-nots. There was enmity between the Greek and the barbarian; that is, enmity between the races. And there was enmity between man and man. These enmities are flourishing today in the enlightened twentieth century as much as they did in the days of Paul.[3]

[2]Take the LSD craze as an example. Not only is the use of LSD widespread on college campuses throughout the United States but it is being used by fraternity men, student leaders and future businessmen. (See Richard Goldstein, "Drugs on the Campus," *Saturday Evening Post*, Part 1, May 21, 1966, pp. 40-62, and Part 2, June 4, 1966, pp. 32-44.) Indeed, the use of drugs is becoming a national problem. James L. Goddard, M.D., commissioner of the U.S. Food and Drug Administration, is reported as saying: "More and more of us are becoming dependent on drugs, hiding from the realities of life—or just using them for thrills. Drug abuse cannot be connected only with narcotic users. The alarming rise in the abuse of stimulant, depressant and hallucinogenic drugs cuts across all strata of society." (Quoted by Roland H. Berg, "Why Americans Hide Behind a Chemical Curtain," *Look*, August 8, 1967, p. 11.)

[3]Take, for example, the race riots which plague the United States. Commissioner George B. McClellan, retiring from his position as head of the Royal Canadian Mounted Police, spoke of the violence and riots in the United States. He said, "How is it that the merest uncorroborated rumor of ill treatment of a black by a white or a white by a black, unconfirmed, unsubstantiated and frequently proved incorrect, can result at once, not in a minor disturbance, not in a peaceful protest, but in what amounts to an armed insurrection—in which whole sections of a major city are destroyed as effectively as if they had been bombed by enemy aircraft or artillery?" ("Respect for the Law—Breaking Down All Over?" From a copyrighted article in *U.S. News and World Report*, August 21, 1967, p. 17.)

The third word for lawlessness in the New Testament is *asotia,* meaning "abandoned." It is used in Luke 15 to describe the prodigal son who, we are told, wasted his substance with "riotous" (abandoned) living. He simply threw everything away, for that is the force of the word. He had no restraint and no regard for decency and no thought for the future.

The fourth word is *anomia* meaning "lawless" or, as it might be paraphrased, "having contempt for the law." It is this word which comes closest to the theme of Romans 13. It is the very word used by the Lord in Matthew 24:12 when He spoke of lawlessness increasing on the earth just prior to His coming.

Think of these sobering statistics for the United States alone. According to the Federal Bureau of Investigation there were almost 3.25 million serious crimes committed in the United States in 1966 including some 11,000 murders. In six years (1960-1966) crime in the United States increased seven times faster than the population. The population increased by 9 percent, crime by 62 percent and the cost of crime to the country reached a new all-time high of twenty billion dollars a year.

In every walk of life there seems to be a breakdown of morals and a decline in respect for the law. A generation which has abandoned the Bible as a rule for life is now paying for its folly in a rising tide of crime. Everywhere we look there is the same abandonment to lust and license.[4]

The worst feature of modern lawlessness, however, is what has become known as "syndicated crime." Billy Graham says, "It ought to shock us that in many countries organized crime is the biggest business of all. In fact, one of America's leading racketeers casually boasted a short time ago: 'Organized crime is bigger than the United States Government.' Crime grosses close to 10

---

[4]Pornography has become big business. Millions of paperbacks dealing with offbeat sex and with the emphasis on the worst forms of deviation flood the newsstands of the world. In one year alone enough filthy pornographic literature was sold in the United States to fill to overflowing more than five Empire State Buildings.

Another example of the rising tide of lawlessness is shoplifting, which has become a national epidemic. Teens dominate this form of theft with youngsters stealing just for the fun of it. They have never been taught that stealing is a crime. Nor is it petty larceny that is involved. Youths are taking expensive skirts and jackets where once they pilfered small items like lipstick and penknives. (See Earl Selby, "Youthful Shoplifting: A National Epidemic," *Reader's Digest,* April, 1967, pp. 95-99. Condensed from the *Christian Herald.*)

percent of the American national income and forms virtually a state within a state. . . . Organized crime, with its syndicates, underworld, racketeering and the Mafia, almost controls some of the world's major cities. In addition, there is unorganized crime, and it is just as bad if not worse. Crime is increasing with such rapidity that we are now close to open rebellion and anarchy."[5]

Governments are responsible before God to protect the community by resisting outlawed members of society. They are to be "a terror . . . to the evil," as Paul puts it. Every Christian must be on the side of law and order and give wholehearted support to those responsible for national safety. Never should a Christian resort to civil disobedience. He should respect and help uphold the law.

"The disheartening truth is," says J. Edgar Hoover, "that too many citizens have become totally unconcerned about the safety and welfare of their fellowman. Many of the vicious assaults which occur take place within sight or sound of individuals who lack the courage to aid the victim personally, or the interest to summon help. There simply are not enough law enforcement officers to constantly patrol all the streets and parks of America; hence, law enforcement must rely on citizens to report potential troublemakers and danger areas."[6]

To these words may be added the warning of retiring Commissioner McClellan of the Royal Canadian Mounted Police: "The phenomenon of public antagonism toward the police is reaching

[5]From *World Aflame* by Billy Graham. Copyright © 1965 by Billy Graham. Reprinted by permission of Doubleday and Company, Inc.
Several years ago J. Edgar Hoover discussed the growth of syndicated crime. It had its roots in the U.S.A. in the bootlegging which was prevalent in the days of prohibition. With the repeal of prohibition the gangs moved into other fields of crime and, being highly organized, soon became powerful overlords of vice. "We now find," said Hoover, "that the overlords of crime have moved out of gang hideouts into the mainstream of American life. These criminals have great wealth, taken in organized gambling, prostitution, the sale of narcotics, the sale of obscene material, and other vices. With that money, they have bought into legitimate businesses or set up their own. They have even infiltrated some labor unions.
"Using this new 'respectability' and their wealth, hoodlums and racketeers have been able to exert real pressure on government, businesses and unions to make possible a further spread of graft and corruption." (From a copyrighted interview with J. Edgar Hoover, "Who's to Blame for the Rising Wave of Crime?" in *U.S. News and World Report,* January 1, 1962, pp. 34-35.)
[6]From a copyrighted interview with J. Edgar Hoover in *U.S. News and World Report, ibid.,* p. 35.

epidemic proportions all over the world, not only in those countries which we are wont to refer to as underdeveloped countries, but in countries which have been and are regarded as some of the most highly civilized in the world."[7]

It is the duty of the law enforcement agencies of a nation to protect the community, and it is the duty of every Christian to obey the laws of the land and so obey the law of God. In its function of protecting the community, it is the duty of government not only to *resist* outlawed members of the community but also to *recognize* outstanding members of the community, particularly those who are good. Paul says, *"Do that which is good, and thou shalt have praise of the same: for he is the minister of God to thee for good"* (13:3b-4a). It is right and fitting that people who render outstanding public service should be given public recognition. Every nation honors its great and its gifted citizens. A wise nation also honors its good citizens.

Whether or not they are recognized, however, the Christian members of the community are to concentrate on doing good. Many Christians neglect the social implications of the gospel because they do not want to be accused of holding a so-called "social gospel." The social gospel, of course, is really no gospel at all, since it places the emphasis on human effort as a means of salvation. The liberal preacher places the cart before the horse. He thinks good works result in salvation and fails to see that salvation results in good works. Unfortunately many Christians who have seen the first truth have failed to grasp the second one. Having said that salvation is "not of works, lest any man should boast," Paul goes right on to say, "For we are his workmanship, created in Christ Jesus unto good works, which God hath before ordained that we should walk in them" (Eph. 2:9-10). Writing to the Philippians on the same theme, Paul says again, "Work out your own salvation with fear and trembling. For it is God which worketh in you both to will and to do of his good pleasure" (Phil. 2:12-13). It is recorded of the Lord Jesus that He "went about doing good" (Acts 10:38). What higher example could we have than that?

Governments are not only responsible to protect the community, they must also (*b*) *punish the criminal.* Paul goes on to say,

[7]From a copyrighted article in *U.S. News and World Report,* "Respect for the Law—Breaking Down All Over?" *ibid.,* p. 17.

"But if thou do that which is evil, be afraid; for he beareth not the sword in vain: for he is the minister of God, a revenger to execute wrath upon him that doeth evil. Wherefore ye must needs be subject, not only for wrath, but also for conscience sake" (vv. 4b-5). In Paul's day provincial Roman magistrates wore a sword. This sword was borne before the magistrate in public processions as a symbol of his right to punish by death. It is said that the emperor Trajan once presented a sword to a provincial governor as he started for his sphere of service. On the sword were engraven the words: "For *me*. If I deserve it, *in* me."

The modern fad seems to be to coddle the criminal rather than to punish him. In 1966, for example, only one criminal was executed in the United States in contrast with 199 executed in 1935. One state after another is abolishing capital punishment. Many arguments are brought forward by humanists who think that the death penalty is barbaric. They claim that capital punishment is "inhumane and unworthy of a civilized society" and that it is useless as a deterrent. Some lawmakers even argue that society actually loses more than it gains when it puts a man to death and point to rehabilitated murderers as proof. It is argued that the law is not infallible and that it is always possible for a mistake to be made and an innocent man executed in error. It is claimed that most serious offenses are committed by those suffering from mental illness or are impulsive in character. It is urged that those executed for capital offenses are usually the poor, the ignorant and the unfortunate. It is maintained that life imprisonment is sufficient protection for society from the menace of murder.[8] All these arguments are put forward in favor of abolishing the death penalty. They all overlook the basic issue—the sacredness of human life in the sight of God. It is a divine decree that has never been rescinded that when a person murders another person, the criminal must pay for his crime with his own life. Modern solutions to the problem of crime do not seem to be working too well when all the facts are in.[9]

[8]See Ernest Havemann, "Capital Punishment Is Not the Answer," *Reader's Digest,* May, 1960, pp. 114-119.

[9]According to one report: "Large numbers of those sentenced to death by courts are never executed. In 1965, for example, 62 death sentences were commuted or reversed on appeal. While the number of executions is declining, the number of murders in this country is increasing. In 1961, for example, there were 8,600 murders in the U.S. In 1965, there were 9,850.

The Old and New Testaments agree in declaring that magistrates are to "bear the sword," and to decry such a decree as "barbarous" is to attack the authority and infallibility of Holy Writ. Society can only set aside God's decrees to its own peril—as we are finding out in America today. Of the thousands arrested in race riots, for example, most go free on probation or get short jail terms. Very few go to prison. So race riots escalate all across the land.

Prominent citizens are taking alarm at the trend toward leniency in dealing with the problem of crime. Former President Dwight D. Eisenhower has given forceful expression to what he thinks about today's trends in crime and punishment. He says: "Law enforcement officials point to the declining rate of criminal convictions as crime itself soars; courts so preoccupied with legal technicalities that they turn vicious criminals loose to roam the streets; undermanned police departments almost everywhere; police salaries which are often lower than those of bus drivers; and the growing number of citizens who assume the right to decide which laws they will obey and which they will not.

"I think that we as a people should be deeply ashamed of all this. . . . I still believe firmly that ours is the best country on earth. Yet today we seem to be plunging into an era of lawlessness, which in the end can lead only to anarchy. And anarchy is a destroyer of nations. . . . All this does not mean, of course, that we have turned into a nation of criminals. But it does mean that there is something seriously wrong with our public and private attitudes toward law and order. Perhaps the basic problem is apathy, plus neglect of certain fundamental moral principles."[10]

Crime of all kinds is rising rapidly. The Uniform Crime Reports of the Federal Bureau of Investigation show this. . . . What is happening is an increase in 'conditional releases'—or paroles—of prisoners before they have completed their full prison sentences. The number of such releases increased by 79.5 percent between 1950 and 1965. In 1965, about 64 percent of all releases from prison were 'conditional'—before completion of the full sentence. What these figures show is a nation-wide trend toward leniency to criminals—less punishment, capital or otherwise." (From a copyrighted article, "Crime Up—Punishment Down," in U.S. News and World Report, April 10, 1967, p. 72.)

[10]From "We Should Be Ashamed," by Dwight D. Eisenhower, Reader's Digest, August, 1967. Copright © 1967 by Dwight D. Eisenhower. Reprinted by permission of Doubleday and Company, Inc. Former President Eisenhower is not the only voice raised in protest against modern leniency toward criminals. The Republican Leader in the House, Representative Gerald R. Ford of Michigan, has called on courts to "uphold the rights of

The Bible, as we have seen, upholds the right of governments to protect the community and to punish the criminal. The punishment must be adequate for the offense. Capital punishment is right and proper because of the sacredness of human life. Paul reaffirms the Old Testament principle in this passage we are considering.[11] The heart of man has not changed with the passing of the centuries. It is just as lawless and rebellious today as it was in the days of Paul, of Noah, or of Cain. During the coming golden age of the millennium, when Jesus reigns from the river to the ends of the earth, His government will be characterized by rigid discipline and swift administration of justice. We are expressly told that He is going to rule the nations "with a rod of iron" (Ps. 2:9). That "rod of iron" is a fitting symbol for His unbending authority.

Governments are not only responsible for national safety, they are also (2) *responsible for national solvency.* Says Paul, *"For this cause pay ye tribute also: for they are God's ministers, attending continually upon this very thing"* (v. 6). Nobody likes paying taxes! However, governments have to pay their officials. The services rendered to the public by the government all cost money. It therefore stands to reason that those who benefit from these services must pay for them and the payment is in the form of taxes.

It is interesting that "ministers" here is the word from which we get "liturgy." The word is used in Hebrews 8:2 of the sacred

the law-abiding citizen with the same fervor as they uphold the rights of the accused." He suggested also that the Supreme Court justices be selected from "judges who have evidenced by their decisions a balanced viewpoint in the area of public protection and individual rights. (See "Johnson's 'War on Crime,'" *U.S. News and World Report,* Feb. 20, 1967, p. 48.)

At a conference of chief justices at Honolulu in 1967 attended by justices from forty-five states, a resolution was passed demanding swift and sure punishment for rioting, looting and arson. Their fourth resolution was "that among the causes of the spreading disrespect for law and its enforcement are the publicly held views that it is inordinately difficult, and many times impossible, to convict those who are guilty of the gravest crimes against our society, and that there are unreasonable and unnecessary delays in the administration of justice; that to the extent these views are supported in logic and fact it requires that we, and all our judicial, executive and legislative bodies and agencies, reappraise the laws and procedures which affect the task of the policeman, the prosecutor and the courts in their effort to protect society, to the end that we will successfully meet the challenge of lawlessness." Their sixth resolution was "that we implore all citizens to deliberately reaffirm their faith in liberty under law."

[11]It is perhaps of special interest to remember that he was writing to the church at Rome—the legislative capital of the ancient world.

duty of the priests in the temple at Jerusalem. It is used in Hebrews 1:14 to describe the duties of the angels. The use of the
word here shows that rulers discharge a God-ordained duty. In a
day and age when it is fashionable to sneer at governmental authority, it is timely to remind ourselves that constituted authorities are "liturgists of God." Not all rulers, of course, conscientiously serve God, but regardless of whether they do or not they
discharge functions which are God ordained.

II. THE RIGHTS OF A NATION'S LEADERS (13:7)

Those who occupy positions of responsibility in a nation are entitled to the support of those they govern. In this closing verse
Paul draws the threads of his argument together and calls on
believers to range themselves solidly on the side of constituted
authority.

A. *Their Right to Our Monetary Support* (13:7)

Paul has just been saying that rulers are responsible for national
solvency. He now shows that believers are to *"render to all their
dues: tribute to whom tribute is due; custom to whom custom."*
Tribute was especially the yearly tax levied on persons or real
estate. It would correspond to our income and property taxes.
What a disgrace it is when a Christian cheats on his income tax
report. Paul tells us we are to pay our taxes. According to Alford,
"Tertullian remarks that what the Romans lost by the Christians
refusing to bestow gifts on their temples, they gained by their
conscientious payment of taxes."[12] *Custom* was an indirect tax on
goods. It would correspond to our sales tax. It also is to be paid
cheerfully by the Christian! Both these taxes were collected in
Paul's day by the publicans. There were flagrant abuses in the
tax system, so much so that the publicans were the worst hated men
in the nation. Paul does not enter into the rights and wrongs of
the taxation system. He simply tells Christians that a nation's
leaders have a right to monetary support; therefore they must pay
their taxes.

B. *Their Right to Our Moral Support* (13:7)

It is possible to keep the letter of the law and not the spirit. So

[12]Henry Alford, *The New Testament for English Readers* (Chicago:
Moody Press, n.d.), p. 956.

Paul adds that in his support of his government a Christian must *"render to all their dues . . . fear to whom fear; honour to whom honour."* *Fear* is a conscientious regard for and awe of those in authority—an attitude certainly not generally conspicuous today. *Honor* is to be given to all set over us, but also to those who are given special distinction by the state. To speak evil of dignities is no part of a Christian's calling (Jude 8-10).

It is perhaps worth repeating here that the emperor of Rome when Paul wrote these words was none other than the notorious Nero. The government of the Roman Empire had for many years been in the hands of a group of Caesars whose private lives were a public scandal and whose administration of justice was one long blot upon the history of Rome. Even a casual reading of Suetonius will reveal this. Besides all this, Paul was a Jew. In his unconverted days he had known that fierce hatred of a foreign occupying power which rankled in every Hebrew heart and which, before long, was to lead his people into a great and fervent uprising against Rome. But he allows no rationalization to dilute his stand. Rulers have their responsibilities imposed on them by God, and to whom, of course, they are answerable. Christians have their responsibilities. They are to give freely of their support to the divinely appointed governments under which they live.

LOVE'S MORAL CONSCIENCE
13:8-14

I. THE COMMANDMENTS OF THE LORD (13:8-10)

    A. Love's Debt (13:8)

    B. Love's Duty (13:9)

    C. Love's Desire (13:10)

II. THE COMING OF THE LORD (13:11-14)

    A. We are to Watch Vigilantly (13:11)

        1. We Are Informed of the Imminence of His Coming

        2. We Are Influenced by the Imminence of His Coming

    B. We Are to War Valiantly (13:12)

        1. An Act of Defiance ("Cast off")

        2. An Act of Reliance ("Put on")

C. We Are to Walk Virtuously (13:13)
   1. The Right Way
   2. The Wrong Way
D. We Are to Wait Victoriously (13:14)
   1. What Is Provided
   2. What Is Prohibited

PAUL HAS BEEN DISCUSSING the laws which govern the various relationships of a Christian's life. He now turns his attention to the highest law of all, the law of love, and shows how love rules supreme in the believer's heart and legislates for every situation of life. He begins this section by speaking of love's moral conscience. Love makes the conscience far more tender than law could ever do.

I. THE COMMANDMENTS OF THE LORD (13:8-10)

The Christian keeps the commandments not because they are commandments of the *law* but because they are commandments of the *Lord*. Love for the Lord accomplishes what fear of the law could never achieve. "He that hath my commandments, and keepeth them, he it is that loveth me," said the Lord Jesus (John 14:21). There are three aspects of this which are all-embracing.

A. *Love's Debt* (13:8)

Love's debt is large. Says Paul, *"Owe no man any thing, but to love one another: for he that loveth another hath fulfilled the law"* (v. 8). Love will always have the interests of the creditor in view. This is not a precept to forbid a Christian from entering into a contractual agreement whereby he obtains a properly bonded loan. It does, however, forbid the Christian to borrow money beyond his ability to repay. It is very easy nowadays to accumulate debts which strain income to the breaking point. The Christian is to avoid this kind of thing. It is just as dishonest to buy more than can be paid for and to keep the creditor waiting for his money, as it is to steal. Nothing will ruin a Christian testimony faster than chronic indebtedness.

Love touches the Christian's conscience and makes him eager to live beyond reproach in this matter of money. The story of Zacchaeus illustrates this. No sooner had this dishonest tax collector

come face to face with the Lord Jesus than he exclaimed, "Behold,
Lord, the half of my goods I give to the poor; and if I have taken
any thing from any man by false accusation, I restore him fourfold." Said Jesus to him, "This day is salvation come to this
house" (Luke 19:8-9). Zacchaeus was not saved because he wanted
to put his financial affairs in order. He wanted to put his financial
affairs in order because he was saved. His personal contact with
the Lord Jesus won his heart and quickened his conscience.

"Owe no man any thing." The injunction goes beyond the interests of the creditor and embraces every obligation. Any pledge
or promise should be regarded as sacred, and should be kept no
matter how irksome or inconvenient it may afterward become.
"Lord, who shall abide in thy tabernacle?" asked David. "He that
sweareth to his own hurt, and changeth not" was the reply (Ps.
15:1, 4). "When thou vowest a vow unto God," said Solomon,
enlarging the theme, "defer not to pay it; for he hath no pleasure
in fools: pay that which thou hast vowed. Better is' it that thou
shouldest not vow, than that thou shouldest vow and not pay"
(Eccles. 5:4-5).

While other debts may be discharged, the debt of love is always
owing. Any payment made on this debt does not release us from
continued indebtedness. "Owe no man any thing, but to love one
another." This is the reason for the Lord's remarkable answer to
Peter when Peter raised the question, "Lord, how oft shall my
brother sin against me, and I forgive him? till seven times?" The
Lord's answer was, "I say not unto thee, Until seven times: but,
Until seventy times seven" (Matt. 18:21-22). When Peter has
forgiven his brother seven times, he has not even begun to discharge his debt of love. He must forgive and forgive and forgive,
realizing that such is the love of God. Love's debt is large.

B. Love's Duty (13:9)

Love fulfills the law as Paul goes on to prove. "For this, Thou
shalt not commit adultery, Thou shalt not kill, Thou shalt not
steal, Thou shalt not bear false witness, Thou shalt not covet; and
if there be any other commandment, it is briefly comprehended in
this saying, namely, Thou shalt love thy neighbour as thyself" (v.
9). The Ten Commandments of the Decalogue (Exodus 20:1-
17) can be divided into two sections. The first section emphasizes

the phrase "the Lord thy God" and the second emphasizes the word "thou." The first summarizes duty Godward, the second summarizes duty manward. The command to obey parents is linked with the Godward commandments because parents represent to their children divine authority. In each of the two sections the commandments deal with the realms of thought, word and deed. The sections can be summarized as follows:

A. Commands 1 and 2—THOUGHT
  B. Command 3—WORD
    C. Commands 4 and 5—DEED
       Each of these commandments is built around the phrase "the LORD thy God."
    C. Commands 6, 7 and 8—DEED
  B. Command 9—WORD
A. Command 10—THOUGHT
       Each of these commandments is built upon the word "thou."

The Lord Jesus reduced the Ten Commandments to two, underlining the heart of each of these sections and placing the emphasis on love rather than on law. "The first of all the commandments is, Hear, O Israel; The Lord our God is one Lord: and thou shalt love the Lord thy God with all thy heart, and with all thy soul, and with all thy mind, and with all thy strength: this is the first commandment. And the second is like, namely this, Thou shalt love thy neighbour as thyself. There is none other commandment greater than these" (Mark 12:29-31). Jesus added, "On these two commandments hang all the law and the prophets" (Matt. 22:40).

Love's duty is to obey the commandments of the Decalogue not because they are commanded under law, for the Christian is not under law but under grace, but because they are love's lasting obligation to God and others. Paul underlines the last five because they deal with love's duty to mankind. When a rich young ruler came to Christ wanting to know what he must *do* to inherit eternal life, the Lord Jesus simply quoted to him these five commandments. When the young man claimed to have kept all these from his youth up, Jesus showed him in a single sentence that he had done nothing of the kind. "If thou wilt be perfect, go and sell that thou hast, and give to the poor, and thou shalt have treasure in heaven: and come and follow me" (Matt. 19:16-22). The young man went sorrowfully away because "he had great possessions." The Lord's swordthrust to his conscience revealed in a flash that he really did not love his neighbor as he loved himself.

A man who loves his neighbor as himself will not defile his neighbor's wife, nor murder him, nor steal from him, nor lie about him, nor covet anything he has.

C. *Love's Desire* (13:10)

Love's desire is for the well-being of men and for the well-pleasing of God. *"Love worketh no ill to his neighbour: therefore love is the fulfilling of the law"* (v. 10). In his great classic on love, Paul explains love's attitude. "This love of which I speak," he says, "is slow to lose patience—it looks for a way of being constructive. It is not possessive: it is neither anxious to impress nor does it cherish inflated ideas of its own importance. Love has good manners and does not pursue selfish advantage. It is not touchy. It does not keep account of evil or gloat over the wickedness of other people. On the contrary, it is glad with all good men when truth prevails. Love knows no limit to its endurance, no end to its trust, no fading of its hope; it can outlast anything. It is, in fact, the one thing that still stands when all else has fallen" (I Cor. 13:4-8).[1]

The underlying principle of the Jewish economy was law. The underlying principle of the Christian economy is love. Imagine love, like that which Paul describes, being turned on one's neighbor! No wonder Paul says that "love is the fulfilling of the law." Love's moral conscience fulfills the law not only out of debt and duty but also out of desire.

II. The Coming of the Lord (13:11-14)

Love prompts the Christian not only to be obedient to the commandments of the Lord but also to be observant of the coming of the Lord. The doctrine of the Lord's imminent return is one of the most wholesome in the Bible. "Every man that hath this hope in him purifieth himself, even as he is pure" (I John 3:3).

[1]J. B. Phillips, *The New Testament in Modern English* (New York: The Macmillan Company. Copyright © by J. B. Phillips, 1958), p. 371.

The prospect of the Lord's near return should be a great incentive to holy living. Paul here tells us four things we need to know and do in view of the fact that at any moment we might be faced with the return of the Lord in glory.

A. *We Are to Watch Vigilantly* (13:11)

Repeatedly in the New Testament we are told to watch for the coming of the Lord. *"And that, knowing the time, that now it is high time to awake out of sleep: for now is our salvation nearer than when we believed"* (v. 11). Salvation in the New Testament is in three tenses. Viewed as to the *past*, it is salvation from the penalty of sin; viewed as to the *present*, it is salvation from the power of sin; and viewed as to the *future*, it is salvation from the very presence of sin. It is this last viewpoint that Paul has in mind here. "Now is our salvation nearer than when we believed." As someone has put it, "Every day we pitch our tent a day's march nearer home."

Because of the soon coming of the Lord Jesus we are to be aware of "the time." That is, we are to know the season in which we live as it relates to the Lord's return; we are to be alert to the significance of the hour. Saints in all ages have eagerly looked for the return of the Lord in their lifetime. Indeed, the Apostle Peter was the only one of the Twelve who had no "blessed hope." He knew that he was going to die before the coming of the Lord (John 21:18-19; II Peter 1:14). Paul, likewise, by the time he came to write his second letter to Timothy, knew that he would fall a victim to Nero's lust for blood (II Tim. 4:6-8). But with only rare exceptions the Christian is not looking for death but rapture. We are to watch vigilantly and read aright the signs of the times.

In most ages of the church's history there have been currents in the tides of time which have seemed to indicate to the watchful that perhaps theirs was the generation of His coming. Those who lived in the days of the Saracen scourge, for example, or those who lived through the horrors of the French Revolution and watched the rise of Napoleon might have thought that these things presaged the Lord's return. In more recent times the meteoric rise of Mussolini led some to the conclusion that the Roman Em-

pire was reborn and that Jesus would soon appear. But in every
past age one or more vital pieces in the puzzle were missing.

How changed are things today! There is probably no area of
prophetic truth which is not flashing out its warning lights to our
generation. Coming events, they say, cast their shadows before
them. If this is so, and if the shadows lying athwart the world
today are what they seem, then everything indicates the immi-
nency of the Lord's return. Take, for example, the return of Israel
to the promised land; the status of Jerusalem; the rise of Russia
and her espousal of the Arab cause; the spread of atheistic ideol-
ogies; the drawing together of the European powers; the apostasy
of the professing Protestant church; the growing influence of
Rome and modern ecumenical trends; the rapid strides of science
and technology; the unleashing of nuclear power; the awakening
of China; the impasse among the nations; the growing empire of
syndicated crime and the general lawlessness of men. The believer needs to watch vigilantly, for the coming of the Lord draws
near. We can "almost hear His footfall on the threshold of the
door." "Watch therefore: for ye know not what hour your Lord
doth come. But know this, that if the goodman of the house had
known in what watch the thief would come, he would have
watched, and would not have suffered his house to be broken up.
Therefore be ye also ready: for in such an hour as ye think not
the Son of man cometh" (Matt. 24:42-44).

B. *We Are to War Valiantly* (13:12)

In view of the near return of the Lord Jesus and the lateness of
the hour, we are to rise and engage the foe. Watching *sights* the
enemy, praying *fights* the enemy. *"The night is far spent, the day
is at hand: let us therefore cast off the works of darkness, and let
us put on the armour of light"* (v. 12). The "casting off" and
"putting on" in each case suggest a definite and complete act.
Imagine a young man reporting for duty at the army headquarters.
He is wearing his civilian clothes. He signs the papers which
make him officially a member of the armed services and is issued
a complete uniform. The company of recruits lines up on the
parade ground the next morning for its first inspection. All the
other soldiers are in full uniform but our friend has on his khaki
pants but otherwise is dressed in a sports jacket, a white shirt and

a green tie! The sergeant major would make short work of him! Once in the army he is to be through with the old dress, radically, completely and once-for-all. In a decisive and complete act he discards his civilian clothes and puts on his uniform. From henceforth he is to be identified by his clothes.

It is just this very thing that Paul has in mind here. Because he is saved the believer is to put off deliberately and decisively, through the power of the indwelling Holy Spirit, the "works of darkness"—all those habits which once marked him out as an unbeliever. In their place he is to put on the "armour of light," and thus arrayed go forth to battle against "the rulers of this world's darkness" (Eph. 6:12-17).

C. *We Are to Walk Virtuously* (13:13)

Paul tells us the right way and the wrong way to "walk." The word "walk," incidentally, has to do with the outward life of a Christian which men see. The *right way* is to *"walk honestly, as in the day"* (v. 13a). Paul told the Thessalonians that we are all "children of light . . . of the day" (I Thess. 5:5). The deportment of a Christian is to be such that none can find fault with it. The word for "honestly" is "becomingly." One is reminded of a dry-cleaning establishment which advertised its services with the words, "If your clothes aren't becoming to you, they should be coming to us!" Is our conduct becoming to us as believers? Can we stand the full light of day shining on our behavior? Are we living beyond reproach? Love's moral conscience, quickened by the thought of the coming of the Lord, will surely guarantee this.

Then Paul spells out the *wrong way* to walk. *"Not in rioting and drunkenness, not in chambering and wantonness, not in strife and envying"* (v. 13b). These sins were once common in the lives of many of Paul's pagan converts, saved as they were out of lives of deep sin. They were to make sure that these sins did not creep back into their lives now that they were saved. Paul was a realist. He knew only too well what dark strongholds the old nature maintains within any believer's heart, what abominable lusts lurk in the shadows of the soul awaiting a favorable moment to leap forth in dreadful force. To be forewarned is to be forearmed. The believer is to walk virtuously, slaying with the Spirit's shining sword the very thought of sin.

D. *We Are to Wait Victoriously* (13:14)

As we seek to make real in our lives these practical injunctions of Paul, each one made more urgent by the truth of the imminent return of the Lord Jesus, we are to observe what is provided for us and what is prohibited to us. *"But put ye on the Lord Jesus Christ, and make no provision for the flesh, to fulfill the lusts thereof"* (v. 14).

When a Christian "puts on" the Lord Jesus he, so to speak, clothes himself in all that Christ is.

> How perfect is His righteousness,
> In which unspotted, beauteous dress
> His saints have always stood.

There is a sense, of course, in which we put on the Lord Jesus when we were saved. Now we must put Him on as to our walk. He is the moral raiment we wear, a raiment which displays His character.

In keeping with this there is to be no provision made for the flesh, no taking thought as to how its evil desires can be gratified. The flesh has endless lusts all wanting to be indulged. There are not only gross appetites but refined carnal attitudes as well included in that word "flesh." All must be denied; provision must be made for none of them. While we await the Lord's return, we are to wait victoriously. If we allow the Holy Spirit to bring His Word to bear upon our lives, love's moral conscience will make us very sensitive to things which will shame us at the coming of the Lord.

LOVE'S MERCIFUL CONDUCT
14:1—15:7

I. ACCEPTING A WEAK BROTHER (14:1-9)
   A. He Is to Be Accepted Confidently (14:1)
   B. He Is to Be Accepted Considerately (14:2-9)
      1. Uniformity Is Not Imperative (14:2-5)
         a. The question of *diet* allows for freedom in one's *personal* religious attitude (14:2-4)
         b. The question of *days* allows for freedom in one's *public* religious attitude (14:5)

Love will see to it that those weaker in the faith than we are, will not be caused to stumble by our behavior. The problem of the "weaker brother" is discussed in this section of Romans. The problem is aggravated by the fact that the weaker brother often thinks he is the stronger brother! The weaker brother is the one who abstains from certains things, judges by appearances and fails to distinguish between the outward act and the inward attitude. Because someone does something with which he disagrees, the weaker brother at once concludes that this person's motives must be wrong.

I. The Question of Accepting a Weak Brother (14:1-9)

Should this type of Christian be received into the fellowship of the local church? There can be no question that a brother who has all kinds of scruples can be a very trying person to have in a local congregation.

A. *He Is to Be Accepted Confidently* (14:1)

Paul leaves no doubt about that at all. He says, *"Him that is weak in the faith receive ye, but not to doubtful disputations"* (v. 1). The idea is that no questions are to be asked about his scruples, nor are those who are strong in the faith to argue with him about them. In the church at Rome, to which Paul addressed this epistle, there were Christians who had been saved out of dark paganism. These were shocked when Jewish Christians ate meat which had been offered to idols. They felt that although this meat was offered for sale in the public marketplace, still those who partook of it were in a definite way contributing to idolatry. Jewish believers, strong in the faith, thought that such scruples were nonsense. To eat meat offered for public sale, even though it had once been offered to an idol, did not constitute idolatry. On the other hand, these Gentile Christians who had come to Christ without any of the background of Judaism with its rites and rituals, its feasts and fasts, its truths and traditions, could not see what bearing Judaism had on Christianity. Their unwillingness to conform to certain days scandalized their Jewish-Christian brethren. Each group was thus perturbed by the other. Each judged and condemned the other. Each thought that his own background was the right one from which to view Christianity. It is an old problem and one which is still with us.

Of course nowadays we are not concerned with the same specifics which plagued the early church. However, we have our own taboos by which we judge our brethren. Paul says that all such externals are not to be made the basis for criticism, especially when they have to do with things about which Scripture is not explicit. People from different cultures have different customs, so where Christianity does not speak specifically, it is best not to be dogmatic. Especially is this true on the mission field.[1] So then, Paul says that the weak brother is to be heartily received, together with his scruples, and he is not to be mocked or martyred by the local fellowship because of his views.

B. *He Is to Be Accepted Considerately* (14:2-9)

Consideration for other people's viewpoints is the outward manifestation of love's merciful conduct. Paul wants us to understand first of all that (1) *uniformity is not imperative.* We do not all have to believe exactly alike, nor do we all have to behave exactly alike. God does not make all people on the same last nor pour them all into the same mold. To show how much room

[1]See Eugene Nida, *Customs and Cultures* (New York: Harper Brothers, 1954).

there is for difference of opinion on nonessentials, Paul deals with the two most vexing questions of the early church—those concerning days and those concerning diets.

In dealing with the problem of *diets,* he shows that there is wide latitude for the exercise of freedom in one's *personal* devotion to the Lord. *"For one believeth that he may eat all things: another, who is weak, eateth herbs. Let not him that eateth despise him that eateth not; and let not him which eateth not judge him that eateth: for God hath received him. Who art thou that judgest another man's servant? to his own master he standeth or falleth. Yea, he shall be holden up: for God is able to make him stand"* (vv. 2-4). The rights and wrongs of eating or not eating is not discussed. It remains an open question. It has nothing to do with salvation or sanctification, at least, not basically. The strong brother is not to despise the weak one as superstitious and narrow-minded, nor is the weaker brother to adopt a censorious attitude toward the stronger brother and label him as worldly and unscrupulous. "God hath received him," says Paul, emphasizing that salvation is not based on any such grounds as the critic assumes. The believer stands not in his own strength, even though he may enjoy greatly his liberty in Christ, but in the upholding power of the Lord Jesus.

In dealing with the problem of *days,* Paul shows that there is wide latitude for the exercise of freedom in one's *public* devotion to the Lord. Some people would like to regiment the church and make all men conform to their ideas about church truth. They are quick to condemn those who will not mouth their "Shibboleths" (Judg. 12:6). But where no vital issue of revealed New Testament truth is involved, there is wide room for difference of opinion. *"One man esteemeth one day above another: another esteemeth every day alike. Let every man be fully persuaded in his own mind"* (v. 5). The motive for what we do is not to be social pressure but personal conviction before the Lord.

What a wide variety of beliefs there is in Christendom as to what days ought to be observed! Some observe the Sabbath, others regard the first day of the week.[2] Some pay special atten-

[2]Seventh Day Adventists and others who nowadays insist on Sabbath observance raise many questions far more serious than whether or not we should keep the Sabbath. The whole question of keeping the law is raised, and that is an issue on which there can be no compromise.

tion to days such as Christmas, Easter, and Pentecost; others pay little or no attention to them at all. Some observe feast days and fast days and divide the calendar into special days about which they revolve all their religious duties. Others regard any such system as legalistic and savoring of Judaism rather than Christianity. Paul says believers are not to quarrel about these things. Uniformity is not essential since the tie that binds is love, not law.

In dealing with this problem of diets and days, then, Paul shows that uniformity is not imperative. Next, he shows that (2) *unity is not impossible.* There is a great deal of difference between uniformity and true unity. The one is cold and lifeless; the other is vibrant, living and warm. But how is unity to be obtained between believers who obviously differ on numbers of things even if they are not vital to true belief? Paul's answer is the lordship of Christ. To begin with, he shows that the lordship of Christ unites believers in *this life.* "*He that regardeth the day, regardeth it unto the Lord; and he that regardeth not the day, to the Lord he doth not regard it. He that eateth, eateth to the Lord, for he giveth God thanks; and he that eateth not, to the Lord he eateth not, and giveth God thanks. For none of us liveth to himself, and no man dieth to himself*" (vv. 6-7). The significance of a person's conduct is not so much what other people think about it, as what the Lord thinks about it. Consider for a moment the spokes of a wheel. Take a movable point on any two spokes. The closer the two points get to the hub, the closer they get to each other; and the farther they get from the hub, the farther they get from each other. The Lord Jesus, so to speak, is the hub of the wheel of Christian fellowship. The important thing is for each to move closer to Him, acknowledging His centrality and sovereignty. The matter of unity will then take care of itself.

The lordship of Christ unites believers not only in this life but also in *that life,* the life to come. "*For whether we live, we live unto the Lord; and whether we die, we die unto the Lord: whether we live therefore, or die, we are the Lord's. For to this end Christ both died, and rose, and revived, that he might be Lord both of the dead and living*" (vv. 8-9). The point of Paul's argument is that the believer is under the control of the Lord. He cannot choose either the manner or the time of his death.

Nor, indeed, does death alter his relationship with the Lord. Differences of opinion fade into insignificance when death enters the picture. Beyond the grave the lordship of Christ is universally acknowledged. And when we get to glory, it will be our greatest joy to cast our crowns at His feet (Phil. 2:9-10; Rev. 4:9-11). Let every believer then maintain in his own life the lordship of Christ and unity will not be impossible.

II. The Question of Accusing a Weak Brother (14:10-13)

The weak brother is to be accepted into the fellowship without discussion or debate, with a mature grasp of the truth that unity, not mere uniformity, is what truly displays the oneness of the body of Christ. There is always the temptation, however, to criticize the scrupulous brother because of areas of difference in his life.

A. *The Desire to Criticize Is Roundly Challenged* (14:10-12)

In the first place, Paul shows (1) *how purposeless it is.* He says, *"But why dost thou judge thy brother? or why dost thou set at nought thy brother?"* (v. 10a). Why indeed! What good does it do? How constructive is it? Gossip and criticism never accomplish anything worthwhile. The weak brother is not to judge the strong brother, nor is the strong brother to despise the weak. Criticism violates the law of love.

Then Paul shows (2) *how presumptuous it is* to criticize another brother. *"For we shall all stand before the judgment seat of Christ. For it is written, As I live, saith the Lord, every knee shall bow to me, and every tongue shall confess to God. So then every one of us shall give account of himself to God"* (vv. 10b-12). There are seven judgments mentioned in Scripture and they must not be confused.[3] The judgment mentioned here is of the believer's works, not of his sins. His sins have been judged at Calvary and are remembered no more forever (Heb. 10:17). However, every work has to be brought into judgment (Matt. 12:36; II Cor. 5:10; Col. 3:24-25). The result of this judgment, which takes place at the return of Christ (Matt. 16:27; Luke 14:14;

[3]These are: the judgment of sin at the cross (John 12:31); the self-judgment of the believer (I Cor. 11:31); the judgment seat of Christ (II Cor. 5:10); the judgment of the nations at Christ's return (Matt. 25:32); the judgment of Israel (Ezek. 20:37); the judgment of the angels (Jude 6); and the judgment of the wicked dead at the great white throne (Rev. 20:12).

I Cor. 4:5; II Tim. 4:8; Rev. 22:12), will be either reward or loss for the believer. Paul solemnly reminds us that criticizing another brother will be called into account at the judgment seat of Christ. It is presumptuous for us to criticize others. If we turn the searchlight within our own hearts, we will find plenty to keep us humble before the Lord without being occupied with other people. We shall have enough to do at the judgment seat of Christ answering for our own behavior without worrying about the actions of our brethren who, for all we can judge motives, were conscientiously following the Lord.

B. *The Desire to Criticize Is Rightly Channeled* (14:13)

Paul is not content with a negative statement in this matter of passing judgment. He has something positive to say. *"Let us not therefore judge one another any more: but judge this rather, that no man put a stumblingblock or occasion to fall in his brother's way"* (v. 13). In view of the judgment seat of Christ, our decision should be to avoid at all costs doing anything which would hinder a brother in the exercise of his faith. Here indeed is a field for judging—ourselves!

The Lord Jesus has wise words on this theme. "Don't criticize people," He said, "and you will not be criticized. For you will be judged by the way you criticize others, and the measure you give will be the measure you receive. Why do you look at the speck of sawdust in your brother's eye and fail to notice the plank in your own? How can you say to your brother, 'Let me get the speck out of your eye,' when there is a plank in your own? You fraud! Take the plank out of your own eye first, and then you can see clearly enough to remove your brother's speck of dust" (Matt. 7:1-5).[4]

Criticizing other people is a sin all too prevalent among God's people. Far too often we are so occupied with other people's sins that we conveniently overlook our own. We judge their behavior but fail to see that our own behavior is just as bad, if not worse, and that by our influence and example we are often leading others astray and causing them to stumble. This is a serious offense in the eyes of the Lord. Think of what He said in Mat-

---

[4]J. B. Phillips, *The New Testament in Modern English* (New York: The Macmillan Company. Copyright © by J. B. Phillips, 1958), p. 14.

thew 18, a chapter which when seen in its context casts a flood of light on the kind of conduct the Lord expects of His people.[5]

In dealing with the reception of believers, Jesus said, "Except ye be converted, and become as little children, ye shall not enter into the kingdom of heaven. Whosoever therefore shall humble himself as this little child, the same is greatest in the kingdom of heaven. And whoso shall receive one such little child in my name receiveth me. But whoso shall offend [cause to stumble, marg.] one of these little ones which believe in me, it were better for him that a millstone were hanged about his neck, and that he were drowned in the depth of the sea" (Matt. 18:3-6). Sobering words! How solemn a thing it is to be responsible for causing someone else to stumble. We are either *stepping stones* or *stumbling blocks*. Says Paul, turn the searchlight upon yourself and in the light of the judgment seat of Christ beware of causing your brethren, the Lord's "little ones," to stumble.

III. THE QUESTION OF ACCOMMODATING A WEAK BROTHER (14:14–15:7)

How far are we to go in seeking to accommodate ourselves to the special quibbles of the weak brother? That is a most difficult question. Paul, however, puts the responsibility on the stronger brother and tells him he is to compromise as far as possible in the spirit of charity and in the spirit of Christ.

A. *The Spirit of Charity* (14:14-23)

The spirit in which we accommodate the weak brother is not that of legalism but that of love. The attitude is not "I have to" or "I ought to" but "I want to." Love for the weaker brother awakens a genuine spirit of helpfulness which overflows in charitable acts toward him.

Paul sets before us three items of consideration in regard to this matter of treating our brethren in the spirit of charity. First he emphasizes (1) *the principles of our liberty in Christ*, and begins by reassuring us of the *rights* of a free conscience. "I

[5]There are two references to "the church" in Matthew. The first is in chapter 16: "upon this rock I will build my church" (v. 18), a clear reference to the *universal* aspect of the church. The second, in chapter 18, depicts the church in its *local* aspect. This chapter deals with (1) the reception of the believer (vv. 1-10); (2) the restoration of the backslider (vv. 11-14); and (3) the reconciliation of brethren (vv. 15-35).

*know, and am persuaded by the Lord Jesus, that there is nothing
unclean of itself: but to him that esteemeth anything to be unclean, to him it is unclean"* (v. 14). Conscience of itself is not an
infallible guide; but nevertheless it is wrong to go against one's
conscience. The stronger brother must not teach the weak one
to violate his conscience. Rather, he should teach him to educate
his conscience by the Word of God. Paul, of course, is not speaking here of that which is morally impure, only of that which is
ceremonially impure. To enjoy one's full liberty as a Christian,
there must be both knowledge and persuasion. To walk in liberty
with a quiet conscience, one must have a mind which perceives
the truth of God and a heart which is persuaded of the truth of
God. And what a blessedness that is, to be delivered from all the
fuss and bother of mere religion! That is the birthright of every
child of God, but one which is usually enjoyed only by those who
have taken their position as adult sons.

The rights of a free conscience are assured, but Paul also reminds us of the *responsibilities* of a free conscience. *"But if thy
brother be grieved with thy meat, now walkest thou not charitably.
Destroy not him with thy meat, for whom Christ died"* (v. 15).
The cry, "Am I my brother's keeper?" came from the lips of a
murderer. The word Paul uses here for "destroy" means "ruin"
or "reduce to uselessness." Every believer is his brother's keeper
and must refrain from anything that would lead him astray. To
have a free conscience in the things we allow is one thing; to
exercise that freedom to the peril of another man's soul is something else. No believer should exercise privilege without regard
to responsibility. "Destroy not him with thy meat for whom
Christ died" gets to the very heart of the matter.

The next thing Paul emphasizes is (2) *the priorities of our
liberty in Christ.* He begins by telling us to guard against *giving
a wrong impression* about the Christian life. *"Let not then your
good be evil spoken of"* (v. 16). If a person exercises his stronger
faith to the detriment of a weak brother and in a way which
prejudices the cause of Christ, then he gives a wrong impression
about the Christian life. He gives unbelievers grounds for speaking against the gospel. It is all too easy for liberty to degenerate
into carnality and worldliness. We do not want to lose our liberty

as Christians, but on the other hand we do not want to abuse
it either.

There is a story frequently told of C. H. Spurgeon that for years
he saw nothing wrong with smoking. To him smoking was no
sin. He could do it in all good conscience—until he found out that
a tobacco firm was advertising "the brand that Spurgeon smokes!"
He had given a wrong impression about the Christian life, and
from that day gave up the habit.

We must not only guard against giving a wrong impression
about the Christian life, we must guard against *getting a wrong
impression* about the Christian life. *"For the kingdom of God is
not meat and drink; but righteousness, and peace, and joy in the
Holy Ghost. For he that in these things serveth Christ is acceptable to God, and approved of men"* (vv. 17-18). The hot issues
of Paul's day (eating and drinking or not eating and drinking)
did not touch the *real* issues. Was it right to eat or wrong to eat?
The answer could be "yes" or "no." One said, "You can eat and
still be of the kingdom of God." Another said, "If you eat you
are not of the kingdom of God." Said Paul, "The kingdom of
God is not meat and drink." The real issues are far deeper than
that and are determined by a man's personal relationship to the
Holy Spirit—righteousness, peace and joy. When we are taken
up with trivial externals, we are in danger of getting a wrong
impression about the Christian life. The things that really matter
are not forms and ceremonies. What counts most is a union with
the Spirit of God so vital that it is expressed in a Christlike walk.
These are the true priorities of our liberty in Christ. Whether a
person eats fish on Fridays or abstains from tea and coffee will
not make him either a better or a worse Christian. Because the
kingdom of God is not concerned with such matters at all.

Finally, Paul emphasizes (3) *the practice of our liberty in
Christ.* The spirit of charity will see to it that *freedom* will be
properly *regulated.* *"Let us therefore follow after the things
which make for peace, and things whereby one may edify another. For meat destroy not the work of God. All things indeed
are pure; but it is evil for that man who eateth with offence. It
is good neither to eat flesh, nor to drink wine, nor any thing
whereby thy brother stumbleth, or is offended, or is made weak"*
(vv. 19-21). During the war, when vessels had to be convoyed

across the Atlantic because of the U-boat menace, all vessels had
to adjust their speed to that of the slowest. This is the idea Paul
is driving home here. Sure, the strong brother could stride ahead,
but love will not permit it. The shepherd must pace the flock
to accommodate the weakest lamb. The Christian must regulate
his freedom to take into consideration the feeble conscience of
the weakest. To do otherwise is to "loosen down" the work of
God and to endanger the spiritual well-being of the weak who,
indeed, should be the special concern of the strong.

In the practice of our liberty not only will freedom be properly
regulated but *faith* also will be properly *regarded*. "*Hast thou
faith? have it to thyself before God. Happy is he that condemneth
not himself in that thing which he alloweth. And he that doubteth
is damned [condemned] if he eat, because he eateth not of faith:
for whatsoever is not of faith is sin*" (vv. 22-23). Faith is not
to be displayed in such a way as to show off one's superiority to
those who have scruples about things. The man whom Paul calls
happy is the one who can eat and drink what he likes without
having any qualms of conscience about so doing. But how can
he be truly happy if the exercise of his liberty is causing a weaker
brother to stumble? Hence the man is doubly happy who not only
has an easy conscience as to what he permits in his life but who
also has an easy conscience knowing that he has truly been his
brother's keeper.

The spirit of charity would sum up Paul's argument thus far
in this way: in essentials, unity; in nonessentials, liberty; in all
things, charity.

B. *The Spirit of Christ* (15:1-7)

But Paul has not finished yet. He has even higher ground to
map out for us. It is a great thing to treat a weaker brother in
the spirit of charity. It is greater far to treat him in the spirit of
Christ. The spirit of Christ demands that we take (1) *the hard
road*. In fact, there are three things about this hard road which
are well worth considering. First, it is *the cross-demonstrating
road*. Says Paul, "*We then that are strong ought to bear the infirmities of the weak, and not to please ourselves. Let every one
of us please his neighbour for his good to edification*" (vv. 1-2).
Selfishness has no part in the Christian life. Paul is not arguing

here that we continually give in to a weak brother's desires. Rather, we are to act in a way which will be to his lasting benefit. We help him carry the cross of his weakness.

Then it is *the Christ-displaying road.* Paul reminds us that *"even Christ pleased not himself; but, as it is written, The reproaches of them that reproached thee fell on me"* (v. 3). The Lord Jesus lived to please God and serve and help men. He died not just for the strong, the steadfast and the scholarly but for the feeble and the faltering as well. He was always going out of His way to bear someone else's burden. He always went the second mile. It was the maimed and halt and blind, the palsied and the deaf who most obviously were the recipients of His grace. He was patient with Peter when he blundered; with James and John when they wanted to call down fire on Samaria; with Thomas when he doubted; and even with Judas when the blood money jingled in his purse. How paltry is any inconvenience we may suffer because of the weak brother in the church when compared with what Christ suffered. The spirit of Christ will make any such burden light.

Then too, it is the *character-developing road.* Paul has just finished quoting concerning Christ from Psalm 69. Now he wants to remind us that the entire volume of Old Testament Scripture is of permanent value and that it should be read and studied. It will point out the road for us, even if it is the hard road. *"For whatsoever things were written aforetime were written for our learning, that we through patience and comfort of the scriptures might have hope"* (v. 4). Do we find the road irksome, this character-developing road of shouldering the weaknesses of others? Are we apt to lose patience with the weak brother and his scruples? The antidote is in the Scriptures. We must get back into the Book and see how God helped others over the hard places and be comforted, for He has not changed. He will help us too.

The spirit of Christ demands that we take not only the hard road but, as it turns out to be, (2) *the high road* too. Paul points out three things about the high road. It leads to *respect* for other believers and consequently to *harmony* in the local church. He says, *"Now the God of patience and consolation grant you to be*

like-minded one toward another according to Christ Jesus" (v. 5).
What a name for God—the God of patience! How patient He has
been with us. As Peter puts it, He is "longsuffering to usward"
(II Peter 3:9). The qualities which make for harmony in the
local fellowship of believers are to be found in God Himself.
If each believer were to get to know the God of patience and of
comfort there would be no strife over nonessentials. The spirit
of Christ would prevail.

The high road leads to *rejoicing* with other believers and consequently to *happiness* in the local church. Paul says, "*That ye may
with one mind and one mouth glorify God, even the Father of
our Lord Jesus Christ*" (v. 6). If the saints would concentrate
on glorifying God, there would be no room for discord or for
criticism.

Then too, the high road leads to the *reception* of other believers
and consequently to true spiritual *hospitality* in the local church.
Paul says, "*Wherefore receive ye one another, as Christ also received us to the glory of God*" (v. 7). So then, the argument
has come around a complete circle. Paul began by telling us that
God has received the weak brother (14:3). He finishes by reminding us that Christ has received us. With all our own foibles
and failures; with all our own weaknesses and wickednesses; with
all our own lack of loveliness, defects of character and spiritual
infirmities, He has received us. How can we close the doors of
fellowship to someone else who is genuinely saved but who has
different problems? The spirit of Christ demands that we extend
to all believers the hospitality of the Lord's Table and the warmth
of the local fellowship.

Let us beware of the spirit of Diotrephes who, as John said,
"loveth to have the preeminence." This man became so inflated
with his own importance that he prated against the aged apostle
with malicious words; "and not content therewith, neither doth
he himself receive the brethren, and forbiddeth them that would,
and casteth them out of the church" (III John 10). What a dog-in-
the-manger attitude! What a reputation to be recorded for time
and eternity in the Book of God! This man would not even receive the Apostle John!

LOVE'S MATURE CONVICTIONS
15:8-13

I. How Christ's Ministry Is Presented to Us (15:8-9a)

A. The Distinctly Jewish Aspect (15:8)

B. The Definitely Gentile Aspect (15:9a)

II. How Christ's Ministry Was Predicted for Us (15:9b-12)

A. The Gentiles Would Be Gladdened by Him (15:9b-11)

B. The Gentiles Will Be Governed by Him (15:12)

III. How Christ's Ministry Is Preserved in Us (15:13)

A. There Is Nothing Hopeless About the Christian Life—We Have Blessed Assurance (15:13a)

B. There Is Nothing Helpless About the Christian Life—We Have Boundless Assistance (15:13b)

It is one thing to give way to the weaker brother on nonessential matters. It is something else to give way when vital issues of faith or morals are involved. Paul was the most conciliatory of men on nonessentials. He was willing to be made all things to all men if the cause of Christ could be furthered (I Cor. 9:20-23). But when it came to a basic issue of fundamental truth, he was adamant. He reminded the Galatians, for example, how that on one of his trips to Jerusalem he had come into conflict with the Judaizing party in the church. "False brethren" he called them, "who came in privily to spy out our liberty which we have in Christ Jesus, that they might bring us into bondage: to whom we gave place by subjection, no, not for an hour; that the truth of the gospel might continue with you" (Gal. 2:4-5). Moreover, when Peter tried to accommodate himself at Antioch, first with one party and then with the other, and that on an issue vital to the faith, Paul "withstood him to the face" (Gal. 2:11-14). Love must manifest its merciful conduct to the weak, but it must also have its mature convictions. It is no part of love's office to compromise vital truth.

So then, Paul next turns his attention in this letter to the question of vital issues, truth which must be held in love but which must at all costs be held. The issue he selects as his example is that of the place of the Gentiles in the church. It was a touchy

enough issue in the early church and one about which Paul held
some very strong convictions. It was relevant to his purpose too
because of the question of reception which has just been discussed and also because he was writing to the capital of the
Gentile world.

In the beginning, the church was entirely Jewish. The conversion of Cornelius (Acts 10) gave the Jewish believers the first
practical intimation that Christianity was not merely a Jewish
sect but something distinctly different. Soon Gentiles began to
be converted in great numbers and before long the center of
gravity moved away from Jerusalem; first to Antioch, and then
to Ephesus, Corinth and Rome. Heated indeed were the debates
in the early days of the church about the reception of Gentiles.
Some thought that Gentiles must become Jewish proselytes before
they could be admitted properly to the church's fellowship. They
wanted to impose on them the burden of the law of Moses with
its intolerable weight of rules and regulations. They demanded
that Gentiles be circumcised, that they keep the Sabbath, that
they embrace all the commandments and customs associated with
Judaism. Others were a little more lenient but still thought that
Christianity was merely an extension of Judaism and believed
that Gentile converts should acknowledge their debt to Judaism
in some way.

Paul was by far the clearest thinker on this issue in the early
church. He would have nothing to do with the notion that Christianity and Judaism were different forms of the same faith. He
could clearly see that the two systems were mutually exclusive.
He saw it even before his conversion. That was why he had
persecuted the church. True, Christians worshiped the same God
as the Jews and turned to the same Scriptures. But there the likeness ended. The cross of Christ was the watershed, the parting of
the ways between the two systems. Judaism was a religion of a
rent veil, and to try to patch up that veil and then stitch Christianity onto it was not only wrong but useless and fatal. Christianity was a new piece of cloth altogether. Jews and Gentiles
who were converted to Christ became members of the church, a
new entity entirely in God's dealings with men. Paul was so completely emancipated from Judaism that, far from wanting Gentiles
to adopt the customs and traditions of his Jewish brethren, he

wished his Jewish brethren could break away from "the beggarly elements" which so sadly hampered and hindered them. He fought tooth and nail for the principle that Gentiles be accepted into the fellowship of the church simply on the basis of their faith in Christ and with no Jewish strings attached.

With Paul, these were love's mature convictions. To unite Jew and Gentile in a new fellowship was part of the ministry of the Lord Jesus and one He had anticipated with evident satisfaction, even before He went to Calvary (John 12:20-24). The bringing in of the Gentile world was the topic of His conversation just prior to His ascension (Luke 24:46-47); and the last recorded words which fell from His lips before the cloud hid Him were, "the uttermost part of the earth" (Acts 1:8). Moreover, the first recorded words of Jesus after His ascension had to do with bringing the Gentiles into the fellowship of the church (Acts 9:6-15), and so were the second (Acts 10:13-14). It is almost as if the Lord Jesus Himself wanted to add His own voice to the urging of the Holy Spirit to speed the infant church on its mission to the Gentile world. So Paul introduces the subject of Gentiles in the church to support his argument that love's mature convictions cannot be compromised for the sake of peace.

I. How CHRIST'S MINISTRY Is PRESENTED TO Us (15:8-9a)

The ministry of the Lord Jesus to the world was twofold. It was "to the lost sheep of the house of Israel" and it was also to those "other sheep" who were "not of this fold." Paul keeps both these ministries very much in mind.

A. *The Distinctly Jewish Aspect of Christ's Ministry* (15:8)

First and foremost the Lord Jesus "came unto his own," and although "his own received him not" the fact remains unaltered (John 1:11). Paul says, *"Now I say that Jesus Christ was a minister of the circumcision for the truth of God, to confirm the promises made unto the fathers"* (v. 8). Elsewhere in this gospel Paul has underlined the fact that God's dealings are with " the Jew first" (Rom. 2:9-10). Alford points out that Christ is called "the minister of the circumcision" nowhere else in the Bible and suggests that Paul used the expression here "to humble the pride of the *strong*, the Gentile Christians, by exalting God's covenant

people to their true dignity."[1] Be that as it may, the Lord's first
concern was for "the lost sheep of the house of Israel" (Matt.
15:24). He came to fulfill the covenant promises made to the
founding fathers of Israel. He came to Israel because God had
pledged Himself by many great and exceeding precious promises
to send the Redeemer to them.

B. *The Definitely Gentile Aspect of Christ's Ministry* (15:9a)

While the Jews were honored by Christ's coming first to them,
they by no means had a monopoly on His ministry. Paul says
that the Lord Jesus also came *"that the Gentiles might glorify
God for his mercy."* While many Old Testament passages fore-
tell the blessings which would come upon the Gentiles through
Christ, it is also true that God entered into no formal contracts
with the Gentiles as He did with the Jews. His dealings with
the Gentiles therefore are an especial expression of His mercy.
The fact that Gentiles now outnumber Jews in the church by
countless millions shows how glorious is the Gentile aspect of
Christ's ministry, how great is God's mercy toward us and how
much He deserves to be glorified by the Gentiles for His grace.
The bearing that all this has on the question of reception is clear.
God has received both Jews and Gentiles without distinction. The
ministry of Christ is the guarantee of that.

II. HOW CHRIST'S MINISTRY WAS PREDICTED FOR US (15:9b-12)

The bringing of the Gentiles into the place of blessing was the
subject of much Old Testament prophecy. Paul selects several
passages to support his argument.

A. *The Gentiles Would Be Gladdened by Christ* (15:9b-11)

Three Scriptures prove his point. He quotes from Psalm 18:49;
Deuteronomy 32:43; Psalm 117:1. Later he quotes from Isaiah
also, thus appealing to the Law, the Prophets, and the Psalms, or
from the three great divisions of the Hebrew Bible.

*"For this cause I will confess to thee among the Gentiles, and
sing unto thy name. And again he saith, Rejoice, ye Gentiles, with
his people. And again, Praise the Lord, all ye Gentiles; and laud*

[1]Henry Alford, *The New Testament for English Readers* (Chicago: Moody
Press, n.d.), pp. 964-965.

him all ye people" (vv. 9*b*-11). In the first quotation, the Lord Himself gives praise to God among the Gentiles; in the second, the Gentiles praise God in harmony with the Jews; and in the third, the Gentiles praise Him without any direct connection with Israel (the expression "all ye people" should read, "all ye peoples").

B. *The Gentiles Will Be Governed by Christ* (15:12)

Having embraced this age of grace, Paul next looks forward to the distant future, to the millennium. *"And again, Esaias saith, There shall be a root of Jesse, and he that shall rise to reign over the Gentiles; and in him shall the Gentiles trust"* (v. 12). It is not only now, during the period when Israel as a nation is set aside, that Christ receives the Gentiles. Even during the coming golden age when Israel will come into its own, the Gentiles will be blessed in Christ. Thus, in his selection of quotations, Paul shows from all parts of the Jewish Bible that the Gentiles are accepted through Christ. This adds weight to love's mature convictions. They are not founded on bias or personal opinion but on the eternal Word of God. Such a truth as the reception of the Gentiles is not to be abandoned at the whim of any brother, weak or strong.

III. HOW CHRIST'S MINISTRY IS PRESERVED IN US (15:13)

Paul has proved his point. He has upheld the rights of the strong and of the weak brother. He has shown that the stronger should give way to the weaker when it comes to nonessentials. The laws of Christian love demand that love express itself in merciful conduct to the weak. But at the same time, those selfsame laws demand that vital truth be held unwaveringly. Mature convictions must be held in love but they must be held.

Paul concludes this whole section by praying that Jew and Gentile in Christ will get along despite differences. It is the Holy Spirit who makes operative in the heart of the individual the ministry of the Lord Jesus. *"Now the God of hope fill you with all joy and peace in believing, that ye may abound in hope"* (13*a*). In other words, (1) there is *nothing hopeless* about the Christian life. We have *blessed assurance.* Joy! Peace! Hope! What mighty cords these are to bind believer to believer in love, mutual understanding and consideration. *"Through the power of the Holy*

Ghost" (13*b*). In other words, (2) there is *nothing helpless* about the Christian life. We have *boundless assistance.*

The way to happiness and harmony in the assembly of God's people is not easy. People are different. They are saved from a multitude of backgrounds—racial and religious, social and educational. It is inevitable that people of different ages and temperaments, abilities and drives, concepts and natures should have trouble adjusting one to another within the fellowship of a local church. But it can be done. It cannot be done by nature, but it can be done through grace. The things that unite us are far stronger than the things that divide us. We are united in Christ by a common *birth,* by precious *blood,* and by one *belief.* "There is one body, and one Spirit, even as ye are called in one hope of your calling; one Lord, one faith, one baptism, one God and Father of all, who is above all, and through all, and in you all. But unto every one of us is given grace according to the measure of the gift of Christ" (Eph. 4:4-7). It is this that makes it possible for us to "keep the unity of the Spirit in the bond of peace" (Eph. 4:3).

When there was strife between the herdsmen of Abram's cattle and the herdsmen of Lot's cattle, Abram's plea to Lot was, "We be brethren" (Gen. 13:8). That was what bound them. The petty things which divided them were scarcely worth a thought. At least, that was Abraham's conviction, and one which he was prepared to carry through with remarkable selflessness and thoroughness.

The story is told of two men aboard an ocean liner. The one was black and the other white. Both were Christians, both felt themselves to be "strangers and pilgrims" amid the gaiety and social frivolity of the voyage. The two men had not met; but one day each was pacing the deck of the ship wrapped in his own thoughts, each with a Bible under his arm. Then they came face to face. They smiled, shook hands, pointed to their Bibles, and tried to exchange a few words. But the barrier of Babel stood between them; they could not speak each other's tongue. Then the white man had an idea. "Hallelujah!" he exclaimed. The black man smiled, and at once replied, "Amen!" Well might we sing:

> Blest be the tie that binds
> Our hearts in Christian love,
> The fellowship of kindred minds
> Is like to that above.

LOVE'S MISSIONARY CONCERN
15:14-33

I. What Paul Commends About His Brethren (15:14)

    A. Their Goodness of Life

    B. Their Grasp of Truth .

    C. Their Gifts of Exhortation

II. What Paul Communicates to His Brethren (15:15-29)

    A. His Underlying Viewpoint of Missions (15:15-21)

        1. The Responsibility for What Has Been Accorded to Him (15:15-16)

        2. The Reality of What Has Been Accomplished Through Him (15:17-21)

            a. He realizes the undeniable limits of his ministry (15:17-18)

            b. He relates the underlying logic of his ministry (15:19-21)

                (1) A complete dependence on God (15:19)

                (2) A clear definition of goals (15:20-21)

    B. His Undying Vision of Missions (15:22-29)

        1. His Desire to See Rome (15:22-23)

        2. His Determination to See Rome (15:24-29)

            a. Where this trip fits into his plans (15:24)

            b. When this trip fits into his plans (15:25-28)

                (1) The prior trip eastward (15:25-27)

                (2) The proposed trip westward (15:28)

             c. Why this trip fits into his plans (15:29)

III. What Paul Commits to His Brethren (15:30-33)

    A. A Share in the Battle (15:30-32)

        1. They Are to Pray Intentionally (15:30)

        2. They Are to Pray Intelligently (15:31-32)

    B. A Share in the Blessing (15:33)

THE LAST TWO CHAPTERS in Romans are of a personal nature yet full of instruction for all that. Chapter 15 contains one of the great missionary passages of the Bible. Here Paul lays bare some of the basic strategy which made him the greatest of all missionaries.

I. WHAT PAUL COMMENDS ABOUT HIS BRETHREN (15:14)

Paul never lost sight of the fact that the church at Rome was not founded by him; so before he plunges into an account of his own missionary philosophy, he tactfully congratulates his brethren at Rome on their own accomplishments.

A. *Their Goodness of Life* (15:14)

To be a good man is to be the very best kind of man that can be. Paul has already reminded the Romans that "for a good man some would even dare to die" (5:7), and now he says, *"And I myself am persuaded of you, my brethren, that ye also are full of goodness"* (v. 14a). What a commendation! This was no mere theoretical goodness either; no goodness merely of abstaining from evil. This was practical goodness manifested in helpfulness to others, in bearing the burdens of the weaker brother.

B. *Their Grasp of Truth* (15:14)

The Roman Christians were diligent students. Paul says that they were *"filled with all knowledge"* (v. 14b) and uses a word signifying knowledge gained by learning, effort or experience. We are not told how they acquired their knowledge of New Testament truth. No doubt Paul's epistle would add to what they already knew, and put into concrete and permanent form some of the truths already imparted by inspired utterance. Perhaps Priscilla and Aquila had taught them "the way of God more perfectly" as once they had Apollos (Acts 18:26; Rom. 16:3). Certainly Rome was strategically placed for the church there to be well informed as to what "the apostles' doctrine" was, both as taught at Jerusalem (Acts 2:10, 42) and in the major Gentile centers of Christianity. Paul commends their grasp of truth. Just as the Roman church made itself familiar with the great doctrines of the faith, so all Christians need to master apostolic truth.

C. *Their Gifts of Exhortation* (15:14)

The church at Rome contained a number of gifted and well-qualified brethren eminently equipped to stir up the saints to their responsibilities. Paul acknowledges that they were *"able also to admonish one another"* (v. 14c). The tendency to settle down is natural and must be fought continually. That is why the ministry of exhortation and admonishment is vital to virile Christianity.

There is a species of jellyfish which lives on a rock from which it never stirs. It feeds on a kind of seaweed which grows in the decayed tissues of its own organism. Hence, the jellyfish does not even have to go in search of food. It has arrived at the ultimate in creature comfort. But this jellyfish is one of the very lowest forms of animal life, the extreme comfort it enjoys being the badge of its degraded position. The Christian must not settle down to a comfortable life. The Christian life is a race to be run, a battle to be fought. It calls for discipline, drive and determination. Hence, the need for exhortation.

II. WHAT PAUL COMMUNICATES TO HIS BRETHREN (15:15-29)

Now Paul has a word of explanation about his missionary philosophy for his fellow believers at Rome. Few if any can speak with such authority about world missions as Paul. The verses that follow get to the very heart of global evangelism.

A. *Paul's Underlying Viewpoint of Missions* (15:15-21)

He begins by explaining his own responsibility before the Lord. He speaks of (1) *the responsibility for what has been accorded to him.* This is the first and foremost aspect of any missionary philosophy—personal accountability for one's own gifts, sphere of influence and opportunities. *"Nevertheless, brethren, I have written the more boldly unto you in some sort, as putting you in mind, because of the grace that is given to me of God, that I should be the minister of Jesus Christ to the Gentiles, ministering the gospel of God, that the offering up of the Gentiles might be acceptable, being sanctified by the Holy Ghost"* (vv. 15-16).

Paul was called to minister to the Gentiles and he regarded his ministry in a most remarkable light. He viewed himself as a spiritual priest to the Gentiles. As God had laid Israel on the heart of Moses, so He had laid the Gentiles on the heart of Paul; he was, so to speak, their "priest." His great function was not to offer up sacrifices for the Gentiles; that had already been done at Calvary. Nor did he regard himself a priest in the Old Testament sense, but rather in a highly figurative sense. The sacrifice he offered as a priest was the Gentiles themselves, and that sacrifice was acceptable to God because it was sanctified and made holy by the Holy Spirit. This is a most exalted view of the responsibility which had been accorded to him. God had called him and he had obeyed. He had dedicated himself wholeheartedly to the task before him. His greatest joy was to see Gentiles saved and then "offered up" as a living sacrifice to God. What a challenge to regard any work to which we have been called of God as a "liturgy," a priestly service, to be discharged until the fragrance of the sacrifice ascends to God.

Paul next speaks of (2) *the reality of what had been accomplished through him.* Paul was not a boastful man. In fact, he could say, "God forbid that I should glory, save in the cross of our Lord Jesus Christ" (Gal. 6:14). On the other hand, he was not afflicted with a self-depreciating false modesty. He speaks freely and frankly about what has been wrought through his missionary zeal.

He realized that there were *undeniable limits* to his ministry. He says, *"I have therefore whereof I may glory through Jesus Christ in those things which pertain to God. For I will not dare to speak of any of those things which Christ hath not wrought by me, to make the Gentiles obedient, by word and deed"* (vv. 17-18). Paul's glorying was not in self but in the Lord. He had much about which he could speak. A long trail of converts and churches marked the lines of his ministry. Telling the story to the glory of God of what God had wrought through him would keep him busy enough. He had no need nor desire to trespass on other people's labors in order to pad out his report or to make it more interesting and impressive. He knew others were working among the Gentiles besides himself. Let them tell their own story; he would tell his. He would recount only what God had been pleased to accomplish through him, realizing at the same time that his was only a part of the story of world evangelism then going forward. Missionaries telling of their work should emulate Paul in this.

He next explains the *underlying logic* of his ministry—a complete dependence on God and a clear definition of goals. *"Through mighty signs and wonders, by the power of the Spirit of God; so that from Jerusalem, and round about unto Illyricum, I have fully preached the gospel of Christ"* (v. 19). His complete dependence on God resulted in spiritual power. Everywhere Paul went he saw results. Even at Athens where they scoffed at his message there were some saved. His preaching was clothed with such irresistible authority, such demonstrations of the Spirit, such miracle-working power that souls were saved in countless numbers. There were hindrances and obstacles. His enemies stirred up opposition. There were times when he was depressed and in doubt. But with it all, there was victory and revival.

Coupled with his dependence on God was a clear understanding of what his objectives should be as a missionary. *"Yea, so have I strived to preach the gospel, not where Christ was named, lest I should build upon another man's foundation: but as it is written, To whom he was not spoken of, they shall see: and they that have not heard shall understand"* (vv. 20-21). His clear definition of goals resulted in specific plans. Paul knew exactly what his basic objective was—the unreached! Why go and poach on someone else's field of labor? The field is vast; it is the world; it is the regions beyond. He was obsessed by the vision he had of the "untold millions still untold." It was that which governed his missionary planning. The text he quotes here from Isaiah 52:15 had become his missionary motto, his driving force.

B. *Paul's Undying Vision of Missions* (15:22-29)

Paul never rested on his oars, never sat back to rest. Time was too short, the task too great, the laborers too few, the issues too grave. To his underlying viewpoint he added undying vision. He saw a lost world, a world which in his day was focused on Rome. And although it was no part of his plan to reside at Rome, it was part of his plan to reach Rome. In explaining the how and the why of this, he gives us a glimpse of his ever-expanding vision of unreached nations.

He speaks of (1) *his desire to see Rome*. He has mentioned this already in his introduction to the epistle, but he comes back to it again. *"For which cause also I have been much hindered from coming to you*" (v. 22). So far he has been too busy in reaching the unreached to fit a visit to Rome into his plans. He has put Rome on his itinerary again and again only to have it blocked out by more pressing interests. For while Paul planned with care, he never became a slave to his plans and always allowed the Holy Spirit to set them aside for better ones.[1]

Thus it was with his plans to visit Rome. Again and again the Holy Spirit postponed those plans until His time was ripe and then He sent Paul there, not as a pioneer but as a prisoner that God might be glorified in his chains and so that Paul, the undaunted, might be a challenge to saved and sinner alike. "*But now*," he says, "*having no more place in these parts, and having a great desire these many years to come unto you . . .*" (v. 23). At last the coast seemed clear and Rome could again be placed on his itinerary, not at the top indeed, but on it nevertheless.

Next he speaks of (2) *his determination to see Rome.* He explains three things about this determination. First, *where* it fits into his plans. "*Whensoever I take my journey into Spain, I will come to you: for I trust to see you in my journey, and to be brought on my way thitherward by you, if first I be somewhat filled with your company*" (v. 24). The pillars of Hercules beckoned to Paul, the westernmost reaches of mainland Europe. He must see Rome, but he must see Spain even more, and Rome could be a convenient posting house on his way. The fact that there were many Jews in Spain probably added incentive to Paul's plans. He would not be able to stay in Rome too long, but at least he would be able to have some fellowship with the believers there.

[1]The book of Acts gives several outstanding examples of this combination of strategic planning and divine leading in Paul's ventures. Take, for example, Paul's original plan to go through Asia, and perhaps on to Ephesus after visiting the churches of Galatia on his second missionary journey. However, under a strange restraint and compulsion of the Holy Spirit ("forbidden of the Holy Spirit to speak the word in Asia," Acts 16:6) he journeyed on until he came to Troas where he received his "Macedonian call" into Europe. Ephesus had looked so obvious a place on the map, strategic, important and vital. Paul's plan was only postponed by the Holy Spirit, not cancelled altogether. Before evangelizing Ephesus, he was directed across the Aegean to Europe where he planted churches in such important centers as Philippi, Thessalonica and Corinth. Then the Spirit directed him back to Ephesus. Thus a circle was drawn around Ephesus and strategic points on that circle evangelized first—Macedonia, Greece, South Galatia. Finally Paul completed his work in that whole area by evangelizing Ephesus at the center. The leading of the Spirit did not spoil Paul's original plans but improved them. (See F. F. Bruce, *Commentary on the Book of Acts* [Grand Rapids: Wm. B. Eerdmans Publishing Co., 1954], p. 328).

Paul then tells *when* this fits into his plans. He has a prior trip eastward before the proposed trip westward. *"But now I go unto Jerusalem to minister unto the saints. For it hath pleased them of Macedonia and Achaia to make a certain contribution for the poor saints which are at Jerusalem. It hath pleased them verily; and their debtors they are. For if the Gentiles have been made partakers of their spiritual things, their duty is also to minister unto them in carnal things. When therefore I have performed this, and have sealed to them this fruit, I will come by you into Spain"* (vv. 25-28). Paul's missionary philosophy of giving was strangely different from what has been current in the church in modern times. The thought underlying the modern missionary movement has been that home churches should send money to the mission field to support infant churches in foreign lands. Paul put things the other way around! The new churches in Gentile lands ought to recognize their spiritual debt to the saints who sent them the gospel and send money to them to relieve *their* poor!

Soon after writing this Roman epistle, Paul left Corinth and took with him a delegation from the various churches he had been visiting which were joining in a gift to relieve the poverty of the Jerusalem Christians.[2] The churches of Macedonia were represented by Sopater, Aristarchus and Secundus; those of Galatia by Gaius of Derbe and Timothy of Lystra; and those of Asia Minor by Tychicus and Trophimus. This party of Gentile Christians was probably already gathering as Paul drew his letter to a close. Soon he would be on his way to Jerusalem to partake in the Passover festivities and then—on to Spain via Rome, or so he planned!

Finally Paul tells *why* the trip to Rome fits into his plans. *"And I am sure that, when I come unto you, I shall come in the fulness of the blessing of the gospel of Christ"* (v. 29). What assurance of victory and of being in the will of God! His great goal was to pour himself into the life and fellowship and testimony of the

___

[2]Paul, of course, had a special concern for the poor saints in the Jerusalem church. Many had been made poor by him when in his unconverted days he had so vigorously persecuted that church. There were widows in the Jerusalem fellowship with whom Paul had to sit down and break bread when he was in their city, widows whose husbands had been slain through him. There were brethren in that church who could hardly lift their heads for very shame because once they had blasphemed Christ—through the activities of Saul of Tarsus. Paul left no stone unturned to do what he could to repay that fearful debt.

Roman church in all the power of the filling and anointing of the
Spirit that was his.

So then, Paul communicates to the church at Rome his underlying viewpoint of missions and his undying vision of missions.
To evangelize the lost, to pioneer new fields, to plan strategically,
to know the Spirit's leading, to be independent of the financial
support of a home church, and, on the contrary, to teach his converts the joy of giving and, above all, to be a constant source of
blessing—these were the things that comprised the missionary
philosophy of Paul. No wonder he turned the world upside down!

III. WHAT PAUL COMMITS TO HIS BRETHREN (15:30-33)

Before closing, Paul wanted to show the brethren in Rome how
they could become partners with him in the great task of evangelizing the world for Christ. They could have a double share in
the work.

A. *A Share in the Battle* (15:30-32)

It is part of the genius of Christianity that any believer can become a warrior in the battle at any time and in any place and
make his influence count to the ends of the earth and high in
heavenly places, simply by engaging in prayer. By praying for
missionaries a believer can place himself in a canoe in the Ama-
zon, in an igloo in the Arctic, in a tent in the Sahara, in a sub-
marine at the bottom of the ocean, in a plane high in the strato-
sphere. He can ward off from the missionary dangers in the
jungle, diseases in the city slum, disasters on the deep. He can
arm the missionary's witness with supernatural power, lift him
from the slough of despond, route the unseen foes that lurk in the
spirit world and strengthen his hand in God. By praying in the
Spirit, the exercised believer can conquer time and space and have
a share in the battle.

Paul suggested to his friends in Rome that they (1) pray *intentionally* for him. *"Now I beseech you, brethren, for the Lord
Jesus Christ's sake, and for the love of the Spirit, that ye strive
together with me in your prayers to God for me"* (v. 30). He
wanted them to definitely and deliberately add him to their prayer
lists and make it a special point to pray for him. Missionaries constantly urge people to pray for them. They know perfectly well

that, for some mysterious reason not fully explained, God is pleased to act in answer to prayer. It is one of the laws of the universe, as fundamental as the laws of gravity and electricity. Paul's request that the Christians pray intentionally for him is practical, for by its very nature prayer has to be a deliberate exercise of the soul. It is not something we tend to do naturally.

Then Paul asked the Romans to (2) pray *intelligently* for him. *"That I may be delivered from them that do not believe in Judea; and that my service which I have for Jerusalem may be accepted of the saints; that I may come unto you with joy by the will of God, and may with you be refreshed"* (vv. 31-32). Paul believed in being specific in prayer. He had three requests he wanted his fellow soldiers to take with them to the throne of grace on his behalf. Each is introduced by the word "that." He wanted them to pray intelligently concerning his safety, his service, and his steps.

It is evident that Paul was aware of the dangers which awaited him at Jerusalem. The unbelieving Jews were thirsting for his blood and he knew it. The believing Jews were cool toward his views on the relationship between Judaism and Christianity and he could not be sure how even they would receive him. He did not want the dangers at Jerusalem to spoil his plans for coming to Rome. We know from the book of Acts how God allowed the perils to mount until finally Paul was arrested at Jerusalem. His forebodings had been well-founded. But then God overruled and used that very captivity as a means for bringing Paul to Rome as "an ambassador in bonds." Thus, all these prayer requests were answered, perhaps not in the way Paul had expected, but answered just the same. It must have been a source of satisfaction to those in the Roman church when finally they went out to meet Paul on the Appian Way (Acts 28:14-15) to know that their prayers for Paul's safety, his service, and his steps had all been answered by God.

B. *A Share in the Blessings* (15:33)

Those who share the battles shall share the blessings. Paul closed the epistle proper with the words, *"Now the God of peace be with you all. Amen"* (v. 33). He breathed his blessing on the church. He was setting his face steadfastly to go to Jerusalem.

He was facing danger, battle, hatred and arrest. He could face
the journey calmly, unruffled, in perfect peace because he knew
"the God of peace." This, perhaps the greatest of all blessings, a
sense of calm in times of storm, Paul bequeathed on the saints of
Rome.

> Peace! perfect peace! Our future all unknown?
> Jesus we know, and He is on the throne.

LOVE'S MANY CONTACTS
16:1-16

I. How Paul Solicits His Brethren at Rome (16:1-2)
   A. They Are to Accept Phebe (16:1-2a)
   B. They Are to Assist Phebe (16:2b)

II. How Paul Salutes His Brethren at Rome (16:3-16)
   A. With Love's Distinctiveness (16:3-15)
       1. Priscilla and Aquila
       2. Epaenetus
       3. Mary
       4. Andronicus and Junia
       5. Amplias
       6. Urbane
       7. Stachys
       8. Apelles
       9. Aristobulus' household
      10. Herodion
      11. Narcissus' household
      12. Tryphena and Tryphosa
      13. Persis
      14. Rufus and his mother
      15. Asyncritus
      16. Phlegon
      17. Hermas
      18. Patrobas
      19. Hermes and the brethren with them
      20. Philologus
      21. Julia
      22. Nereus and his sister
      23. Olympas and the saints with them
   B. With Love's Demonstrativeness (16:16)

PAUL WAS A MAN with many friends. His great heart embraced all the people of God, and his love for them provoked him to take a keen interest in them. Every contact was a potential friend and Paul had many contacts. Somehow, in a day and age which knew nothing of modern communications, Paul was able to keep in touch with the church universal. It would not be hard to imagine Paul in Corinth haunting the harbor at Cenchrea and accosting mariners from all parts of the Roman world. "Where are you from, sailor? Rome? Do you by any chance know a sail maker by the name of Aquila?" It is easy to picture Paul cross-questioning merchants from the east as they pass through Corinth. "You've just come from Ephesus? Were you at Antioch in Syria? Antioch in Pisidia? Troas?" And never a Christian could enter Corinth but that Paul would pounce on him for at least a quick report on the church at Philippi, at Berea, at Thessalonica, at Jerusalem, Alexandria or Samaria.

So Paul, with his heart full of love for the people of God, had many contacts. He was able to keep himself informed of the state of the church in Rome. He knew many of the leading Christians by name. They were all down in his prayer book, and now he checks them off one by one as he draws his letter to a close.

I. How Paul Solicits His Brethren at Rome (16:1-2)

First he has to commend to the church at Rome a sister from the church at Cenchrea, the port of Corinth, who is planning a trip to the capital.

A. *They Are to Accept Phebe* (16:1)

It was a wise custom in the early church, and one still widely practiced today, to furnish believers leaving one locality for another with letters of commendation to the church in the new vicinity (II Cor. 3:1). It insured for the traveler a friendly reception in the strange city and helped the church there in its reception of believers from other places. *"I commend unto you Phebe our sister, which is the servant of the church which is at Cenchrea: that ye receive her in the Lord, as becometh saints"* (vv. 1-2a). Nothing else is known of Phebe beyond the fact that Paul calls her a "succourer of many" (v. 2), implying perhaps

that she made it her ministry for the Lord to be helpful especially
to strangers in Cenchrea and Corinth. Her name, however, is
immortalized by her faithful service to the apostle, to the church
at Rome, and to the ages from then till now in carrying this epistle
to Rome.

B. *They Are to Assist Phebe* (16:2)

It is a great ministry of local Christians to put themselves and
their service at the disposal of visiting saints from other parts of
the world. Those who have traveled extensively know what a
blessing it is to be in the fellowship of the church and find helpful
brothers and sisters in all parts of the world. *"Assist her in whatsoever business she hath need of you,"* writes Paul, *"for she hath
been a succourer of many, and of myself also"* (v. 2*b*). The word
for "assist" means "to stand by" and is used by Paul when he says
that the Lord Jesus stood by him at his trial before Nero (II Tim.
4:17). The world knows nothing of the fellowship, friendship and
helpfulness which is to be found within the family of faith. No
lodge or club on earth can begin to provide for its members such
a bond of helpfulness as exists between truly saved believers.

II. HOW PAUL SALUTES HIS BRETHREN AT ROME (16:3-16)

Thirty-five persons are named in these concluding sections of
Romans. Nine were with Paul in Corinth when he wrote; eight
men and one woman. Twenty-four were at Rome; seventeen of
them men and seven of them women, all affectionately greeted by
Paul. In addition there are two households in Rome that are mentioned, as well as some unnamed brethren. There are also two unnamed women. It is a notable list. There is something strangely
attractive about it and about these shadowy names which appear
for a flash upon the page of Scripture and then are gone back into
the black night of obscurity. They flare up before our gaze like
bursts of flame and then burn down to a little handful of white
ashes. And there they are, names forever immortalized by the pen
of Paul, names that represent people who lived and loved long,
long ago and who live forever in the power of an endless life.
There they are, people dear to the heart of Paul, carrying the
gospel banner high in the world's capital and one by one sum-

moned into the spotlight to be tenderly, lovingly mentioned and greeted by Paul.

A. *He Salutes Them With Love's Distinctiveness* (16:3-15)

He doesn't lump them all together and say, "Greetings to all the saints at Rome." Love delights to single out its objects and recall them one by one. Love particularizes. "He calleth his own sheep by name," said the good Shepherd describing His intimate knowledge of each one (John 10:3). Just so Paul, the great under-shepherd, shows here what a true pastor-heart he had.

There were *Priscilla* and *Aquila*. Here, in Acts 18:18 and in II Timothy 4:19 the wife's name comes first, intimating perhaps that she was the dominant of the two when it came to spiritual things. Aquila was a Jew, a native of Pontus and a tentmaker by trade. Paul first met this couple on his second missionary journey. At that time they were plying their profession at Corinth. He lived with them for awhile, being of the same trade, and quite possibly led them to the Lord. When Paul left Corinth they accompanied him to Ephesus and did the spadework for the gospel in that city so that when Paul arrived back there a little later, it was ripe for revival. While awaiting Paul's return, they were able to instruct another gifted evangelist, Apollos, in "the way of God more perfectly." Now they were in Rome, and their home was once more a center of evangelism. Some years later they appear to have returned to Ephesus, for Paul greets them as being there during his second imprisonment, just prior to his martyrdom. (See Acts 18; I Cor. 16:19; II Tim. 4:19.) Here he says to the Roman church, "*Greet Priscilla and Aquila my helpers in Christ Jesus: who have for my life laid down their own necks: unto whom not only I give thanks, but also all the churches of the Gentiles. Likewise greet the church that is in their house*" (vv. 3-5). When they jeopardized their own lives for Paul's sake is not known; but since the news had evidently spread abroad among all the Gentile churches, some time must have elapsed.

The practice of holding Christian assemblies in private homes is illustrated in a passage from the Acts of the Martyrdom of St. Justin. "The answer of Justyn Martyr to the question of the prefect (Rusticus), 'Where do you assemble?' exactly corresponds to the genuine Christian spirit on this point. The answer was, 'Where each one can and will. You believe, no doubt, that we all meet together in one place; but it is not so, for the God of the Christians is not shut up in a room, but, being invisible, He fills both heaven and earth and is honored every where by the faithful."[1]

Next in Paul's list comes *Epaenetus*. "*Salute my well-beloved Epaenetus, who is the firstfruits of Achaia unto Christ*" (v. 5). The American Standard Version reads "Asia" instead of "Achaia." That this man should be the first of Paul's converts in Asia would make him especially dear to the apostle. Paul had seen a great revival in proconsular Asia, particularly at Ephesus. The fires had spread to Smyrna, Pergamos, Thyatira, Sardis, Philadelphia, Laodicea, Colossae, Hierapolis and other cities. But he never forgot his first convert.

None of the names found in verses 5-15 are mentioned elsewhere in Scripture, except perhaps Rufus. At the head of the list is Epaenetus. He is followed by *Mary*. "*Greet Mary*," says Paul, "*who bestoweth much labor on us* [you]" (v. 6). There are a half dozen Marys in the New Testament—the mother of the Lord, Magdalene, the sister of Lazarus, the wife of Clopas, the mother of John Mark, and this unknown saint at Rome. There are also two forms of the word "Mary" in the New Testament, one being Miriam, and thus Jewish, and the other Maria, a Gentile name. Opinions differ as to whether this Mary was a Gentile or a Jewess. Mary of Rome, however, whoever she was, had worn herself out for the Christians in that city. The word for "labor" is the same as that used for the Lord when "*wearied* with his journey" He sat down by the well (John 4:6). It is the same word used of the disciples when after a fruitless night's fishing they told the Lord that they had "*toiled* all night" (Luke 5:5). Mary of Rome, then, joins the ranks of the multitudes who for the cause of Christ and on behalf of His people have worked their fingers to the bone and not grown weary in well-doing. Her sisters are with us still.

"*Salute Andronicus and Junia, my kinsmen, and my fellowprisoners, who are of note among the apostles, who also were in Christ before me*" (v. 7). It is not certain whether the latter name should be "Junias" (masculine) or "Junia" (feminine). The word "kinsman" can mean either fellow countryman or blood relative. In

[1]Cited by Henry Alford, *The New Testament for English Readers* (Chicago: Moody Press, n.d.), p. 970.

this verse it is at least likely that Paul is referring to actual relatives. It is an attractive thought! One can well picture this couple, saved before Paul, moving in the highest of church circles, greatly concerned about the fanaticism and blood lust of young Saul, urgently longing for his conversion and for the consecration of his unquestioned talents and great zeal for the Lord, mightily laying hold of the throne of grace on his behalf. One can picture, too, their joy and gratitude to God for the manner of Saul's conversion and for the spectacular results of his preaching, pioneering and penmanship. If it is correct to believe that Andronicus and Junia were indeed Paul's relatives, what a bond must have been theirs in Christ! There are reasons for believing that the great apostle had been disinherited by his family and was no longer welcomed at his ancestral home in Tarsus.[2] If this was so, he must have found special consolation and satisfaction in the fellowship of at least two of his relatives who were not only saved but saved before him and high in the esteem of the apostles.

It is not clear from the text whether Andronicus and Junia were themselves apostles or simply highly regarded by the apostles. It would seem from the New Testament that while the Twelve occupied a special position, the word "apostle" was not restricted to them by the early church. Thus Barnabas, James the Lord's brother, Silas, and others are called apostles. (See Acts 14:4, 14; I Thess. 2:6.) In any case, Andronicus and Junia were "of note" in apostolic circles. The thought seems to be that they had the mark of greatness upon them; they were illustrious.

It is interesting how the Spirit of God passes over in silence so much that we would like to know. What made this couple so great in the early church? We shall never know until that great day when all the saints are gathered around the throne of God and are there publicly honored for their deeds of distinction. Then Andronicus and Junia, along with all the other unsung multitude of God's worthies, will come into their own. The day is coming when great David's greater Son will read out the roll of honor and recite the names of His mighty men. Then this couple will get their reward. In the meantime, all we know of them is that Paul calls them his "fellowprisoners," the literal interpretation of which

[2]F. F. Bruce has a note on this. See his *The Book of Acts* (Grand Rapids: Wm. B. Eerdmans Publishing Co., 1954), pp. 240-241.

means "war captives." Perhaps they had shared one of his imprisonments. One day we shall know.

"Greet Amplias my beloved in the Lord," says Paul. "Greet Urbane, our helper in Christ, and Stachys my beloved" (vv. 8-9). To be loved by Paul, to be counted as one of his helpers—these are distinctions indeed. These unknown saints flash for a moment in the reflected light of Paul's greatness. Yet the humblest of the children of God, beloved by the Lord and one of His helpers, is just as surely known, honored and remembered. The day is coming when each one will be given a place in the sun to reflect His glory for every eye to see for all the ages of eternity.

"Salute Apelles approved in Christ" (v. 10). Here was a saint who had won his spurs. He had in some way been put to the test and had won the approval of his brethren. It is instructive to note how this word "approved" is used elsewhere in the New Testament. (1) It is rendered "tried" in James 1:12: "Blessed is the man that endureth temptation: for when he is tried [approved], he shall receive the crown of life, which the Lord hath promised to them that love him." ((2) Paul uses the same word in his discussion of a believer's attitude toward the weaker brother. The man who looks out for his brother's interests and who recognizes that "the kingdom of God is not meat and drink; but righteousness, and peace, and joy in the Holy Ghost" (Rom. 14:17), will win the approval of his brethren. Paul says, "For he that in these things serveth Christ is acceptable to God, and approved of men" (14:18). (3) Writing to the Corinthians Paul says, "For there must be also heresies among you, that they which are approved may be made manifest among you" (I Cor. 11:19). We know too that there were heresies threatening the saints at Rome, because later in this chapter Paul tells the believers how to handle false teachers (16:17-18). (4) Another essential of winning approval is modesty about one's own accomplishments. "For not he that commendeth himself is approved, but whom the Lord commendeth" (II Cor. 10:18). (5) In his last letter, written to young Timothy, Paul says, "Study to shew thyself approved unto God, a workman that needeth not to be ashamed, rightly dividing the word of truth" (II Tim. 2:15). The same Greek word for "approved" is used in each of the above examples. In some such way perhaps Apelles was raised to a place in the esteem of his brethren. These are ways open to any of God's people.

"Salute them which are of Aristobulus' household. Salute Herodion my kinsman. Greet them that be of the household of Narcissus, which are in the Lord" (vv. 10b-11). In both the above instances the word "household" does not appear in the original, a fact which is evident even in the Authorized Version where the word occurs in italics indicating it has been supplied by the translators. Because of this the suggestion has been made that those saluted were the household slaves of Aristobulus and Narcissus and that it does not necessarily follow that either of these men were themselves Christians. Lightfoot maintained that Aristobulus should be identified as a grandson of Herod the Great, brother of Herod Agrippa of Judea.[3] Alford discusses the possibility of Narcissus being a well-known freeman of Claudius. While concluding that this could hardly be true because that particular Narcissus was executed in the very beginning of Nero's reign and prior to the writing of Romans, he does admit the possibility that the family of Narcissus could still be known by his name even after his death.[4] Herodion probably belonged to the Herod family also, and was a fellow countryman of Paul, that is, a Jew.

"Salute Tryphena and Tryphosa, who labour in the Lord. Salute the beloved Persis, which laboured much in the Lord" (v. 12). Tryphena and Tryphosa were most likely sisters. Persis is assumed to have been a more elderly sister in Christ because her labor is referred to in the past tense. How careful Paul was to shun all appearance of evil. When speaking of those he loved in the Lord who were brethren he called them "my beloved" (see v. 9); but when speaking of sisters in Christ, he used the more formal expression "the beloved."

"Salute Rufus chosen in the Lord, and his mother and mine" (v. 13). This Rufus may have been the son of Simon the Cyrenian, the man who carried the cross for Christ (Mark 15:21). Certainly Mark, who wrote his gospel for the Romans, describes Simon as the father of Alexander and Rufus, the likelihood being that this man was the Rufus known in the Roman church. Possibly too Simon of Cyrene was the same Simon mentioned in Acts 13:1 as

[3]J. B. Lightfoot, *St. Paul's Epistle to the Philippians* (London: Macmillan and Co., 1878), pp. 174-175.
[4]Alford, *op. cit.*, p. 971.

one of the elders of the Antioch church who played a part in com-
mending Paul and Barnabas to the mission field. F. F. Bruce suggests that Paul's reference in Romans to "Rufus, his mother and
mine" might possibly refer to Paul's days in Antioch when perhaps he was a guest in their home.[5] Dan Crawford, in comment-
ing on the Lord's promise: "Verily I say unto you, There is no
man that hath left house, or brethren, or sisters, or father, or
mother, or wife, or children, or lands, for my sake, and the gospel's,
but he shall receive an hundredfold now in this time, houses, and
brethren, and sisters, and mothers, and children, and lands, with
persecutions; and in the world to come eternal life" (Mark 10:29-
30), quaintly says, "All along the line of pursuit, devils' hue-and-
cry notwithstanding, the saint has been the gainer, here finding a
fresh mother, and there a whole Bethany of sisters and brothers!
Rufus may have a mother; but Paul says she is 'his mother and
mine.' One of Paul's twenty thousand mothers! Is not this the
whole purport of Romans 16, yea, this the precise divine reason
for the long list of friends recorded there? And this, to show how
wisely and how well Christ has *kept* that old 'hundredfold' promise to His own."[6]

*"Salute Asyncritus, Phlegon, Hermas, Patrobas, Hermes, and
the brethren which are with them"* (v. 14). One group of saints
met in the house of Priscilla and Aquila. Here is a second group
meeting in like simplicity.

*"Salute Philologus, and Julia, Nereus, and his sister, and Olym-
pas, and all the saints which are with them"* (v. 15). Some have
thought that Philologus and Julia were husband and wife and that
Nereus and his sister were their children, while Olympas was of
the same family household. This is the third assembly of believers
in Rome mentioned in the chapter. With this group Paul brings
his salutations of the Roman Christians to a close. He has, however, one more thing to say. Having saluted them with love's distinctiveness, he suggests a practical way love can be shown.

B. *He Salutes Them With Love's Demonstrativeness* (16:16)

Love is not cold and formal. Love is warm and affectionate. So
Paul says, *"Salute one another with an holy kiss. The churches of*

[5]Bruce, *op. cit.,* pp. 259-260.
[6]Dan Crawford, *Thirsting After God* (London: Pickering and Inglis, n.d.),
pp. 78-79.

Christ salute you" (v. 16). This direction is repeated five times
in the New Testament (I Cor. 16:20; II Cor. 13:12; I Thess. 5:26;
I Peter 5:14). In the East, a kiss was and is a sign of respect and
affection. It was the traditional Oriental greeting, but it would be
wrong to dismiss the injunction merely as an Orientalism. "A
hearty handshake" would give the idea in our culture. A warm
handclasp conveys the idea of love, respect, fellowship and
warmth. It is just this that Paul had in mind.

This page of worthies is no mere relic from the past. As Bishop
Moule writes, "It is a list of friendships to be made hereafter, and
to be possessed forever in the endless life where personality indeed shall be eternal, but where also the union of personalities in
Christ shall be beyond our utmost present thought."[7]

LOVE'S MIGHTY CONQUESTS
16:17-20

I. WATCH VIGILANTLY AGAINST SEDUCTION (16:17-19)

    A. Seduction From Without (16:17-18)

        1. How False Teachers Betray Themselves (16:17)

            a. We are to recognize them (16:17*a*)

            b. We are to reject them (16:17*b*)

        2. How False Teachers Behave Themselves (16:18)

            a. Their real god (16:18*a*)

            b. Their real goal (16:18*b*)

    B. Seduction From Within (16:19)

        1. The Dynamic Witness of the Assembly (16:19*a*)

        2. The Dangerous Weakness of the Assembly (16:19*b*)

II. WAR VICTORIOUSLY AGAINST SATAN (16:20)

    A. Satan Is to Be Bruised

    B. Saints Are to Be Blessed

MARK THEM! AVOID THEM! This is Paul's advice for dealing with
those who would undermine the faith with false teachings. From
earliest times the church has been plagued with heresy. More
than one of Paul's letters takes up the cudgels against unscriptural
doctrines. The church at Galatia was plagued with legalism, the

[7]Handley G. C. Moule, *The Epistle of St. Paul to the Romans* (New York:
Hodden and Stoughton, n.d.), p. 430.

church at Colossae with gnosticism, the church at Thessalonica with false eschatalogical teachings. Peter, John and Jude stood shoulder to shoulder with Paul in combating teachings which were subversive of the truth. It is therefore not surprising to find that at Rome, the great magnet of the world, false teachers were on the prowl. Paul has two parting words of advice on the subject of Satanic subversion of the doctrines of the faith.

I. WE ARE TO WATCH VIGILANTLY AGAINST SEDUCTION (16:17-19)

Heresy is always stealthy. It is like water that presses against a dyke. It probes for a weak spot through which it can enter, in a trickle at first but later like a flood.

A. *Seduction From Without* (16:17-18)

We are to notice how false teachers (1) *betray themselves.* Once we recognize them, we are to reject them. It is no part of love's sphere to tolerate seduction. *"Now I beseech you, brethren, mark them which cause divisions and offences contrary to the doctrine which ye have learned; and avoid them"* (v. 17). "Divisions" comes from a word meaning "dissention" or "discord" and is translated "seditions" in Galatians 5:20, where it is listed as one of the works of the flesh and where it keeps close company in the text with "heresies." "Offences" comes from a word meaning "trapstick." One authority gives the etymology of this word *skandalon* as "a crooked stick on which a bait is fastened, which, being struck by the animal, springs the trap; a trap, a gin, a snare; hence, anything which one strikes or stumbles against, a stumblingblock, especially a cause of stumbling."[1] In other words, it suggests an impediment placed in the way, causing the unwary to stumble and fall. In Romans 11:9 Paul uses the same word, only there it is translated "stumblingblock." It well describes the activity of the cultist.

The believer is to be on his guard against teachers who come to divide and destroy the local church. They deliberately seek to snare and trap those who are not watching vigilantly against sedition. Paul's warning to the Roman church against such heretics, even though it appears almost as an afterthought, inserted between two lists of names, was actually most timely. History attests

[1]E. W. Bullinger, *A Critical Lexicon and Concordance* (London: Samuel Bagster and Sons Ltd., n.d.), p. 547.

how badly the warning was needed at Rome and how little it was heeded.

The way to detect error is to lay the subversive teaching alongside the straightedge of divine truth—"the doctrine which ye have learned." In Romans 6:17 Paul uses the same word "doctrine." "God be thanked," he says of the Romans, "ye have obeyed from the heart that form of doctrine which was delivered you [unto which you were delivered]." Heresy will make little progress in a church that is rooted and grounded in the "apostles' doctrine" (Acts 2:42). Mormons, Jehovah's Witnesses and other modern-day cultists find their most fruitful field for recruits in the ranks of those who have some smattering of "religion" but who are largely ignorant of the broad and basic tenets of the Christian faith.

"Shun them!" says Paul. It is good advice. There is a time and a place to confront the heretic. There is a way to expose error both privately and publicly. But that is no task for the average church member. It is a task for the theologian and the Spirit-taught believer. All too often the untaught and the unspiritual engage the cultist in debate and find themselves badly beaten in the discussion. For one thing, the errors propounded are never simple but subtle. Also, the door-to-door emissaries of the cult are usually well trained and have been primed on the best ways to turn aside the usual objections made to their teachings. When an untaught believer tries to meet such in debate, he is in danger of himself being led astray.

Paul's injunction "mark them . . . avoid them" is very practical and is a wise rule for the average believer. The writer knows personally of one family which failed to heed the apostle's words with disastrous results. He received a phone call one day from a woman he knew attended a local Bible-believing church. Whether the woman and her husband were truly saved, it is difficult to say in view of what followed. The woman asked on the phone, "Can you tell me where I can get a Greek Bible?" "A Greek Bible?" was the astonished reply. "Why do you want a Greek Bible?" (The woman was no student—certainly no student of Greek!) "Well," she said, "you can understand the Bible better when you go back to the original." At this point the writer's suspicions were aroused. "Have you been talking to a member of the Jehovah's

Witness group?" he asked. It turned out that the woman and her husband had not only been talking to Jehovah's Witnesses but had been allowing them into the home to give Bible instruction. Things had progressed so far that the couple were attending various meetings at the Kingdom Hall. When he hung up the phone, the author called the woman's pastor and suggested a pastoral visit would be in order; but the pastor seemed reluctant to get involved. The writer therefore called a friend of his, a well-taught Christian worker and an experienced controversialist, and then made arrangements for them both to meet with the woman, her husband and their Jehovah's Witness instructors. A royal battle followed, lasting late into the night. The cultists finally left, and the woman and her husband professed to be convinced that they had been led astray. They refused, however, to destroy the books they had bought from the cult and, although they did go back to their old church for a short while, the poison was still at work. Eventually they began meeting again with the Jehovah's Witnesses, cancelled their membership in the fundamental church, were baptized as Jehovah's Witnesses and became zealous propagandists for the cult. True, their pastor was not blameless. Evidently the couple had been neither properly taught nor cared for in their own church. But their fascination with and ultimately their seduction by the Russellites all began because they did not "mark" and "avoid" the cult's missionaries. The "trap-stick" was carefully laid at their door. It was well baited with plausible words and friendly overtures. They were unwary and the trap was sprung. The fear of Armageddon entered into their souls and they became "Watchtower slaves."

False teachers, then, betray themselves by seeking to divide and destroy. Paul next tells how false teachers (2) *behave themselves.* He exposes their real god and their real goal. *"For they that are such serve not our Lord Jesus Christ, but their own belly; and by good words and fair speeches deceive the hearts of the simple"* (v. 18). False teachers are motivated by their own base interests. It is striking that Paul should say that they serve "their own belly." Later on, writing to the Philippians he warns of those who are "the enemies of the cross of Christ: whose end is destruction, whose God is their belly, and whose glory is in their shame, who mind earthly things" (Phil. 3:18-19). It does not necessarily

follow that the false teachers are sensualists, although of course
they may be. The reference to the belly is a contemptuous way
of drawing attention to the low motives, their real god, their self-
seeking spirit. They use plausible arguments. They flatter. They
have a suave and polished style. They thoroughly deceive the
"simple," the guileless. Above all, they "serve not our Lord Jesus
Christ."

They have a Christ in the cults but he is not our Lord Jesus
Christ. The *modernist*, for example, has a Christ, but he was not
virgin born. He was a man so good that his deluded followers
mistook him for God. He was the world's greatest ethical teacher,
divine only in the sense that all men are divine. The Christ of the
modernist performed no miracles, those recorded in the New
Testament being merely legendary exaggerations of events expli-
cable by natural causes. The modernist's Christ did not rise from
the dead. He is not "our Lord Jesus Christ."

The *Mormons* have a Christ but he was the son of Adam-God
and Mary. He was a polygamist, secretly married to the Marys
and to Martha at Cana. His atonement had to do only with the
sins of Adam and is not sufficient for our personal sins. Their
Christ is not ours.

The *Jehovah's Witnesses* have a Christ but he was not the second Person of the Godhead. He was merely "a son of God." Before he came into the world he was a created angel, namely,
Michael the archangel. When he entered this life he became a
perfect human being, nothing more. The ransom he offers does
not guarantee eternal life to any man. Nor did he rise from the
dead. According to the Watchtower people, we do not know what
happened to the body of Jesus in Joseph's tomb. The Christ of
the Russellites is not "our Lord Jesus Christ."

The *Christian Scientists* have a Christ but he is not God. He is
merely a divine ideal. His blood was of no more avail when it was
shed on the cross than when it flowed through his veins. He ac-
commodated himself to the immature ideas of his contemporaries
and made great concessions to popular ignorance. He is not "our
Lord Jesus Christ."

The *Spiritualists* have a Christ but he is nothing more than a
medium of high order. He was not divine but is now an advanced
spirit in the sixth sphere. His death had no atoning value. In fact,

Jesus was simply a Jewish enthusiast who met an untimely death.[2]
The Christ of the Spiritualists is not "our Lord Jesus Christ."

All the cults have a Christ but he is not the Christ of the Bible.
The Christ of the Bible is the second Person of the Godhead. He
was supernaturally conceived of the Holy Ghost and was born of
the virgin Mary. He lived an immaculate life, claimed to be God,
performed amazing miracles, and proved that claim. His teachings
were sublime, perfect, flawless. He foretold His death exactly and
was crucified just as He predicted. His death was vicarious; He
suffered for the sins of the world, and He imparts eternal life to
those who trust in Him. He rose again physically and literally the
third day and ascended bodily into heaven. He is seated today at
God's right hand, from whence He will return to judge all men.
This is "our Lord Jesus Christ." The Christ of the cults is unknown to the Bible—unless, perhaps, he is the Antichrist.

B. *Seduction From Within* (16:19)

So much then for the cult! Thus far apparently, it had not made
its inroads into Rome, for Paul speaks of (1) *the dynamic witness
of the assembly at Rome. "For your obedience is come abroad
unto all men. I am glad therefore on your behalf"* (v. 19a). Paul
has already spoken three times of obedience in this epistle. First,
in the introduction of the letter he speaks of his own "obedience
to the faith among all nations, for his name" (1:5). Second, sum-
marizing the sin question, Paul contrasts Christ's obedience with
Adam's disobedience. "For as by one man's disobedience many
were made sinners, so by the obedience of one shall many be
made righteous" (5:19). Third, speaking of the life of victory
won for the believer by Christ at Calvary and the practical outworking of that victory in our lives, Paul says, "Know ye not, that
to whom ye yield yourselves servants to obey, his servants ye are
to whom ye obey; whether of sin unto death, or of obedience unto
righteousness" (6:16). It is a great word, that word "obedience."
It is at the heart of our service, our salvation and our sanctification
as Paul's previous references to it in Romans reveal.

[2]See Keith L. Brooks, *The Spirit of Truth and the Spirit of Error* (Chicago:
Moody Press, 1963), for further details on the above-mentioned cults.

> Trust and obey,
>   For there's no other way
> To be happy in Jesus,
>   But to trust and obey.

The Romans had earned a wide reputation for their obedience. It was a true Roman characteristic. Rome's vast empire was held together by obedience. The Roman Christians had carried over into their faith the most outstanding feature of their national culture and had become renowned for their obedience. Paul was proud of them for it; the thought of their obedience made him glad.

However, he has a word of warning. He speaks of (2) *the dangerous weakness of the assembly at Rome.* The believers there were at the very heart of worldly and sophisticated things. There was danger that these things might creep into the church, for the great world revolved around Rome. Into her markets poured the multitudes of earth and the merchandise of the world. Her citizens and nobles were polished, cultured, proud, and had vast wealth, enormous power and boundless privilege. There was abject slavery too, and grinding poverty, and hopeless misery, for cruelty and oppression were part of the pattern of life.. Thousands were slaughtered at a Caesar's whim or to make a "Roman holiday" for the plebian mob. Vice was taken for granted. It was elevated in pagan religions as the very essence of worship. And from all these various backgrounds the Christian believers of Rome had come. Many of the believers carried with them from their past a sophistication regarding evil which, if uncrucified, could wreck and ruin the church. So Paul says, *"Yet I would have you wise unto that which is good, and simple concerning evil"* (v. 19b). Only divine grace can wash the mind of its memories and free the heart from the fetters of a past deep knowledge of the world and its ways, and impart instead a guilelessness, a simplicity, an innocence regarding evil.

A striking example of the change God can work in a man is given in the life of Moses. In the providence of God, Moses received a very thorough education in "all the wisdom of the Egyptians" (Acts 7:22). Then, when it seemed that his prospects were boundless and even the throne of the Pharaohs might possibly be within his grasp, he made his decision for Christ (Heb. 11:24-26). Determined to cast in his lot with the people of God, he struck what he considered to be a blow for God and for the emancipation of the Hebrews. But by slaying the Egyptian he acted in the flesh and according to the spirit of the world. Instead of becoming a missionary, he became a murderer. His forty years in Egypt learning to be somebody had to be followed by forty years in the wilderness as a humble shepherd learning to be nobody. It took God but a moment to get Moses out of Egypt, but forty years to get Egypt out of Moses! In the stillness of the desert, however, Moses gradually unlearned the Egyptian spirit. He emerged no longer proud, headstrong and self-confident, but humble, submissive and meek.

This is what God wishes to do with each of His saints. As long as the spirit of the world activates us, we are a potential danger to the church with which we meet. Paul urged the Romans to be watchful against seduction from within—a worldly spirit, which if allowed free reign would finally open the door to every kind of error. History has proved how right he was to warn the Roman church of these things.

II. WE ARE TO WAR VICTORIOUSLY AGAINST SATAN (16:20)

The devil, "the father of lies," lurks behind all the systems of deception that plague mankind. At the very heart of Satan's plot against the human race is a thoroughgoing deception. He is the weaver of all the various religious delusions with which fallen men clothe the nakedness of their souls. It is not surprising, therefore, that Paul turns abruptly from a description of the cultist to an unmasking of the evil one who inspires their teachings. He treads with an iron heel on the adder's head.

A. *Satan Is to Be Bruised* (16:20a)

That God permits Satan a measure of freedom to pursue his evil designs against the human race is part of the mystery of iniquity. We can be quite sure, however, that God makes no mistakes and that He is following out His own perfect plans with the unfaltering wisdom of omniscience. In the meantime, God has Satan on a leash. Satan may be the instigator of strife and division, but God is "the God of peace," and as Paul says, *"the God of peace shall bruise Satan under your feet shortly"* (v. 20a). This bruising will actually be an utter and complete crushing of the serpent. The saints are going to share with Christ in His final absolute triumph over the evil one (Gen. 3:15).

B. *Saints Are to Be Blessed* (16:20b)

We do not have to wait the final crushing of the serpent, however, in order to enter into the blessings and benedictions of grace. We can enjoy them now. Paul says, *"The grace of our Lord Jesus Christ be with you. Amen"* (v. 20b). Each one of Paul's epistles ends with a benedictory prayer. Here he takes the key thought of the epistle—the thought of grace—and pours it like fragrant spikenard on the heads of the saints of God.

Then he adds a resounding "Amen!" It is his second "amen" in the epistle. He will use the word twice more before finally putting down the pen. It almost seems as though he can hardly tear himself away from this communication with his friends and fellow believers at Rome.

Heretics, then, may plague the church. Satan may scheme to defile it and destroy it. But the grace of the Lord Jesus is sufficient, and in that grace we may triumph now, and in that grace we shall surely triumph by and by.

LOVE'S MARVELOUS COMPANIONSHIPS
16:21-24

I. GREETINGS CONVEYED FROM THE SAINTS OF GOD (16:21-23)
   A. Timotheus
   B. Lucius
   C. Jason
   D. Sosipater
   E. Tertius
   F. Gaius
   G. Erastus
   H. Quartus

II. GRACE CONFERRED BY THE SON OF GOD (16:24)

PAUL WAS AT CORINTH when he wrote to Rome. At the close of his third missionary journey he spent three winter months in

Greece, mostly at Corinth, where he stayed in the home of his friend Gaius. He was busy making final preparations for his trip to Jerusalem and bringing together representatives of the various churches which were contributing to the gift of money for the poor in the Jerusalem church. The Macedonian churches and those of Galatia and Asia were all to be represented. By the time Paul came to sign this epistle to Rome, several of the delegates were with him.

The church at Corinth was one which had given Paul much trouble. Yet it was a gifted church and one which contained a host of very capable brethren. Some of them are mentioned here in Paul's final salutations to Rome.

I. Greetings Conveyed From the Saints of God (16:21-23)

The first who joins his greetings with that of Paul is his dear young friend *Timotheus* (v. 21). Of all Paul's companions, this remarkable man is one of the best known. His mother and grandmother were pious Jews and had diligently trained the boy in the truths of Scripture. His father was a Gentile, and probably on this account Timothy had never been circumcised and was therefore, so to speak, only half Jewish.

Probably Timothy was living at Lystra when Paul visited that city on his first missionary journey. It seems likely that young Timothy was converted at that time (Acts 14:6; 16:1; II Tim. 1:5). When Paul came back to Lystra on his second missionary journey, the spiritual elders of the church drew his attention to Timothy as a most promising young man. Paul, disappointed in John Mark, turned with interest to Timothy. Because of the bitterness of the Jews and because Timothy was already half Jewish, Paul circumcised him before admitting him to the missionary team (Acts 16:3). He was then set apart as an evangelist by the church, who expressed their confidence in Timothy and their fellowship in this new development by the laying on of hands (I Tim. 4:14; II Tim. 4:5). From that point on, Timothy became one of Paul's closest and most constant companions.

At Philippi Timothy's loyalty and zeal became increasingly conspicuous (Phil. 2:22). When Paul was forced out of Philippi, he seems to have left young Timothy behind to help in the care of the infant church. He followed Paul to Berea, where once again he was left behind by Paul, this time in company with Silas, to minister to the new church. But not for long!

He picked up Paul's trail to Athens where he rejoined his chief only to be entrusted with another errand. This time he was sent back north to Thessalonica to encourage and strengthen the church there (Acts 17:14; I Thess. 3:2). By the time this mission was accomplished Paul had left Athens and was pioneering in Corinth, so to that great city Timothy came and we find his name associated with that of Paul in both his letters from Corinth to Thessalonica.

Nothing is known of the next five years in Timothy's history. He must have been with Paul, however, for at least part of his stay at Ephesus on his third missionary journey, for at some point in that period Paul sent Timothy to Corinth and expected him to return to Ephesus (I Cor. 4:17; 16:10). When Paul arrived in Corinth after the completion of his work at Ephesus, Timothy was with him, for as we see here in Romans, he joins in sending greetings to Rome. When Paul's work in Macedonia and Greece was over and he made final preparations to go to Jerusalem, Timothy was one of the party sent on ahead to await Paul's arrival at Troas (Acts 20:3-6).

Once again Timothy drops out of the Bible story until we see him again with Paul at Rome during Paul's first imprisonment. He was with Paul at Rome when the letters to Philippi, Colossae and Philemon were written. It appears, too, that after Paul's release from his first imprisonment that he and Timothy visited proconsular Asia together. Then Paul continued on to Macedonia, leaving Timothy behind at Ephesus—in tears at having to part with Paul—to deal with various disorders in the Ephesian church (II Tim. 1:4). The duties placed upon him were onerous indeed as we learn from I Timothy; so much so that Paul became anxious for the steadfastness of his beloved friend and earnestly longed to see him again (II Tim. 4:9, 21). It is interesting that the last recorded words of Paul were addressed to Timothy. It is no wonder that Paul heads the list of those who send greetings to Rome with the name of this illustrious disciple.

"*Timotheus my workfellow, and Lucius, and Jason, and Sosipater, my kinsmen, salute you*" (v. 21). The last three mentioned were fellow countrymen of Paul. *Lucius*, in all probability, was the one surnamed the "Cyrenian," one of the "prophets and teachers" at Antioch who commended Paul and Barnabas to the mission field (Acts 13:1). *Jason* is most likely the Jason who entertained Paul and Silas in his home when first they came to Thessalonica with the gospel. He had shared in Paul's persecutions in that city, his house having been mobbed and he himself dragged off before the magistrates, who released him on bail (Acts 17:5-9). The name *Sosipater* and the name Sopater of Acts 20:4 apparently designate the same person. If so, he was one of Paul's converts at Berea and one of the delegates Paul took with him to Jerusalem.

"I Tertius, who wrote this epistle, salute you in the Lord" (v. 22). There is some evidence that Paul was afflicted with an Oriental eye disease, *ophthalmia,* contracted in the lowlands of Pamphilia on his first missionary journey and which brought on almost complete blindness (Gal. 4:13-15). Because of this, the apostle found it necessary to dictate his letters to a secretary, an amanuensis. It was characteristic of Paul's courtesy that he allowed his penman to insert his own personal greeting to the Roman Christians, some of whom had migrated to the capital from Corinth. For Paul to have dictated to Tertius his own salutation would have been to treat him like a mere machine.

"Gaius mine host, and of the whole church, saluteth you. Erastus the chamberlain of the city saluteth you, and Quartus a brother" (v. 23). Among the ancient Romans a person was usually given three names. First there was the *praenomen* corresponding to our first name, then there was the *nomen* and finally the *cognomen,* or family name. (Occasionally a person was given an *agnomen* as well, an additional name given either to honor some personal achievement or else to show adoption.) The full name of the *Gaius* mentioned here was probably Gaius Titius Justus. According to F. F. Bruce such a name would suggest that Gaius was a Roman citizen and "perhaps a member of one of the Roman families settled in Corinth at the time when Julius Caesar made it a Roman colony."[1] Probably he is the same Gaius mentioned by Paul in I Corinthians 1:14 as one of the few Corinthian converts whom he baptized with his own hands.

[1]See F. F. Bruce, *Commentary on the Book of Acts* (Grand Rapids: Wm. B. Eerdmans Publishing Co., 1954), p. 371.

Erastus was the chamberlain of the city. This position, possibly that of city treasurer or city manager, was one of considerable importance. Erastus is usually identified with the Erastus who was with Paul at Ephesus and who was sent by Paul, along with Timothy, into Macedonia while the apostle remained in Asia (Acts 19:22). When Paul wrote his last epistle, Erastus was still at Corinth (II Tim. 4:20), so this was probably his usual place of abode.

All we know of *Quartus* is that he was "a brother." This is a scanty enough description, but what a wealth of warmth is included in it. How dear those become to us to whom we are linked by the ties of grace! Indeed often we have more, much more, in common with our brothers and sisters in Christ than we have with those who are our kin by nature.

So then, Paul conveys these greetings from the saints of God linking the family of faith together with the bonds of Christian love. These names remind us of love's marvelous companionships, of the blest tie that binds believers together in the family of God.

II. GRACE CONFERRED BY THE SON OF GOD (16:24)

Paul repeats the benediction of verse 20: *"The grace of our Lord Jesus Christ be with you all"* (v. 24). The grace of our Lord Jesus Christ is defined for us in II Corinthians 8:9: "Ye know the grace of our Lord Jesus Christ, that, though he was rich, yet for your sakes he became poor, that ye through his poverty might be rich." That is "our Lord Jesus Christ"! From His highest heaven He never ceases to pour out upon His own inexhaustible riches of His grace. Well might we sing, "Hallelujah, What a Saviour," and bask in the grace He confers. For of all love's marvelous companionships, this is the most marvelous of all!

EPILOGUE
16:25-27

I. The Work of God Is Declared (16:25-26)

   A. It Is Within His Power to Establish That Work (16:25*a*)

   B. It Is Within His Purpose to Establish That Work (16:25*b*-26)

      1. Divinely Revealed to New Testament Saints (16:25*b*)

      2. Divinely Concealed from Old Testament Saints (25*c*-26)

II. The Wisdom of God Is Declared (16:27)

Paul has come to the end of his letter. It just remains for him to conclude with his customary benediction and to lift the thoughts of the saints to a contemplation of God and His ways. And what a magnificent doxology this is with which he adds the finishing touch, maybe taking the pen from Tertius to write the closing words in his own hand, and adding his last amen. The doxology draws the attention of the Romans to the work and the wisdom of God.

I. The Work of God Is Declared (16:25-26)

Salvation is the work of God from start to finish. The work was finished by Christ at Calvary and no mortal hand can add anything to that divinely finished work.

A. *It Is Within God's Power to Establish His Work* (16:25*a*)

Paul comes straight to the point on this. *"Now to him that is of power to stablish you,"* he says. The word "stablish" takes us back to the beginning of the epistle. One of Paul's stated reasons for wishing to come to Rome was "to the end ye may be established" (1:11). He acknowledges that only God can accomplish this. To root and ground believers in the things of God is as much

282

and as solely a work of grace as to bring sinners to a saving knowledge of Jesus Christ.

An internationally famous evangelist was once challenged in a great European capital by one of that nation's own evangelists. "Sir," demanded the national, "do your converts stand?" "Sir," retorted the other, "do yours?" It is a great joy to see souls saved, but to be able to come back to them in later years and see how they have developed and grown, this is what brings the deepest joy to the heart.

The work of establishing the saints is well within God's power. Power to do this is inherent in God. Not all the powers of the pit, not all the allurements of the world, nor the wiles of the devil, nor the weakness of the flesh can hinder Him. "Being confident of this very thing," said Paul in a letter he wrote when he finally arrived at Rome, "that he which hath begun a good work in you will perform it until the day of Jesus Christ" (Phil. 1:6).

B. *It Is Within God's Purpose to Establish His Work* (16:25b-26)

This is good news. It is divinely revealed in the New Testament, both in the Gospels and the Epistles, and the truth lies latent also in the Old Testament. Note the threefold repetition of the phrase "according to" in these verses.

That God cannot be hindered in the outworking of His purposes is (1) *divinely revealed in the New Testament*. Paul says that it is *"according to my gospel"* (that embraces the Epistles) *"and the preaching of Jesus Christ"* (that embraces the Gospels). Paul's gospel was his own in the sense that he had not been taught it by men (Gal. 1:11) but had received it by direct revelation from God. It was not essentially different from the gospel proclaimed by others, but it did show a much fuller and wider development.

Paul's gospel was a Christ-centered gospel, for that is what the phrase "according to . . . the preaching of Jesus Christ" primarily implies. In its substance and essence it was a proclamation of the person and work of Christ.

There are those who would have us believe that the magnificent Christology of Paul was superimposed by him on the simple preaching of the early church. They would have us believe that Paul's epistles represent a radical departure from the simple message proclaimed by the Lord Jesus Himself. But these charges are false. For example, a study of the names and titles attributed to the Lord Jesus in the early sermons recorded in Acts will show that from the very beginning the highest and loftiest ideas were entertained concerning the person of the Lord. Then too, Jesus proclaimed Himself to be the Son of God in the sense of being absolute Deity, and declared that He was the man's sole Saviour from sin. That is what Paul preached too. These are the truths that not only save but "stablish." Even such an abstract concept as being "in Christ" (one which comes to the very heart of the matter when the establishing of the saints is in view), which is a theme developed in one way or another in all Paul's epistles, did not originate with him. The truth is found first in Christ's preaching. It is developed most thoroughly by the Lord, for example, in His teaching concerning the true vine (John 15). So then, the good news that God intends to establish His work is revealed in the New Testament both in the Epistles and in the Gospels. Paul's gospel has its roots in Christ's.

That God cannot be hindered in the outworking of His purpose concerning the church is (2) *divinely concealed in the Old Testament*. It is almost trite to say concerning the two Testaments that "the Old is in the New revealed; the New is in the Old concealed." The statement is very largely true. However, some truths connected with what Paul calls "the mystery" were certainly a New Testament revelation, and if they existed in the Old Testament types at all it was only in the vaguest and most shadowy way. The Old Testament saints could not discern these "mystery" truths in their Scriptures. We can see them, or at least some of them, only as we think through the Old Testament in the light of the greater revelation of the New Testament.[1]

Paul says that God's purpose to establish His work is "*according to the revelation of the mystery, which was kept secret since the world began, but now is made manifest, and by the scriptures of the prophets, according to the commandment of the everlasting God made known to all nations for the obedience of the faith*" (vv. 25b-26).

---

[1]The truth concerning the bride of Christ is latent in what we are told of some of the brides of the Old Testament. Some of the truths concerning the church as a building can be read back into the tabernacle and the temple. But it is doubtful if the truth concerning the body of Christ is found in the Old Testament, unless perhaps it is hinted at in Psalm 139:16.

The greatest and most important of the New Testament mysteries is the mystery of the church, the joining of Jew and Gentile in the body of Christ.[2] "The relation of Jew and Gentile was the burning question in the church in Paul's day. Nothing could be settled till it was settled. This question was the foe of stability and well-nigh wrecked the churches of Galatia. Paul knew the might of the disturbing currents sweeping around the churches, and that nothing but God's power could establish the Romans comfortably with a preaching that accorded with this mystery, so hateful to the zealous but unbelieving Jew, who knew Moses but had only hate for what Peter calls 'the present truth' (II Peter 1:12)."[3]

God's purpose was to establish the saints in this great mystery, a mystery made manifest "by the scriptures of the prophets." These prophets are evidently not the Old Testament prophets but the New Testament prophets through whom these new truths were revealed and by whose instrumentality they were being committed to writing. It is through the Bible, the New Testament in particular, that God works out His perfect plan to mature the saints and bring to complete stability His church.

He is "the everlasting God" and pursues His goals from age to age. Christians may be feeble and frail, but He is strong. The church may look weak and divided, but it is the body of Christ and linked to Omnipotence. Whatever else may fail, the work of God cannot. There remains but for Paul to close with a word about the wisdom of this eternal God.

[2]Scofield gives a description of the New Testament mysteries. He says: "A 'mystery' in Scripture is a previously hidden truth, now divinely revealed. . . . The greater mysteries are: (1) the mysteries of the kingdom of heaven (Matt. 13:3-50); (2) the mystery of Israel's blindness during this age (Rom. 11:25, with context); (3) the mystery of the translation of living saints at the end of this age (I Cor. 15:51-52; I Thess. 4:13-17); (4) the mystery of the New Testament church as one body composed of Jew and Gentile (Eph. 3:1-12; Rom. 16:25; Eph. 6:19; Col. 4:3); (5) the mystery of the church as the bride of Christ (Eph. 5:23-32); (6) the mystery of the inliving Christ (Gal. 2:20; Col. 1:26-27); (7) the 'mystery of God even Christ,' i.e., Christ as the incarnate fullness of the Godhead embodied, in whom all divine wisdom for man subsists (I Cor. 2:7; Col. 2:2, 9); (8) the mystery of the processes by which godlikeness is restored to man (I Tim. 3:16); (9) the mystery of iniquity (II Thess. 2:7; Matt. 13:33); (10) the mystery of the seven stars (Rev. 1:20); (11) the mystery of Babylon (Rev. 17:5, 7)" (The Scofield Reference Bible, 1909, p. 1014).

[3]James M. Stifler, The Epistle to the Romans (Chicago: Moody Press, 1960), p. 253.

II. THE WISDOM OF GOD IS DECLARED (16:27)

"To God only wise, be glory through Jesus Christ for ever. Amen." The title draws out our thoughts to Him whose loving counsels foresaw the fall of man, provided for it before the foundation of the world, foreknew us, loved us into the kingdom, and who arranges for all things to work together for our good and His eternal glory. It draws our thoughts also to the Son of His love, our blessed and glorious Saviour, the Lord Jesus Christ. And having engaged our thoughts, our hearts, our wills to Him, Paul puts down his pen.